LEARNING DISABILITIES

Learning Disabilities:

The Challenges of Adulthood

EDITED BY

James R. Patton
and
Edward A. Polloway

pro·ed
8700 Shoal Creek Boulevard
Austin, Texas 78757-6897

Portions of this material previously appeared in the
Journal of Learning Disabilities

pro·ed

8700 Shoal Creek Boulevard
Austin, Texas 78757-6897

Library of Congress Cataloging-in-Publication Data

Learning disabilities : the challenges of adulthood / edited by James R. Patton and Edward A. Polloway.
p. cm.
Includes articles that previously appeared in the Journal of learning disabilities, v. 25, no. 7 and 8, 1992.
Includes bibliographical references and index.
ISBN 0-89079-581-9 (pbk.)
1. Learning disabled—Education. 2. Learning disabled—Services for. 3. Learning disabled—Employment. 4. Learning disabilities. I. Patton, James R. II. Polloway, Edward A.
LC4818.L43 1996 95-14293
371.91—dc20 CIP

Printed in the United States of America

1 2 3 4 5 6 7 8 9 10 00 99 98 97 96

Contents

Preface

As we progress through our own adult journeys, we recognize the inherent complexities of everyday life. We are constantly made aware of our shortcomings and, in an effort to rationalize them, we find fault in how we were prepared for adulthood. Unfortunately, the issue of planning for the demands of adult living was and continues to be a missing component of the educational programs of most students.

As the field of learning disabilities truly becomes one based on a life-span perspective, it becomes apparent that we must attend to issues from infancy to old age. School-age children and youth who have learning disabilities have received attention because there was no avoiding it: Federal mandates required action, and the large number of students classified as learning disabled provided additional motivation.

The scenario is much different for young adults with learning disabilities who have exited the formal school system through graduating, completing a program, dropping out, or aging out. There is no mandate for services for the young adult, and the same types of supports that existed in high school probably will not be available. Although some demands may stay the same (i.e., deadlines), other demands of adulthood will create new stresses for the individual with learning disabilities who is trying to navigate through daily adult life.

It is plain and simple: Adulthood places many new demands on a person at a time when there may be fewer supports to help deal with the resulting complexities. For this reason, the study of adulthood and persons with learning disabilities is warranted. Several professionals in the field of learning disabilities have been interested in adult issues for some time; however, the professional literature has not reflected this interest until recently (see Chapter 1). Our first attempt to write about this topic occurred in the fall of 1977, and the resulting product was pitiful at best. It reflected both a dearth of information on the topic at that time and our limited writing skills. However, it was an important undertaking for us because it anchored us to this subject and directed some of our later writings.

This book evolved from a series of articles on adults with learning disabilities that appeared in the *Journal of Learning Disabilities* (Vol. 25, Nos. 7 and 8, 1992). All of the original articles, plus four additional chapters that were not part of the series, are included in this volume. The new material covers adult development, transition, postsecondary education assessment practices, and resources. We believe that this book represents a comprehensive set of topics that is particularly relevant to adults who have learning disabilities.

We are honored to have been part of this project concerning such an important topic. Along with the other books and articles covering adulthood and learning disabilities, this volume is intended to contribute to the knowledge base and reflects the efforts of a wonderful group of professionals.

1. Adults with Learning Disabilities: An Emerging Area of Professional Interest and Public Attention

JAMES R. PATTON AND
EDWARD A. POLLOWAY

As the field of learning disabilities (LD) has matured, so also have the individuals who inspired those professionals who selected this field as their career focus. Thus, a field that once had as its primary concerns early identification and elementary curriculum and methods has increasingly changed its focus (by both choice and necessity) to incorporate the challenges faced by adults with learning disabilities.

We can surmise from a review of chronologies of the field (e.g., Hammill, 1989; Wiederholt, 1974) that the students who helped launch the field of learning disabilities are no longer children. The original "Strauss Syndrome" children (Strauss & Lehtinen, 1947) would now be considered middle-aged. Cruickshank's students who were at the elementary level in the early 1950s are today's baby boomers. Students who were beginning school careers when Kirk suggested the term *learning disabilities* in 1963 are now thirtysomething. Those students who entered formal education at the time of the initial implementation of Education for All

Reprinted, with changes, from "Learning disabilities: The challenges of adulthood," by James R. Patton and Edward A. Polloway, *Journal of Learning Disabilities,* Vol. 25, 1992, pp. 410–415, 447.

Handicapped Children Act of 1975 (P.L. 94-142) may be recent high school graduates and are now facing the challenges of community and/or postsecondary environments. Finally, not only are individuals with learning disabilities becoming adults, but the field of learning disabilities has also "grown up"; Levine (1989) referred to this as the "early adulthood of a maturing concept" (p. 1).

Learning Disabilities and Adulthood

As Zigmond (1990) noted, a limited body of literature addressed the needs of adolescents prior to the passage of P.L. 94-142. Even less was written on adults. However, this neglect in the literature did not imply that learning disabilities did not exist at these age ranges but, rather, that these adolescents and adults were not perceived as a "distinct population with distinct characteristics and programming needs" (Zigmond, 1990, p. 1).

Professionals acknowledge that trend as our collective advancement in knowledge tries to keep pace with the needs of these individuals (i.e., as our field matures with the population; Levine, 1989). Have we responded sufficiently? One way, though by no means the only way, to measure the field's response is to consider the level of commitment to adulthood issues in professional journals. In Figures 1.1 and 1.2, a trend of emerging interest is illustrated for the *Journal of Learning Disabilities* (JLD) and *Learning Disability Quarterly* (LDQ), two journals that have been published over a time frame sufficient to illustrate a trend.

What implications can be drawn from the data in these figures? Clearly, the focus on adults in the literature has increased over the 13 years represented therein. Although the relationship has not been a linear one, there are several noteworthy illustrations of the increased commitment in these two journals (for example, the significant attention given in LDQ in 1990 [28%] and the relatively stable attention in JLD over the period 1987 to 1990 [8% to 13%]).

The data in Figures 1.1 and 1.2 provide a superficial, quantitative view of the attention given to learning disabilities in adulthood. Perhaps the qualitative nature of this literature base is more significant. As human service professionals began to explore learning problems in adulthood, their initial focus was frequently on revisiting childhood problems. Consequently, the knowledge base regarding learning disabilities in adults tilted primarily toward research and case histories from follow-up studies of children variously labeled as learning disabled, hyperactive, and reading disabled, or as having minimal brain dysfunction. Certainly that research offered some insight into the problems of specific groups of

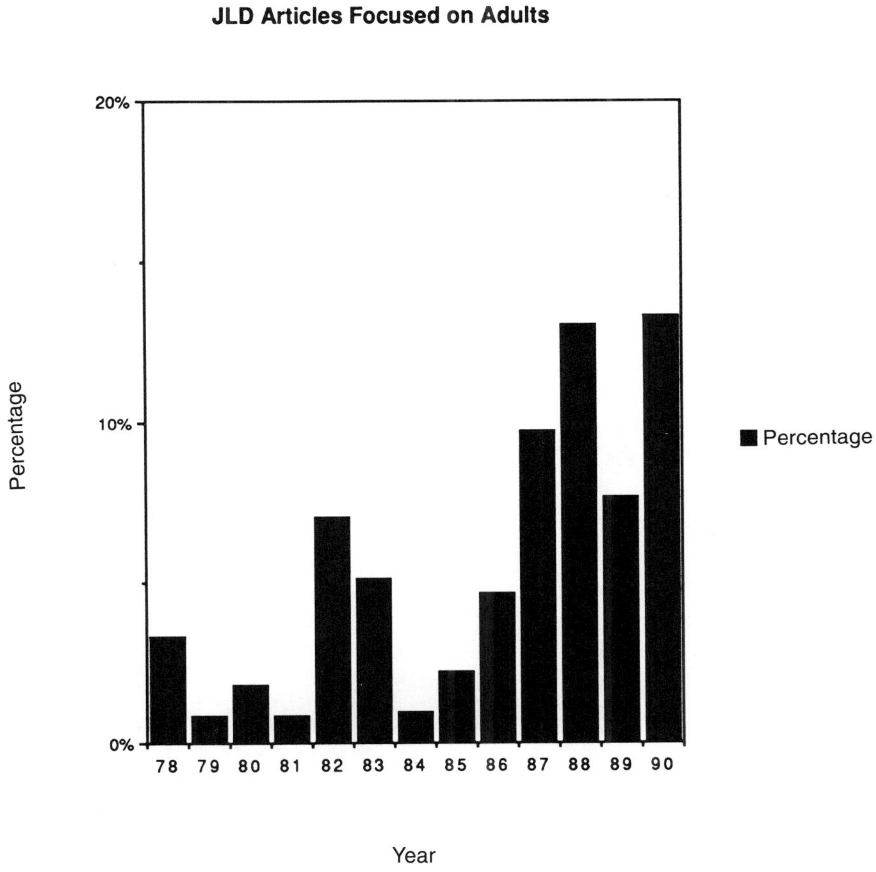

Figure 1.1 *Journal of Learning Disabilities* articles focused on adults.

adults with learning disabilities (Patton & Polloway, 1982). However, although the follow-up studies were initially successful in shifting attention to adults, such an approach often inadvertently resulted in a comparison of the adult with his or her own childhood—that is, a review of common characteristics and specific behaviors (e.g., impulsivity, hyperactivity) that may have been exhibited years earlier, followed by an assessment of whether those problems persisted into adulthood (Polloway, Smith, & Patton, 1984).

Although the nature of the problems that students with learning disabilities face in their youth may continue when they reach adulthood, the nature of the demands placed upon these individuals clearly changes with age. An overfocus on childhood is likely to be narrow in scope, encourage a return to childhood disability models that no longer serve

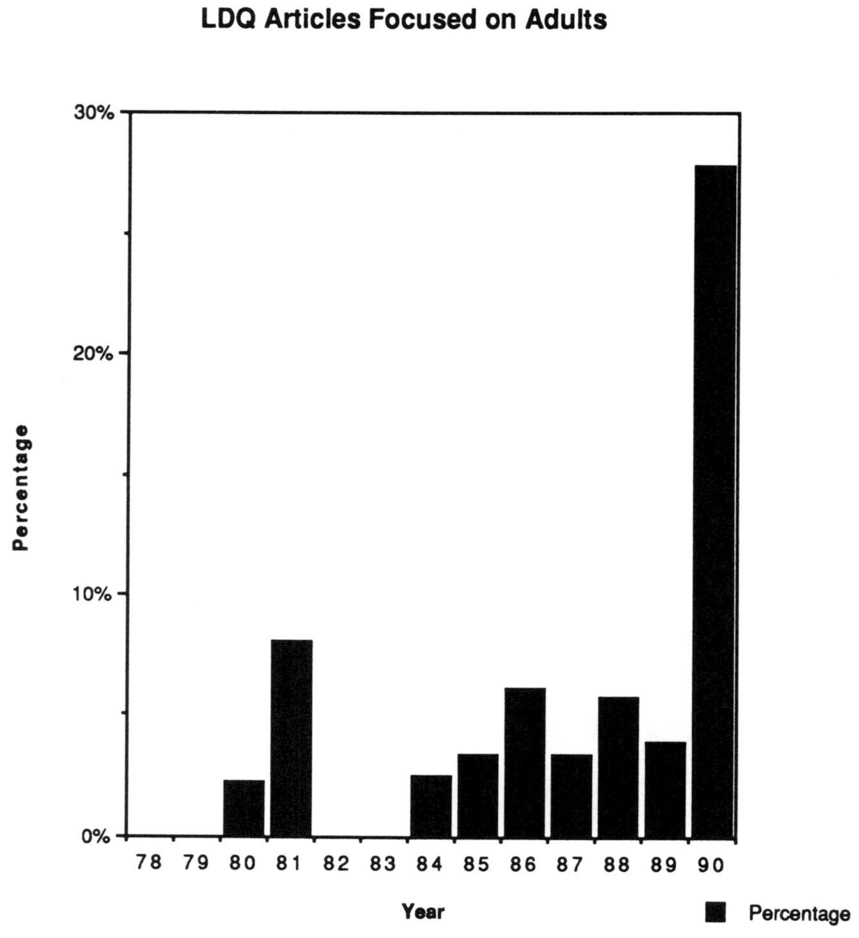

Figure 1.2 *Learning Disability Quarterly* articles focused on adults.

useful purposes, and possibly lead to or ignore concomitant problems of adulthood (Polloway et al., 1984). It also can result in professionals overlooking the essential fact that "learning disabilities are expressed differently in different developmental periods" (Keogh, Major-Kingsley, Omori-Gordon, & Reid, 1982, p. 69). In short, adults with learning problems should not be viewed simply as "children with LD grown up."

Adulthood is a time when most persons strive to achieve personal, social, and occupational competence. For adults with LD, as for any of us, these general objectives may be difficult to obtain. In a simplified sense, we adjust to adult life in one of three ways: (a) by achieving a stable, successful life-style, (b) by experiencing significant problems but dealing with them in a covert fashion, or (c) by encountering major difficulties with overt negative ramifications (Patton & Polloway, 1982). Many individuals who were identified as learning disabled in their youth adjust quite well to the demands and complexities of adulthood; these individuals may provide a guide for us in our efforts (Gerber & Ginsberg, 1990; Gerber, Ginsberg, & Reiff, see Chapter 9 of this book). Nevertheless, there are numerous persons, particularly those with more severe problems, for whom adulthood poses many problems and for whom successful adjustment can remain quite elusive. To better understand both individuals who are successful and those who may struggle, it is useful to consider an adult development perspective.

Adult Development Models

A negative myth that has molded the conception of adulthood for many generations of Americans is that to be an adult is to be a finished product (see Note). Children and adolescents grow up thinking that when they are "grown up" they will have finished the developmental period of their lives and will be prepared for anything they might face in life. From such a view, adults are not expected to grow, develop, or change; adults only age. This thinking results in adulthood being viewed as a single-lane drive down a long hill (Smith, 1991).

During the 1980s, developmental psychology textbooks changed from reflecting the above attitude to a life-span approach, subsequently including topics on adult life. There are several reasons for the increasing recognition of adult development. Certainly the dramatic lengthening of life that has occurred in the United States and elsewhere during this century has had a significant effect. During the late nineteenth century and early twentieth century, when psychology was being formulated as a science and personality theories were first being constructed, the average life span in Europe and the United States was significantly shorter than it is today. When the average life span fell somewhere between four and five decades, there was much less concern about phases or stages of adult life. Surviving childhood was an accomplishment and adults were seen as the fortunate products of that survival. Indeed, when Freud was doing his pioneering work on personality formation, even adolescence had not clearly been defined as a unique or valid period of development (Smith, 1991).

The changing demographic age distribution created by the "baby boom" cohort and their parents has also surely been important in the change in developmental thought in recent years. It has created a "market" for adult development literature and adult development services. Longer lives, better health, early retirement, and greater affluence have all certainly contributed to an environment that makes adult life more interesting to more people. These factors have also created a need for more insight into the changes and challenges that may characterize the respective stages of adult life.

One of the most common ways of viewing adult life has been through stage theories. It was with stage models that Freud and other pioneers of developmental psychology attempted to understand the anatomy of the personality. This approach has continued to be employed as greater attention is paid to the full life span. Some of the most notable stage theorists who address adult development include Erikson, Havighurst, Levinson, and Gould. For a complete presentation of their research, readers are encouraged to obtain the original works: Erikson (1950, 1968), Havighurst (1972), Levinson (1978), and Gould (1978). For more information about how these specific stage theories relate to learning disabilities in adulthood, readers are referred to Bassett, Polloway, and Patton (1993).

Applying an Adult Development Model

Polloway and colleagues (1984) posited that a life-span developmental view provides the foundation for an understanding of the adjustment challenges of adults with learning disabilities. For our purposes, it is sufficient to note at this time two overriding concepts that assist in applying such a model: the basic assumptions of life-span development and the major mediating variables that influence development.

Baltes, Reese, and Lipsitt (1980) identified four major assumptions about life-span developmental psychology. First, development is seen as a lifelong process, actively ongoing from birth to death. Second, development is seen as the expression of biological and socialization processes that are dependent on age and are modified by the influences of historical factors, such as cohort changes between generations (e.g., the changes noted in the baby boomer cohort in the 1960s).

Third, development is pluralistic and, therefore, adulthood is viewed as multidirectional (rather than as unidirectional, as seen in models of child development). Constancy of change is thus a basic element. Specific periods of life can be perceived through such questions as, What changes are occurring? When are they occurring? Why are they occurring? and How are they occurring? Based on a life-span model, adult development becomes a process of increments and decrements over time and reflects an individual's response to various influences during life, such as biological and psychological variables tied to chronological age, historical events (e.g., economic depression, war), and specific, nonnormative life events, such as divorce, promotion, and loss of job.

The fourth assumption is that a life-span developmental view offers an integrative framework by providing a basis for combining knowledge derived from various developmental periods and promoting a perspective on how life tasks and challenges should be considered within life-span contexts. Considering these four assumptions, the argument can be forwarded that a life-span model provides an important perspective for viewing the problems faced by adults with LD while focusing attention on specific characteristics that have merit for understanding life adjustment.

The second concept that facilitates the application of a life-span model is that of *mediating variables*. Polloway et al. (1984), building on the concept of resources to facilitate adaptation to life events advanced by Lieberman (1975), Hultsch and Deutsch (1981), and Vaillant (1977), stressed the role that such variables may play. The four variables they identified included biological and intellectual variables (e.g., physical health, energy, attention, memory), personal and social variables (e.g., social relationships, support systems), past experience and anticipatory socialization (i.e., the role of past experiences as a basis for responding to current tasks—specifically, the influence of previous successes or failures), and locus of control (i.e., perception of the degree of control one has over life events). Each of these broad areas has implications for a variety of challenges (e.g., vocational, financial, personal, social) that are faced during adulthood.

Adjustment Within Adult Contexts

An inspection of the growing number of adult outcome studies conducted with students who have learning disabilities results in an alarming picture. The scenario for many young adults is characterized by unemployment and/or underemployment, low pay, part-time work, frequent job changes, nonengagement with the community, limitations in independent functioning, and limited social lives. Although other, more personal outcomes (i.e., happiness, self-esteem, sense of achievement) have not been adequately studied, it is likely that many individuals with learning disabilities may not fare well in these areas, either.

Cronin, Patton, and Polloway (1991) concluded that many individuals who were formerly in special education programs were not prepared adequately for the multidimensional demands of adulthood. They suggested that the major life demands of adulthood can be categorized into six domains: employment–education, home and family, leisure pursuits, community involvement, emotional and physical health, and personal responsibility and relationships. Although arbitrary, these domains provide a framework for examining the successful adjustment of young adults with learning disabilities as well as a "top-down" strategy for curriculum development.

Clearly, adjustment problems in any of the six areas can have a significant impact on both the choices one makes in life and how successful one is within a chosen path. Within a life-span perspective, the relative importance of selected domains will change throughout an individual's life, while the absolute importance of all domains remains constant.

For most of us to achieve a positive quality of life, appropriate supports must be available to enhance the likelihood of successfully dealing with the demands of adult life. We use the word *supports* because it is a broader term than *services* and has particular relevance for adulthood. The concept moves beyond the idea of special services located within the school context and includes, most importantly, personal supports within the individuals themselves and natural supports from the environment (e.g., family, friends, neighbors). Thus, although agency services are important, they may not necessarily prove to be the key variables in determining success for an individual in an adult-relevant context. To highlight some concerns regarding supports and services, we will briefly address two topics: transition planning and adult service delivery.

Transition Planning

The literature in special education has become replete with references to transitional programming, especially for adolescents with disabilities. With the passage of Individuals with Disabilities Education Act of 1990 (IDEA; P.L. 101-476), transition plans now must be included within IEPs by no later than age 16 and on an annual basis thereafter. Although we chose not to fully review the literature here, the reader is referred to Clark and Kolstoe (1990), Ludlow, Luckasson, and Turnbull (1988), Clark and Knowlton (1987), and Trapani (1990) for more detailed discussions.

We chose to focus on the overriding principle of transition from a relevant educational perspective. To facilitate adult adjustment, curriculum orientation at the secondary level (as well as at the earlier levels) must be future-focused. That is, as children get older, curriculum should shift to a more preventative and less *remedial* approach. To be truly preventative, curriculum design at the high school and postsecondary levels for students with learning disabilities should reflect considerations *down* from the goal of successful adjustment, rather than simply *up*, such as from an elementary curriculum focused primarily on the remediation of basic skills. An example of this orientation was described by Cronin and

Gerber (1982), who based their efforts on the model developed by Knowles (1978) illustrating how adult concerns could be integrated into curricular design for secondary students. This concept has been further developed within Polloway, Patton, Epstein, and Smith's (1989) differentiated curriculum model and within the adult outcomes orientation increasingly advocated by special educators (e.g., Cronin & Patton, 1993; Cronin et al., 1991; Edgar, 1990; Patton, Cronin, Polloway, Robinson, & Hutchison, 1989; Wiederholt & Wolffe, 1990), particularly for those students who are not planning to enroll in higher education.

Adult Service Delivery

Until relatively recently, most services afforded to persons with learning disabilities terminated when they exited from high school. With the increasing acknowledgment of the adult-relevant needs of individuals with disabilities, however, a broader range of services has become a reality. As a consequence, postsecondary education and vocational and social support systems are now viable options.

If adults with disabilities desire to further their education, they may choose from a number of options: adult education classes, 2- and 4-year colleges, trade schools, and private agencies. Successful functioning in any of these settings depends on a number of learning-related variables that may prove particularly problematic for some individuals. The extent of efforts to address some of these potential problems varies greatly across settings. Many institutions of higher education have sought to address the needs of college students identified as learning disabled (Blalock & Dixon, 1982; Brinckerhoff, Shaw, & McGuire, see Chapter 6 of this book).

Adults with learning disabilities now can access a range of vocational training opportunities. They are eligible and can qualify for both federal and state vocational rehabilitation services (Dowdy, Smith, & Nowell, see Chapter 5 of this book; Gerber, 1981). There is a continuing need for increased publicity to make sure that persons are aware that vocational services are available (Fafard & Haubrich, 1981). It is interesting to note, however, that in spite of an increased school and rehabilitation services commitment, many adults with LD find jobs via their natural support network (i.e., family and friends) rather than through agencies or teachers.

For social support, adults with disabilities have available to them the same services that all citizens have, such as mental health agencies and private psychiatric/psychological/counseling agencies. Furthermore, self-help groups for people with learning disabilities have been established throughout the nation. It is particularly significant that adults with learning disabilities have consistently rated other persons who are disabled as being most helpful to them. The ability to draw on such resources may well be fundamentally related to the ability to analyze life problems and generate possible solutions (noted earlier as a key concern). This is underscored by Gerber and Ginsberg's (1990) finding that successful adults with LD both had support available and accepted it. It further emphasizes that natural supports, as opposed to governmental services, are key contributors to quality of life.

This brief discussion on service delivery for adolescents and adults can be summarized as a search for the appropriate matching of needs with supports. The incredible heterogeneity of this population results in the need for an equally broad spectrum of available supports and services. By addressing adult characteristics within the context of a model of needed supports, we seek to dispel the deficit model, with its overemphasis on irrelevant (i.e., child-oriented) characteristics, and substitute instead an orientation that stresses adult-referenced needs tied to effective systems of support.

The chapters in this book add significantly to the existing literature base on adults with learning disabilities, providing a measure of the state of practice in the early 1990s and an index for what must still be done. The book also emphatically makes the point that continued research, program development, and support must be directed toward this population if we are to maximize the quality of these individuals' lives.

Note

The authors acknowledge the assistance provided by their colleague, J. David Smith, relative to many of the concepts in the life-span developmental model that are presented herein.

2. *Adult Development Theories: An Overview and Reflection on Their Relevance for Learning Disabilities*

J. DAVID SMITH

There is a limiting concept in our society that has shaped the views of many generations on the subject of adulthood. This concept has encouraged us to believe that to be an adult is to be a finished product. Many children and adolescents have been taught that "growing up" means completing their developmental years. They have also been led to believe that being an adult means having to be prepared for anything that they might face in life. In the view of many people, adults are not expected to grow, develop, or change; they only age. From this perspective, adulthood really does mean being "over the hill."

In recent years, however, developmental psychologists have evolved from perpetuating a negative attitude on adulthood toward a new view of human development. Many now take a "life span" approach to development and often include in their textbooks several chapters on adult life. There are several reasons for the increasing recognition of adult development. The dramatic lengthening of life that has occurred in the United States and elsewhere during this century has certainly made a difference. This is in sharp contrast to the late 19th and early 20th centuries, when the average life span in Europe and the United States fell to somewhere between 4 and 5 decades, and there was much less concern about phases or stages of adult life. During that period, surviving childhood was viewed as an accomplishment and adults were seen as the fortunate products of this survival. Indeed, during the late 19th and early 20th centuries, when Freud was doing his pioneering work on personality formation (Freud, 1914), even adolescence had not yet been defined as a unique and valid period of development.

The changing demographic age distribution created by the "baby boom" generation and their parents has also been instrumental in the change in developmental thought because it has created a market for adult development services and literature. Longer lives, better health, early retirement, and greater affluence all have certainly contributed to an environment that makes the study of adult life more interesting than ever before. The same factors have also created a compelling need for more insight into the changes and challenges that characterize each period of adult life.

The importance of adult issues for those with learning disabilities is being recognized more frequently by professionals in the field. The notion that a learning disability has lifelong implications for an individual is receiving increased emphasis and attention. In 1985, the National Joint Committee on Learning Disabilities (NJCLD) developed a position paper on adults with learning disabilities that reflected a concern for lifelong needs.

> Learning disabilities are both persistent and pervasive throughout an individual's life. The manifestation of the learning disability can be expected to change throughout the life span of the individual. . . . Adults with learning disabilities may experience personal, social, and emotional difficulties that may affect their adaptation to life tasks. (NJCLD, 1994, p. 28)

A framework based on adult development models rather than on child-based models is warranted to better understand the adult needs of those with learning disabilities. An attitude that promotes adulthood as a time of continued development and learning must be applied to those who are learning disabled as well as to those who are not. With such a perspective, it will be possible to study and improve the quality of life of those adults who continue to struggle with their disabilities.

Professionals commonly view adult life through stage theories. It was through stage models that Freud (1949) and other pioneers of developmental psychology attempted to understand the structure and function of the human personality. This approach has continued to be employed as greater attention is paid to the concept of the full life span. The many different stage theories that have been applied to adult life differ greatly in constructs and emphasis. However, most of these theories assume the following:

1. Everyone passes through life stages in basically the same manner; there is a fundamental universality to the human development experience;
2. Everyone passes through the life stages in the same order; there is a basic sequentiality to the human experience;
3. There are adaptive (positive) ways and maladaptive (negative) ways of going through the sequence of stages.

These basic assumptions are included in a discussion of stage theories by Lillian Troll (1982). In her book *Continuations: Adult Development and Aging,* Troll has also identified two additional assumptions that she believes characterize stage theories. The first assumption states that these theories assume a predetermined end point to development; that is, the life sequence leads toward a goal. Troll's second assumption states that the adaptive or positive ways of going through the life stages, as identified by various theorists, tend to be in tune with middle-class values contemporary with the formulation of a particular theory.

The focus of this chapter is to briefly examine selected stage theories of adult development that have implications for understanding adults with learning disabilities. Although the theory of Erik Erikson will receive particular attention, other theories will be discussed in relation to the assumptions outlined by Troll.

Stage Theory of Erik Erikson

Erik Erikson was the first personality theorist to systematically extend the concepts of development into adult life. Although he based his theory on Freudian principles, he felt that the psychosocial interactions at each stage were more important than psychosexual development as described by Freud. This is illustrated in Erikson's book *Childhood and Society* (1950), where he introduced his theory of eight life stages. Each stage involves tension between possibilities, a psychosocial crisis that must be resolved before further development may proceed. Erikson's eight developmental stages, along with the crisis (challenge) associated with each stage, are listed in Table 2.1. Although Erikson originally conceptualized each stage as being closely related to a specific age period, he has subsequently explained, with the help of Joan Erikson (Erikson & Erikson, 1986), that the stages are not bound to age but are really the threads that form the woven fabric of life. For example, basic trust was originally presented as strictly an infantile stage; later, however, the Eriksons reconceptualized

TABLE 2.1
Erikson's (1950) Stages of the Life Cycle

Stage	Challenge	Ideal result
Infancy	Trust	Hope
Early childhood	Autonomy	Will
Preschool	Initiative	Purpose
School age	Industry	Competence
Adolescence	Identity	Fidelity
Young adulthood	Intimacy	Love
Maturing adult	Generativity	Care
Older adult	Integrity	Wisdom

basic trust as a lifelong concern that must usually be revisited at many junctures in the life span.

Although all of Erikson's stages have been reconceptualized as important forces throughout the life span, four of these stages have been particularly helpful to adult developmentalists in viewing the unique aspects of psychological development during the adult years of life. These four stages (or factors) are *identity, intimacy, generativity,* and *integrity.* A brief discussion of each of the four stages is appropriate, given their continuing importance in the adult development field.

Identity

According to Erikson, adult identity is quite different from the childhood identifiers we often equate with who we are. A newborn is usually given a name out of the love, hopes, and/or affiliations of his or her parents. In a similar way, a child's neighborhood, school, and church are determined for him or her. The key aspect of establishing an adult identity is choice. An adult identity consists of the goals, values, manners, and relationships that are chosen as part of the way that a person wishes to be defined. Although Erikson originally conceptualized the quest for identity as an adolescent process, he subsequently observed that the search for an adult identity may indeed last a long time. Additionally, he has commented that, for the average middle-class American, the process may last well into one's 30s. Indeed, an adult's identity must be refined and redefined repeatedly throughout the adult years.

Marcia (1967) analyzed Erikson's theory of identity and compared it with his own observations. In doing so he concluded that there are four ways in which people contend with the challenges of developing an adult identity. Each of these, according to Marcia, involves ways of encountering or avoiding two central issues of identity formation: *crisis* and *commitment.* Crisis is the perceived need for developing one's own identity, and the discomfort of knowing that independent choices need to be made. Commitment is the risky effort of actually making a personal investment in these choices—it is the dynamic aspect of identity formation. Marcia described the four ways that crisis and commitment may be addressed, or avoided, as "identity statuses," which are listed in Table 2.2.

In Status 1, *identity diffusion,* the person appears to have no sense of crisis or urgency about identity and no action is usually being taken in making choices toward an adult identity. Little interest is shown in choices concerning vocational direction or other adult goals. In Status 2, *identity foreclosure,* a commitment to identity has been made, but not on the basis of a personal exploration or perceived need to do so. No crisis has occurred, but a commitment has been made to the values of another party. Often this involves commitment to parental values that have been handed down in an authoritarian fashion. In Status 3, *identity moratorium,* the person experiences a sense of crisis about establishing an identity, but has made a decision to continue exploring alternatives before a commitment can be made. Status 4, *identity achievement,* is arrived at through experiencing the uncertainty and uneasiness of an identity crisis and meeting this challenge through making commitments to chosen goals, values, and identifications (Marcia, 1967).

Although identity development is a lifelong process, it may certainly be an important focus during adolescence and young adulthood. During this period physical, emotional, intellectual, and social development may cause a particularly emphatic push toward making critical vocational and personal choices. Conversely, this surge of development may lead to a sense of being overwhelmed, and a young person may then feel com-

TABLE 2.2
Identity Statuses Proposed by Marcia (1967)

Status 1: Identity Diffusion
No crisis of choice has been experienced and no commitments have been made.

Status 2: Identity Foreclosure
No crisis has been experienced, but the person has come to commitments, usually forced on him or her by parents or some other authority figure.

Status 3: Identity Moratorium
Considerable crisis is being experienced, but no commitments are yet made.

Status 4: Identity Achievement
Numerous crises have been experienced and resolved, and relatively permanent commitments have been made.

pelled to foreclose or declare a moratorium on making choices, or give in to a sense of diffusion regarding decision making. An individual's decisions during this period, however, do not necessarily last a lifetime. Indeed, a person who achieves an identity during young adulthood will need to remain open to change and adaptation across a life span. He or she will have to find ways of adapting to changes in relationships, vocation, social environment, and self. Most people seem to find that the quest for an identity is a lifelong process rather than a stage encountered once and then left behind.

Intimacy

Although the word *intimacy* is often associated with romance and sexuality, Erikson's conceptualization of this term as a stage of adult development goes beyond these typical associations. For Erikson, intimacy is the willingness, indeed the eagerness, to fuse one's identity with the identity of another. From this perspective, intimacy is the capacity to commit to affiliations and partnerships, and the ability to develop the strength to abide by these commitments despite the fact that they require sacrifices and compromises (Erikson, 1950). Thus, although heterosexual courtship and marriage may epitomize intimacy for many people, there appear to be other relationships that enable people to achieve intimacy. Erikson described the opposite of intimacy as *distantiation,* which he defined as the isolation of oneself from others. Distantiation can occur physically, emotionally, or socially.

Don Hamachek (1990) defined the characteristics he observed in people who have achieved the capacity for intimacy in their adult lives. These characteristics include (a) the willingness and ability to trust others and themselves in the relationships they form, (b) tolerance and acceptance of the differences perceived in other people, (c) the ability to form close emotional bonds without fearing the loss of one's own identity, and (d) the ability and willingness to commit to relationships that involve sacrifice and compromise.

Generativity

Unlike identity and intimacy, *generativity* is a term unfamiliar to most people and, therefore, is a bit more difficult to comprehend as a developmental period. Erikson's own words may be helpful in this regard:

> Mature man needs to be needed . . . Generativity, then, is primarily the concern in establishing and guiding the next generation, although there are individuals who, through misfortune or because of special and genuine

> gifts in other directions, do not apply this drive to their own offspring. And indeed, the concept of generativity is meant to include such more popular synonyms as productivity and creativity. . . . (Erikson, 1950, pp. 266–267)

Although in his earlier work Erikson emphasized the parental role as a model of generativity, it is important to note that the concept has been increasingly broadened to encompass the many ways that adults care about people, institutions, traditions, their work, and other facets of the culture in which they live. It is through this type of caring that adults are able to share their creativity and productivity with others.

John Kotre (1984), in *Outliving the Self: Generativity and the Interpretation of Lives,* contended that the full spectrum of generativity can be understood by recognizing four types. The first is biological generativity, which he described as the "begetting, bearing, and nursing of children" (p. 11). Although this is the most fundamental type of generativity, Kotre believes that it is imperative that we understand the other outlets for generativity that are open to people.

Distinct from biological generativity is parental generativity. This is expressed in "feeding, clothing, sheltering, loving, and disciplining offspring, and initiating them into the family's traditions" (Kotre, 1984, p. 11). Within the context of Erikson's theory, these are the family activities that preserve its continuity and produce trust, autonomy, and initiative in children.

The third type of generativity, according to Kotre, is technical generativity. This is expressed through the caring instruction that adults give to those who are less skilled or knowledgeable in certain areas of life than themselves. In describing the adult who is generative in this sense, Kotre stated, "The skills they teach are myriad: how to read, how to fish, how to fight, how to steal, how to program a computer, how to perform a healing ritual, how to write a legal brief, and so on" (1984, p. 13). However, technical generativity does not consist just of teaching isolated skills. It also involves the transmission of culture; the teacher is passing along the "stuff" of the culture.

When teaching goes beyond the technical aspects of a culture, however, it passes into the fourth form of generativity, the cultural form. This type of generativity is most directly concerned with ideas. Kotre commented that:

> When a teacher turns from how to do it to what it means, when she speaks of the idea of music or healing or law, when she brings to the fore the symbol system that stood in the background and offers her student the outlines of an identity, she becomes culturally generative. She is no longer a teacher of skills but a mentor, and her apprentice has become a disciple. (1984, p. 14)

Integrity

According to Erikson, the final adult psychosocial crisis that must be resolved is the tension between a personal sense of worth and acceptance in life, which he called *integrity,* and a sense of disappointment and embitterment, which he termed *despair.* In Erikson's own words, integrity is achieved when there is "acceptance of one's one and only life cycle as something that had to be, and that, by necessity, permitted no substitutions" (1963, p. 268). On the other hand, despair is "signified by fear of death . . . (and) expresses the feeling that the time is now short, too short for the attempt to start another life and to try out alternate roads to integrity" (p. 269).

In a list of characteristic behaviors of people who have achieved a sense of integrity, Hamachek included the following traits: (a) many of the positive ego qualities associated with earlier stages, such as trust, autonomy, initiative, industry, and identity; (b) the belief that who they are and what they have become are largely the consequences of their own choices; (c) the acceptance of the idea that this is their one and only life, and that what has happened is largely of their own doing; (d) acceptance of death as an inevitable part of the life cycle; and (e) an approach to the final stage of their lives that has a sense of personal wholeness.

In his original narrative on the life span in *Childhood and Society,* Erikson (1950) beautifully expressed the relationship between the stages of life. He wrote:

> *Webster's Dictionary* is kind enough to help us complete this outline in a circular fashion. Trust (the first of our ego values) is here defined as "the assured reliance on another's integrity," the last of our values. I suspect that Webster had business in mind rather than babies, credit rather than faith. But the formulation stands. And it seems possible to further paraphrase the relation of adult integrity and infantile trust by saying that healthy children will not fear life if their elders have integrity enough not to fear death. (p. 269)

This statement seems to be a clear indication that Erikson's theory does, to a large degree, meet the assumptions about stage theories made by Troll (1982). Here Erikson appears to believe that all people pass through these stages and that there are adaptive and maladaptive ways of encountering each stage. He also seems inclined to see the stages as being sequential, although he does express flexibility in this assumption. He also seems to believe that life is lived toward an end point, the achievement of integrity. Whether he has defined his stages according to middle-class standards is arguable, although again he has shown flexibility in the interpretation of how successful growth through each stage may be achieved.

Seasons of Life

Another influential stage theory is the one developed by Daniel Levinson and his colleagues, which was initially presented in the book *The Seasons of a Man's Life* (Levinson, Darrow, Klein, Levinson, & McKee, 1978). As the title implies, the data on which this theory was based came entirely from the study of adult males. Subsequent research has been conducted with women and the results are expected to be published in the near future in a book to be titled *The Seasons of a Woman's Life.* Levinson's theory, however, has continued to be primarily grounded in the original study of 40 men. These men, in four groups of 10, represented different levels of education and a variety of social and economic backgrounds. Ten of the men were university professors, another 10 were novelists, 10 more were industrial managers, and the final group was composed of production workers. The initial report on this research focused on the early and middle years in the lives of these men, and the theory is still more concerned with those periods rather than later adult life.

Levinson and his collaborators (Levinson et al., 1978) discovered that, regardless of education or background, all of the men went through a similar sequence of social and emotional experiences. These common experiences, or stages, are presented in Table 2.3. In each stage, Levinson found that there were certain routine life tasks that became important to these men. The accomplishment—or lack of accomplishment—of these tasks appeared to be quite important to the life satisfaction of each individual. For example, the tasks during the "novice" phase of early adulthood (which encompasses those stages shown in Table 2.3 for a man's 20s and 30s) include developing a dream of the possibilities for adult life, establishing a mentoring relationship with a supportive and more experienced adult, finding a special mate, and embarking on an occupational pursuit. Levinson found that problems with any of these tasks could lead to difficulty in moving on to subsequent stages of development.

Another important aspect of Levinson's (1978) theory of adult development is his emphasis on transitions between the periods of development themselves. He found that these transition periods tend to last several years and are critical in preparing the individual for the next stage of life. During what he calls "young adult transition," for example, he found that people cling to many of the characteristics of adolescence and childhood while "trying on" the characteristics of adulthood. For a while, an individual's persona contains characteristics of both child and adult identities, but is not fully child nor fully adult. Transitions tend to be dynamic times of great challenges and opportunities. Much of what has been attributed to the "mid-life crisis," according to Levinson, is truly characteristic of the transition in life between early and middle adulthood. At this time one discovers that one is neither precisely young nor

TABLE 2.3
Levinson's (1978) Stages of Adult Development

Transition to Adulthood (Adolescence to Early 20s)
This is a period that encompasses the establishment of psychological distance from the family of origin and the beginning of an independent adult identity.

Entering the Adult World (Early to Late 20s)
This is a period of exploration and tentative commitments to adult occupational, personal, and social roles. It is the period when the overall adult life structure is beginning to be formed.

Settling Down (Early 30s)
This is a period of more serious commitment to occupational and family identifications and responsibilities.

Becoming One's Own Person (Middle to Late 30s)
Period of less need for encouragement and support from a mentor. During this time the independent early adult identity is achieved and solidified.

Transition to Mid-Life (Middle 40s)
A period of transition which brings on an awareness of changes in appearance and physiology.

Middle Adulthood (Late 40s)
A period of a new identity, new challenges, and new opportunities.

middle-aged but somewhere in between. An individual has characteristics of both stages of life, and it takes time to develop a new identity and lifestyle. This period can also, however, be a time of great growth and need not necessarily be the stereotypic "crisis" of middle age.

Levinson's theory of adult development also meets the assumptions of Troll (1982) concerning stage theories. His findings do indicate that all people pass through the same stages, and that they may do so in either adaptive or maladaptive ways. He also seemed to believe that the stages of life are sequential, and must be experienced in a certain order if the individual is to live in the most personally satisfying manner. Finally, Levinson felt that the individual does develop by means of a process that culminates in greater *individuation.* Levinson defined this term as the process of a person becoming more aware and expressive of his or her individual and unique character as the developmental journey continues.

Adaptation to Life

A third theorist who engaged in the exploration of adult development theories is George Vaillant. Vaillant (1977) actually constructed his theory around that of Erik Erikson. Although Vaillant endorsed Erikson's stages of development and the sequence of those stages, he placed more emphasis on the idea that not every individual moves as far or as fast as others along this continuum of stages. Vaillant was particularly interested in how people cope with anxiety along this path of development, and how anxiety may either be dealt with effectively or become a barrier for further growth. Vaillant believed that the means one uses for dealing with anxiety are, in a sense, always attempts at "health." Some strategies, however, are more effective than others. Vaillant referred to those methods as *adaptive mechanisms.* The manner in which he described these mechanisms is very reminiscent of Freud's concept of defense mechanisms (Freud, 1949), but Vaillant preferred to see them as functional attempts at adaptation rather than merely defensive efforts. The four levels of adaptive mechanisms that Vaillant described are *psychotic, immature, neurotic,* and *mature.*

According to Vaillant (1977), psychotic mechanisms are very low-level attempts at dealing with anxiety. They are frequent and normal in children, but when they are used excessively by adults, this behavior may be labelled psychotic. At various times, all of us use mechanisms at all of the levels, even the psychotic level. Denial, for example, is a psychotic mechanism but it may be considered a normal reaction to extreme anxiety (such as the anxiety experienced after the death of a loved one).

Immature mechanisms are most frequently used by adolescents. When used excessively by an adult, however, they may cause the individual to be viewed by others as very disordered. Passive aggression and escape into fantasy are examples of these mechanisms.

Neurotic mechanisms are common in all of us. In stressful situations, all adults may use these mechanisms. Some examples include the repression of unpleasant information and the displacement of feelings.

Mature mechanisms are the most effective attempts an individual makes at dealing with anxiety. By using these mechanisms, adults are most likely to produce effective and relatively lasting outcomes. Examples of mature mechanisms for dealing with anxiety are humor and altruistic service on behalf of others.

Vaillant has found that the people who are most likely to achieve Erikson's generativity stage are those who primarily use mature mechanisms. Those who continue to use predominantly immature mechanisms and few mature mechanisms as they progress through their adult years are the least likely to successfully achieve an identity or to form truly intimate relationships. In his book *Adaptation to Life,* Vaillant (1977) reported on his longitudinal study of the adaptive mechanisms used by a sample of men over a 25-year period. He found that those men who were still using predominantly immature mechanisms in mid-life were at highest risk both for relationship difficulties and vocational problems. He referred to this group as the "perpetual boys." The men who used mature mechanisms more frequently were found to be happier in their relationships and more productive in their work at mid-life. Vaillant described them as the "generative men."

In most people's lives, according to Vaillant (1977), there is a process of gradually adding more types of mature mechanisms in the course of development, and an increase in the frequency of use of those mechanisms. Vaillant believed that there is a corresponding inclination to use immature mechanisms less frequently as we live longer. He posited that, in this sense, there is a tendency for life to be therapeutic; one tends to get better at it the more one does it. He argued, however, that individuals vary in the degree to which they will mature, and that those who mature the least are at greatest risk for unhappiness in their personal and professional lives.

Vaillant's (1977) theory is developmental. He was obviously concerned about the growth of people to higher levels of maturity, and he did accept Erikson's stages and the idea that they are sequential. He emphasized most clearly, however, that it is the effect of adaptive or less adaptive mechanisms for dealing with the "slings and arrows" of life that influences how far a person may progress along this developmental continuum. Additionally, Vaillant's theory meets Troll's assumptions for a stage theory of adult development, in that it views the achievement of maturity and the resulting happiness that this may bring through meaningful relationships and satisfying work as the ultimate goal in dealing with the anxieties of living.

Implications for Adults with LD

The assumption that Troll (1982) delineated concerning the reflection of middle-class values in adult development theories indeed seems to be valid for the theories of both Levinson (Levinson et al., 1978) and Vaillant (1977). Although some might argue that Erickson's stages are universal, an equally convincing position can be developed for the culturally bound definitions that he gives to identity, intimacy, generativity, and integrity. Yet this question of the grounding of adult development in cultural values should be an important reminder to us that adults with learning disabilities are actually challenged and frustrated by their difficulties in achieving valued cultural standards of literacy, job performance, social skills, and communication skills. The fact that adults with LD have difficulty achieving valued adult developmental milestones may lead others to view adults with LD, or adults with LD to view themselves, as somehow being less "valuable." The risk of finding themselves in this socially and culturally devalued position may be the very core of the issue of learning disabilities in adulthood. Thus, it may be of great importance that we professionals examine theories of adult development most carefully to learn what values and expectations they reflect about the course of what the literature defines as normal adulthood. Such examination may provide insights concerning how people come to be perceived as disabled, and may suggest ways for us as professionals to help adults with LD understand this process. Most important, it may enable professionals to assist people with LD in making choices about what is truly valuable for them and to what ends they wish to work in making changes in their lives.

3. Transition of Youth with Learning Disabilities to Early Adulthood

GINGER BLALOCK

Youth with learning disabilities face the same challenges as their nondisabled peers in their movement toward adult life activities. These hurdles are physical and psychological "growing pains" that include psychological and physical separation from parents, economic struggles, serious decision making about the future, evolution of a solid self-identity, and establishment of lasting relationships. High school students without disabilities generally deal with those challenges with varying but adequate degrees of success; family and friends assume that these students will triumph and move forward, and this (typically unspoken) expectation seems to play an important role in spurring on the general adolescent population. The challenges are cultural rites of passage that everyone is expected to meet and surpass.

In contrast, the presence of learning disabilities (LD) may hinder significant others in the student's life from solidly communicating those same expectations of ultimate success and, as a result, may impede the individual's actual triumphs. Numerous studies have documented the difficulties encountered by students with LD in making the transition from school to adulthood (e.g., deBettencourt, Zigmond, & Thornton, 1989; Sitlington & Frank, 1990; SRI International, 1992; White, Chapter 4 of this book; Zigmond & Thornton, 1985). Students with LD comprise 50.1% of all those served by federal special education funds and 13.6% of students served by federal general education funds (U.S. Department of Education, 1991). They can be found in a variety of environments (see Table 3.1), including outside school, as the dropout rates in Table 3.2 suggest. According to SRI International's (1992) National Longitudinal Transition Study, only about 1% of youth with LD pursue higher education, a much lower figure than that suggested by previous studies (Rogan & Hartman, 1990; Sitlington, Frank, & Cooper, 1989).

Professionals in the fields of special education and rehabilitation have now come to realize that a successful passage into adulthood must be by design, not by accident. Struggles by students and their families to move toward adult adjustment have generated a wealth of isolated, fragmented supports (i.e., services, programs, people) over the past 2 decades that cemented parts of the post-school puzzle (e.g., work–study, prevocational programs, survival skills curricula). Only recently, however, have the entire programs of many students been organized with a future

TABLE 3.1
Students with LD and Their Educational Environments, 1988–1989

Environment	Students (%)
General classroom	19.6
Resource room	57.9
Separate class	20.9
Separate school	1.3
Residential facility	0.1
Homebound/hospital	0.1

Note. Source for data: U.S. Department of Education (1991), p. 27.

TABLE 3.2
Basis of Exit for Students with LD, 1988–1989

	Number	Percentage
Diploma	66,156	50.1
Certificate	9,149	6.9
Maximum age	1,683	1.3
Drop out	35,269	26.7
Status unknown	19,790	15.0
TOTAL	132,047	100.0

Note. Source for data: U.S. Department of Education (1991), p. 31.

focus long before graduation, through individualized transition planning—a concerted, integrated effort that can support the student in reaching her or his work, community, school, and personal goals. The term *transition* as used in special education and rehabilitation has come to mean an outcome-oriented process that helps youth with disabilities move successfully to adult life activities. Everson, Moon, Barcus, and Morton (1987) reminded us that

> Transition is an interagency planning and implementation process which takes place at the local level and results in new and different outcomes for youth with disabilities. Effective transition planning and implementation is more than the development of ITPs; it is also an evaluation of local programs and services and a coordinated and cooperative effort by all involved agencies to bring about systems change. (p. 214)

The long-range failures of many students with LD cited in follow-up studies have led professionals and parents to begin to address the full composition of the process necessary to support those youth. When the Education for All Handicapped Children Act of 1975 (P.L. 94-142) was reauthorized and renamed the Individuals with Disabilities Education Act (IDEA; P.L. 101-476) in 1990, new mandates were included to address the future life needs of youth with disabilities in a comprehensive fashion. The IDEA requires that individualized transition planning occurs

- for *all* students served in special education (not just those with severe disabilities)
- no later than age 16, and earlier for some students (i.e., in more complex situations)
- in a way that involves parents, the student, and all pertinent parties (including postsecondary institutions and adult agencies).

IDEA places the major responsibility for transition on the public schools, as it should be, because preparation for transition must begin much earlier than a student's senior year in high school. Individualized Transition Plan (ITP) teams may determine that a student does not need specialized transition services and simply focus on the Individualized Education Program (IEP), but they must document that they have considered her or his need for transition support. The federal law defines *transition services* as follows:

> Transition services means a coordinated set of activities for a student, designed within an outcome oriented process, which promotes movement from school to postschool activities . . . (and which) shall be based upon the individual student's needs taking into account the student's prefer-

> ences and interest and shall include instruction, community experiences, development of employment and other postschool adult living objectives, and when appropriate acquisition of daily living skills and functional vocational evaluation. [Section 602(a), 20 U.S.C. 1401(a)(19)]

The ITP, typically found as an attachment to or a part of the IEP, must project vocational, educational, and other life goals in order to develop and monitor such an integrated service program for each special education student, if appropriate. These goals are generated by the student and parent(s) foremost, with assistance from teachers and others who serve or will serve the student Outcomes toward which the ITP aims may include any or all adult life activities: postsecondary education, vocational training, integrated employment, continuing adult education, adult services, independent living, or community participation. Therefore, IDEA now forces school systems to reach out and collaborate with adult service providers. Cobb and Hasazi (1987) stressed that students with mild disabilities need curricula to include employment placement or postsecondary education placement outcomes as well as academic achievement outcomes. In fact, adult level services for persons with LD, *if available at all,* have emphasized the postsecondary education and work outcomes. Unfortunately, our systems have virtually ignored the independent living and community participation components of life, which remain problematic for many individuals with more severe levels of LD.

The federal government has had other significant influences in addition to mandated transition planning within IDEA. Federally funded demonstration projects spread across the United States have directly served over 127,000 youth with disabilities, more than half of whom have a learning disability (Wehman, 1992). On the basis of the demonstrated needs of youth with disabilities found in the follow-up studies, the components listed in IDEA, and the outcomes of state and federal demonstration projects, a number of elements appear critical for an effective transition program at the local level (Blalock, 1990; Cobb & Hasazi, 1987):

1. Appropriate student and community assessments, to identify strengths, needs, and priorities;
2. Administrative and community support;
3. Trained transition teams at school and community levels;
4. Parental involvement in the transition program;
5. Individualized transition planning;
6. Functional curricula, including community-based training and supervised work experiences;

7. Vocational education/special education collaboration;
8. Interagency collaboration and post-school options;
9. Follow-up studies.

Each of these elements will be detailed in the sections that follow.

Appropriate Assessment: Students and Their Environments

Two types of assessment are cornerstones for determining the best directions for an effective transition program. First, student assessment, particularly in regard to life skills, can identify the critical present and future needs of youth with LD. Second, community needs assessments can ensure local input and accurate, comprehensive data for use in decision-making and planning.

Student Assessment

According to McCue (1989), a comprehensive assessment for students with learning disabilities must expand the kinds of typical assessment components (psychoeducational, neuropsychological, medical/neurological) in order to identify students' functional abilities. Vocational assessment strategies must be implemented in order to identify functional limitations, vocational interests, and local possibilities. Competent vocational evaluators are able to combine existing diagnostic evaluations with their own functional assessments to provide a profile of potential occupational areas suitable for the individual to explore. In addition, these vocational assessments actually include descriptive data regarding social/behavioral and independent living skills addressing all major life areas. These data and the areas they target are then used as the basis for individualized transition planning—both informal and formal—throughout middle and high school; they also can help in rehabilitation counseling and in the development of Individualized Written Rehabilitation Plans (IWRPs; McCue, 1989).

Some urban districts are fortunate enough to have positions for vocational evaluators and even more fortunate to find qualified persons to fill those positions. Smaller districts typically are not so blessed. However, some small school districts, often with the support of their special education cooperatives, have created a system for informal and formal vocational assessment that allows teachers and others to team up with the scarce expert evaluators (Blalock, 1990). Depending on their backgrounds, teachers are trained in the areas with which they are unfamiliar (e.g., aptitude testing, getting local world-of-work information) and encouraged to form a team with those who have expertise they do not (e.g., counselors, vocational educators). Vocational assessment specialists may be employed part- or full-time by a cooperative or district or may be hired contractually as needed. This level system is outlined in Table 3.3. Timelines for implementing vocational assessment are contained within

TABLE 3.3
Levels of Vocational Assessment

Level	Procedures	Sample	Responsible parties
Informal	Individual interview Simple interest test Self-reported abilities	Students with LD at all levels	Teachers, counselors, or vocational evaluator
Outcome: 4-year plan for high school			
1	Individual interview Interest inventory Aptitude test Learning styles inventory Curriculum-based assessment Observations (work, home)	Students with LD at all levels	Special education teachers with counselor or with vocational education teacher; vocational evaluator
Outcome: List of recommendations for ITP/IEP			
2	All of above, plus: McCarron-Dial System Situational assessments	Students with moderate LD, or with neurological problems; seniors referred to VR	Vocational evaluator
Outcome: Vocational assessment report			
3	All of above, plus: Work samples Job tryouts	Students with severe LD, or with neurological problems; seniors referred to VR	Vocational evaluator
Outcome: Vocational evaluation report			

Note. LD = learning disabilities; ITP = Individualized Transition Plan; IEP = Individualized Education Program; VR = vocational rehabilitation.

timelines for transition planning as presented in Table 3.4 (see Note). One final note: The IDEA emphasizes that assessment should focus on student (and family) interests and goals, rather than operate from a deficit model.

Community Needs Assessment

Finding out what employers, parents, consumers, and school personnel think are transition needs and strengths in their own communities has been identified as a critical initial step in local transition planning (Blalock, 1990). Frequently, parties in one role have little knowledge of what the other parties do (Smith, 1992). Everson et al. (1987) listed several components of local needs assessments, in which responsible parties should

- identify and assess secondary and postsecondary vocational training programs

TABLE 3.4
Transition Planning Team Process and Timelines

8th grade	Training about high school and beyond Informal vocational assessment (interest, self-reported skills, goals) Individual interview Develop 4-year plan for exit IEP meeting
9th–10th grades	Formal vocational evaluation Completion of Transition Planning Guide with student, by counselors and special education teachers ITP development meeting as part of annual IEP meeting
10th–12th grades	Implement ITP through secondary school and adult service provision, as per local agreements Update vocational assessment as needed Update ITP annually (during IEP meeting) and implement annual follow-along procedures —Increase adult agencies' involvement during junior and senior years —ITP copies provided to all responsible parties
12th grade	Informal Transition Review in fall Exit transition meeting in spring

Note. IEP = Individualized Education Program; ITP = Individualized Transition Plan.

- identify and assess adult employment services
- identify and assess secondary curricula in all areas of adult preparation
- identify and assess other pertinent adult services (e.g., postsecondary special services, special recreation program)
- identify and assess generic community programs which could be accessed with or without support
- conduct follow-up studies of former secondary students with LD
- share findings locally and with state departments of education

The community transition team may design the formal or informal needs assessment instrument and procedures themselves or may hire or ask an expert (such as state-level Department of Labor specialists or educational researchers) to do so, with team input. The format for data collection could be designed to meet the needs of all involved agencies (Cobb & Hasazi, 1987).

Gaining Administrative Support for a Transition Process

Lindsey and Blalock (1992) described a few of the strategies used by one rural multicultural project to gain administrative support for development and implementation of a new transition process. In each of the target districts, the special education director was part of the local and school transition teams and participated in both team planning and staff development activities. In addition, other levels of support that rallied to assist the small communities included the local university, the special education cooperative, and the state department of education, which in turn motivated the district- and building-level administrators to support the program.

Three major areas required administrative support. First, release time and substitute teachers were needed occasionally, so that local teams could meet during the day. Daytime meetings worked well for the employers and parents involved and were especially important for the rural teachers who also served as bus drivers and coaches, held outside jobs, or had children. Second, the roles and duties of the special educators needed to change to accommodate job placements after school hours, the transition teams' activities, more time to be spent working directly with families, and additional time needed for revising curricula to include more employability skills. Finally, full implementation and long-lasting changes depended upon administrative involvement and ongoing support.

Developing and Training Transition Teams

Two major projects (Everson et al., 1987; Minnesota Department of Education, 1990), among others, have carefully outlined procedures for developing interdisciplinary, interagency transition teams. Their "Ten Cs of Teamwork" include communication, cooperation, collaboration, confronting problems, compromise, consensus, coordination, consistency, caring, and commitment. These guides offer many ideas for strategic management of groups, to help them accomplish common goals at the state or local level.

At the local level, Lindsey and Blalock (1992) described the process that helped small multicultural communities develop transition programs that were tailored to their strengths and needs. "Collaborative ethic," or the commitment to work together toward a common goal, was eventually achieved by diverse members of both school and community transition teams after a great deal of effort and planning. The components described by Phillips and McCullough (1990) that were necessary to build collaborative ethic included administrative support, participant ownership, multilevel planning and decision making, staff development (including parents), and format feasibility. One key event that helped all parties commit to working on change was a visit to a successful transition program in a similar rural area with equally limited employment options. Members of the team who traveled to this "model" site included three administrators, two parents, three teachers, and a paraprofessional. They all participated in a crossdisciplinary training session, a visit with parents, and observational visits to job sites.

The importance of crossdisciplinary (and in this case cross-agency) training involving all team members has been promoted by several projects working on collaboration (e.g., Blalock, Bassett, & Donisthorpe, 1989; Everson et al., 1987). Knowlton and Clark (1987) decried the typically academic preparation of most secondary-level educators and promoted a major role revision that focuses on transition goals and activities.

Many communities find that local interagency agreements help to formalize shared missions and provide to directors the necessary rationale for staff to spend time on transition program efforts. These agreements generally detail activities for which various team members are responsible and which generally fall within the scope of their work anyway. Except in a few very progressive states, waiting for the state-level organizations to develop statewide interagency agreements has often proven to take far too long, because lawyers may spend months determining the legal ramifications of agencies' proposed commitments. These local agreements should be evaluated and updated regularly.

Three levels of teams typically evolve in local districts as they establish their transition programs. Table 3.5 outlines the overlapping composition of such teams. In addition, Everson et al. (1987) recommended establishing a state-level Transition Task Force that would study transition and evaluate or develop state interagency agreements.

TABLE 3.5
Levels of Teams Involved in Transition Services

Level 1: Individualized Transition Plan (ITP) Committee	
Usually:	*As Appropriate/Infrequent:*
Special education teacher/department head	Postsecondary special services
Vocational evaluator/transition coordinator	Vocational rehabilitation
Student	Adult
Vocational agency representative	
Parent(s)	(if appropriate)
Counselor or administrator	Social services representative
General education teacher/department head	Juvenile probation officer
Level 2: School or Building Transition Committee	
Principal or assistant principal	
Teachers/department heads: special education, general education, vocational education	
Counselors/other administrators	
Work-study/COOP/DECA coordinator	
Feeder middle school representatives	
Parents (sometimes)	
Level 3: Community Transition Team	
School administrator	Adult vocational agency representatives
Parents	Vocational rehabilitation counselor
Students/consumers	Department of Labor counselor
Special educator(s)	Chamber of Commerce representative
Vocational educator(s)	Employers/professional organization representatives
Transition specialists/coordinators	Postsecondary special services
School board member	County extension agent
Juvenile corrections representative	Social services representatives
Social Security Administration representatives	

Parental Involvement

Every transition model project in the United States has emphasized the crucial role played by parents in successful transitions. School districts repeatedly cry for greater family involvement in transition services, but unfortunately many parents have become tired of dealing with school issues by the time their children reach adolescence. In addition, many local education agencies actually act in ways that repel parents. This section describes activities that parents can do to contribute to their child's successful passage into adulthood. Strategies are also listed for educators and human service professionals to use to increase parental involvement.

Struck (1987) has developed a set of parent handbooks on the topic of transition from school to adult life. The modules explain what transition is and describe its importance, a transition planning process, postschool options, and available support resources. The last module describes parents' role in transition and arms them with questions to ask of employers, training institutions, and service providers. Highlights of Struck's "Transition Tips" include the following:

1. Support the school's effort to provide job training;
2. Make sure vocational training is part of your (child's) IEP;
3. Help identify employment and living options in your community;
4. Help identify your (child's) needs and interests;
5. Work on social skills at home;
6. Let your (child) prepare meals, go shopping, or make a budget;
7. Join advocacy groups;
8. Encourage your (child's) participation in community activities;
9. Ask questions. (p. D-2)

Elksnin and Elksnin (1990) outlined a framework for using collaborative consultation techniques to build partnerships for transition. These techniques follow problem-solving and communication steps similar to those used by professionals. A number of ideas also have been provided by Husted (1992) as strategies for professionals to use to enhance parent involvement:

1. Start the transition plan in middle school;
2. Use the IEP as a report card, to monitor progress toward goals;

3. Focus on early interests as a guide for career directions, to get everyone involved to think about the broad skills needed;
4. Encourage parents to talk a lot;
5. Ask specifically for what you need from the parent(s);
6. Communicate positives as much as negatives;
7. At IEP/ITP meetings, focus on present levels of performance rather than deficits;
8. Get teachers, parents, and students to plan IEPs/ITP together, in advance of the formal meeting;
9. Don't expect parents to do something you wouldn't do.

Husted (1992) cautioned that it is not the school's responsibility to do all the transition planning, and that parents need to make themselves available to help so the school gets used to having parents involved.

The ITP Process

Target areas for transition planning include employment and/or vocational training, postsecondary education, independent living, community participation, income, medical, and transportation goals. Detailed checklists for activities in each area and for connections with adult services are also provided by Everson et al. (1987).

A number of criticisms and cautions regarding ITPs have been leveled by Stowitschek and Kelso (1989) in four major areas of concern: (a) As districts develop their ITPs, care must be taken to ensure that the goals and objectives have maximum *relevance* to work and community life, and are measurable and specific—single coordinators were recommended to maintain the *quality* of a district's ITPs; (b) *accountability* of ITPs can be protected by connecting ongoing vocational assessment with transition goals and objectives and by specifying responsibilities of school staff, local adult agency personnel, students, and family members; (c) factors that enhance the *feasibility* of successful transitions (e.g., family involvement, ongoing assessment, and subsequent revisions of plans) must be carefully incorporated into the planning process; and (d) *preparedness* of the key players in the transition process (teachers, adult service providers, and parents) must be accomplished through a variety of training strategies and experiences.

Table 3.4 presents a framework for the transition planning team process for individual students, modeled after one created by Albuquerque Public Schools and modified by Gallup-McKinley (New Mexico) County Schools. A set of procedures for conducting and evaluating ITP meetings was suggested by Everson et al. (1987).

Various ITP forms are now ubiquitous and usually appear as an attachment to the IEP. Practitioners seem to find it most beneficial to develop the ITP first, so that its future focus can drive the development of the IEP. The ITP attachment used by the Santa Fe, New Mexico, public schools includes all the essential components in an easily understood format (see Figure 3.1). In addition, many districts use transition planning guides to prepare for ITP development (see, e.g., Missouri Linc, 1991–92; Struck, 1992).

Development of Functional Curricula Linked to Community (K-12)

A wealth of data now exists that supports a movement toward more functional curricula grounded in community experiences for the majority of students with disabilities, including many with LD. Recent findings from SRI International's (1992) longitudinal follow-up study suggest that taking vocational education classes or spending more time in general education during the last year of high school led students to be much more likely to continue their education. Among students with LD, 64.3% were found to have taken vocational education. All students with LD need some form of informal or formal career/vocational instruction.

Recent research has brought a number of important factors to light regarding the impact of school preparation on post-school outcomes. Blalock, Mahoney, and Van Dyke (1992) found that the single most important predictor of employment after school was a paid job during high school. They also discovered a significant relationship between driver's licenses and competitive employment. SRI International (1992) indicated that students from affluent backgrounds, suburban dwellers, men, and younger exiters (e.g., 18-year-olds) were better at locating employment. The latter finding suggests that schools may be doing a better job of career development in recent years.

Wehman (1992) made the case for functional, community-based instruction for all students with disabilities:

> It has become abundantly clear to those professionals in the field, as well as concerned family members, that truly the only way to alter this disturbingly high unemployment and drop-out rates is to significantly emphasize work opportunities and work experiences in the schools. The public schools must go through critical self-examination of the curriculum offerings that are provided. (pp. 112–114)

Date of Meeting: __________ School: __________

Student Name: __________ D.O.B.: ______ Grade: ____

I. Graduation Plan (check one):

( ) Standard Plan (23 required credits & pass NMHS Competency Exam)

( ) Modified Plan (IEP graduation as per district policy)

( ) Certificate of Completion (complete planned course of study)

Anticipated Date of High School Graduation: __________

II. Need (check one):

( ) The Transition Team has determined that this student is not in need of special transition services/support beyond what is available to all students in the public school.

( ) The Transition Team has determined that this student is in need of special transition services and/or support.

III. Transition Services/Support Needs (check each area that applies):

( ) Vocational Assessment	( ) Employment
( ) Career/Vocational Guidance	( ) Medical
( ) Career/Vocational Education	( ) Transportation/Mobility
( ) Residential/Independent Living	( ) Leisure/Recreation
( ) Socialization/Community Integ.	( ) Income Support
( ) Postsecondary Education (Academic/Vocational)	( ) Guardianship/Advocacy
	( ) Other: __________

Transition Area	Goals & Objectives (actions to be taken)	Responsible Persons (parent/school/agency)	Time Line

Figure 3.1 Santa Fe Public Schools Special Education Services Individual Transition Plan (Attachment to IEP, Grades 8–12).

According to SRI International (1992), dropouts might have stayed in school if they had been given vocational education, tutoring, and personal counseling.

Curricula that offer a continuum of academic and functional options have been developed by a number of districts and universities to prepare students for real-life demands. The most comprehensive examples begin in kindergarten, with very general skills appropriate for that age group, and proceed to postsecondary training or experiences, as appropriate for the individual (see Figure 3.2).

Two of the most widely used functional curricula, both of which can be used or modified for students with LD, are Project CERES (Ceres Unified School District, 1988) and the Life-Centered Career Education (Brolin, 1991). Both of these are infusion curricula that present objectives and activities for Grades K through 12, working on domains that include daily living, social skills, and occupational skills. CERES, designed for general education students, also focuses on citizenship, leisure activities, and academic content areas. Cronin and Patton (1993) have created a life skills curriculum that focuses on adult domains (based on major life demands), integrates those with academic and social skills appropriate for school instruction, and then infuses that instruction into new and existing life skills courses. Examples of courses include Personal Finance, Practical Math, Health and Hygiene, Practical Communication, and Career Development.

Husted (1992) suggested guidelines for implementing transition activities at the elementary level that are appropriate for all special education students. These include (a) provide a sense of time (e.g., "Shopping for new clothes takes about 2 hours, but sewing new clothes takes about a week") and a sense of closure ("You've just finished the social studies project on Mexico. It took you three weeks to complete it, and you did a thorough job"); (b) provide a reason for doing the task (e.g., "If you plan how to include others in your game, you will make more friends"); (c) provide natural opportunities, logic, and realism (e.g., shopping for upcoming events, discussing the need for various items of clothing and their multiple uses); (d) make sure the location of the activity is reasonable and not forced (e.g., use the library to look up information about recreation events).

White (1993) outlined the "Skills Employers Want" originally generated by Carnevale, Gainer, and Meltzer (cited in White, Chapter 4 of this book). The list includes (a) basic skills (as they relate to dealing with information and problem solving), (b) organizational/leadership skills, (c) self-esteem/goal-setting/motivation for developing self and career, (d) interpersonal/teamwork skills, (e) problem solving/creative thinking, (f) oral communication skills, and (g) learning strategies and generalization skills. The message from employers is that successful employees

GR1 GR6 GR7 GR8 GR9 GR10 GR11 GR12 Postsec.

Career awareness . .
Academic skills. . . . .
Personal behaviors. . . . .(more as needed)
Work attitudes. . . . .(more as needed)
Dependability . . . . (more as needed)
Punctuality . . . .(more as needed)
Responsibility . . . .(more as needed)
Organization . . . .(more as needed)
Self-help skills . . . . . . (more as needed)
Social skills . . . .(more as needed)

Integration into community . . . . (more as needed)
Career education. . .
Prevocat./vocat. skills.
School work stations. . . .
C-BI field trips . . . .
C-BI instruction . . . . . .
(include vocational
placements for more
severely disabled students)

INFORMAL TRANSITION PLANNING/
4-YEAR PLANS
Domestic skills. . . . (more as needed)
Consumer skills. . . . (more as needed)
Independent living skills. . . . .
Leisure/recreational skills. . . .
Systematic vocational training
Systematic work experiences
(1 hr/wk = mild/moderate)
(more time = S/PH students
(continual lengthening of work
period; rotated experiences)

FORMAL TRANSITION PLANS

EXIT TRANSITION
MEETINGS

Figure 3.2 Transition contents/events timeline created by Los Alamos High School teachers and assistants.

have to be able to "think on their feet" and think ahead, and those do not tend to be the approaches taught in secondary school curricula. Social skills continue to be a critical factor in getting and keeping jobs.

A most promising approach used to prepare students with LD for independence has been one that teaches students about their own learning disabilities and provides them with skills to advocate for themselves (Phillips, 1990). Transition programs that prepare students in this manner for postsecondary training or education have proliferated in recent years. These programs tend to start early in helping youth identify their own strengths, weaknesses, interests, and educational and vocational goals. Seminars that teach the characteristics of effective learners provide the framework for assisting those students in identifying their own learning profiles, so they can then pinpoint which specific accommodations, if any, they will need to succeed in a postsecondary environment. Subsequent units teach ways to search for and communicate effectively with 2- or 4-year colleges, universities, and trade schools to determine available support services, application procedures, and other important topics such as financial aid or work opportunities.

Some transition-to-college programs have emphasized mostly academic preparation (e.g., Webb, 1988), whereas others included personal/social skill development and follow-up (e.g., Brandt & Berry, 1991). In addition, new federally funded self-determination projects offer hope for teachers in the forms of new curricula and motivational strategies that help students verbalize their disabilities, their rights and responsibilities under the law, and their specific academic needs (University of Colorado, 1992).

Posthill and Roffman (1991) described The Threshold Program, a post-school transitional training program for adults with learning disabilities at Lesley College in Cambridge, Massachusetts. The Threshold Program serves adults with low-average intellectual functioning through a 2-year program that emphasizes vocational, social, and independent living skills training, as well as remediation of practical academics. This program is similar to others at Adelphi University in New York State and the City University of New York, where students live on campus, undertake supervised field placements in the occupation in which they are training (typically early childhood or human services paraprofessionals), receive tutoring in academic topics related to their vocational training, participate in weekly group counseling, and take advantage of creative electives. The Threshold Program also offers a Transition Year Program, which gives students who have completed the 2-year training outreach support in the form of independent living advisors who visit homes regularly, vocational advisors who help with job-seeking and initial training, and a weekly "real world" seminar. A recent follow-up study (Posthill & Roffman, 1991) found that four cohort groups of Threshold graduates were holding their own, with 61% employed in fields for which they were trained. Over half had held their jobs for a minimum of 1 year, 75% were living independently, and 84% of the latter group had kept an apartment for over a year.

Vocational Education/Special Education Collaboration

Integration into regular vocational education has been cited by many as a critical element in appropriate transition programming for students with mild disabilities (Blalock, 1990; Cobb & Hasazi, 1987). Districts vary widely in terms of the access to vocational education by students with disabilities, but professionals agree on its importance in secondary curricula. In a recent nationwide follow-up study, 64.3% of students with LD had some form of vocational training, contrasted with 72.1% of students with mental retardation and 55.8% of youth with speech impairments (SRI International, 1992). The study did not differentiate vocational coursework provided by general or special education. Projects that focus on transition typically include inservice training designed to break down the historical barriers that exist between the two disciplines and to provide collaboration and mainstreaming strategies through crossdisciplinary training (Blalock, 1993).

Interagency Collaboration/Postschool Offerings

Connections with post-school options, as well as availability of those options, are a major component of successful transitions. Establishing and nurturing those connections are major functions of the local transition team. The Minnesota Department of Education (1990) offered guidelines and checklists to organize a team's information on available options. As described earlier, those community team meetings provide an avenue to solve problems and share information so that existing options can be fully used and new options can begin to develop. A major issue is collaboration in lobbying for additional funding at the adult service level, so that greater numbers of communities can offer vocational training and employment programs. Traditionally, such funding has served those with more severe mental, physical, and multiple disabilities. Only more progressive urban agencies have deliberately focused at least part of their services on youth and adults with LD (e.g., Gaylord-Ross's Career Ladder Program in San Francisco; see Siegel et al., 1993).

Carl Perkins Vocational Education Act dollars have been used widely to implement special services programs at postsecondary institutions (typically community and vocational–technical colleges). However, many deficits in addressing the needs of adults with LD remain in our nation's systems of postsecondary education. Efforts to respond to those growing needs are the subject of several of the chapters in this book.

Follow-up Studies

A critical strategy in addressing transition needs of youth with LD is to investigate their outcomes after they exit school programs. The primary purpose for such studies is to identify the factors related to successful transitions to adult life activities, particularly employment. In addition, such findings can and should provide ammunition for major changes in district offerings. Particularly, data about postschool employment, independent living, postsecondary training, and social networks has direct bearing on the quality and relevance of secondary programs. Indications of whether these studies have generated more work experience opportunities, functional curricula, community-based instruction, and transition planning have not yet appeared. An upcoming special issue of *Career Development for Exceptional Individuals* will discuss the impact that follow-up studies have had on their respective states and communities.

White (1993) reminded professionals in education and rehabilitation that conducting and using follow-up studies is a two-pronged effort:

> Researchers must be diligent in providing current information about the demands adults will face both in the workplace and in everyday life, and teachers must be prepared to seek out this information and make the necessary adjustments in the curriculum. It is not enough to review the follow-up literature and feel disappointed that more adults with learning disabilities are not doing better. (p. 455)

Although longitudinal data (such as SRI International, 1992) provide more realistic long-term pictures of former students' achievements, having data from even 1 year after students leave school is much more helpful than having none. Rural districts often have an easier time keeping track of their constituents, but regardless of difficulty of implementation, such studies need to be built into annual budgets and district practices. Also, studies should begin to incorporate nondisabled peers and dropouts for more accurate comparisons (Affleck, Edgar, Levine, & Kortering, 1989; Karpinski, Neubert, & Graham, 1992). Bruininks, Wolman, and Thurlow (1989) have offered very helpful considerations in designing follow-up studies for special education programs.

Conclusion

A menu of components critical for effective movement of youth with learning disabilities to adult life activities has been described. The literature is replete with data suggesting less successful outcomes among students than school programs had planned or hoped for. However, numerous model and local projects are developing frameworks, guidelines, and activities for filling in the gaps. These models and strategies promise to provide the necessary tools to empower youth with disabilities to take greater advantage of the adult options ahead.

Note

Readers are referred to McCue (1989) and Powers (1991) for more-thorough discussions of vocational assessment for persons with LD.

4. The Postschool Adjustment of Persons with Learning Disabilities: Current Status and Future Projections

WARREN J. WHITE

Most people would probably agree that the central purpose of American schools is to "prepare young people to take their places as adults in society" (Clark & Kolstoe, 1990, p. 366). Although there may be some disagreement about what "their places as adults" means, many persons would agree that it can be reduced to three basic criteria: An adult is self-supporting, an adult can function in the community without supervision, and an adult behaves in ways that are neither threatening nor unacceptable to others (Clark & Kolstoe, 1990). Considerable attention has been given in recent years to the status of numerous groups of young adults, especially young adults who had significant academic and/or behavioral difficulties when in school. In particular, young adults with learning disabilities have been studied to determine the degree to which they are self-supporting, functioning without supervision, and behaving in ways that are deemed acceptable; in fact, several reviews of the literature are now available.

Reprinted, with changes, from "The postschool adjustment of persons with learning disabilities: Current status and future projections," by Warren J. White, *Journal of Learning Disabilities,* Vol. 25, 1992, pp. 448–456.

This chapter is another review of that literature, but with a different intent than most reviews. I will attempt to relate what is known about adults with learning disabilities (LD) to the current knowledge base about the changing economic and technical realities of the society in which they will be living and working in the 1990s. That is, given what is known now about adults with learning disabilities, what are the possible implications for the future? This is important for several reasons. First, one of the functions of postschool-status studies has been to facilitate the evaluation of current education programs in order to make adjustments in curriculum areas in which the adults seem to be having the most difficulty. Although this seems logical, it may no longer be a sufficient foundation upon which to base curriculum decisions. Without a clear understanding of the changes society is undergoing, curriculum modifications based solely on follow-up studies may be already outdated by the time they are fully instituted.

Second, an understanding of the relationship between the current status of adults with learning disabilities and potential future occupational and social environments may have important implications for policy decisions. Transition services for youth with handicaps have been a federal priority since 1984 (see Will, 1984). Since then, millions of federal dollars have been spent every year on new transition personnel preparation programs, clearinghouses for transition information, transition demonstration projects, and so forth. Further, the Individuals with Disabilities Education Act of 1990 (P.L. 101-476) adds rehabilitation counseling to the definition of related services, adds a definition of transition services, and requires that all Individualized Education Programs (IEPs) include a statement of needed transition services for students beginning no later than age 16. The rationale for these additions to P.L. 101-476 was largely based on the results of follow-up studies that showed less-than-optimal postschool adjustment by many young adults with handicaps, as well as on literature reviews that summarized these studies. However, most of the follow-up literature provided only a snapshot of what had already occurred—in some cases, many years before—with little sense of how these results fit into the larger societal context, now or in the future. For example, it is not unusual for literature reviews of the adult status of individuals with learning disabilities to include case studies from the early 1960s, yet school programs, occupational skill requirements, and vocational options (among other things) are radically different now than they were then. For federal and state transition policy to be effective, it must address not only current conditions but also future possibilities.

The following criteria were used to determine which studies would be included in this review: The study must contain quantitative data (i.e., no case studies); the study must have appeared in the literature since

1975; the sample population must have been diagnosed as learning disabled, dyslexic, or specific learning disabled (not mildly handicapped, LD/BD, retarded reader, hyperactive, etc.); and the sample population must have been adults (post–high school) at the time of follow-up. A review of the major special education journals since 1975 was conducted and, using these criteria, articles were selected.

There has been considerable discussion in the literature about the quality of follow-up research. The frequent lack of control groups, questions regarding how representative of the original population a given sample might be, and the reliance on information from old school files to make identification decisions are frequently noted as problems. The following sections discuss some of the concerns a reader should keep in mind when trying to interpret follow-up research.

Methodological Considerations in Follow-up Research

There have been a number of different approaches to studying adults with learning disabilities. Some investigators have studied vocational outcomes only, while others have studied a broad range of outcomes, including social and marital status and leisure time use. Some subjects were sampled from populations still in school, some from persons referred to vocational rehabilitation agencies, others from volunteers from a prison population, while one represents a stratified random sample of all school districts in the United States. Terms used to identify individuals in these studies have also varied widely, ranging from *learning disabilities* to *dyslexia* to *retarded readers*. These different approaches, populations, and definitions have yielded a hodgepodge of results that are difficult to aggregate, compare, and interpret. The following sections address some of the methodological considerations that should be taken into account when analyzing adult outcome studies.

Follow-up Versus Follow-along

Halpern (1990) stated that two dimensions distinguish between follow-up and follow-along strategies:

> (1) Follow-up studies are cross-sectional, collecting information on outcomes at only a single point in time, whereas follow-along studies are longitudinal, collecting outcome information at multiple points in time;

> and (2) follow-up studies are usually retrospective, collecting information at the same time that outcome information is collected, whereas follow-along studies are usually prospective, collecting predictor information at one point in time and outcome information at subsequent points in time. (pp. 14–15)

Follow-along strategies are generally superior to follow-up strategies because of their ability to relate to changes in status across time. Follow-along studies are able to establish a baseline of adjustment at the subject's time of leaving school, so the effect of receiving adult services and the stability of adjustment can be measured. Follow-up studies must collect school-based information retrospectively from existing school records, many of which are old and incomplete, so that the effects of receiving adult services and the stability of adjustment can only be inferred (Halpern, 1990). Only one of the studies in this review was designed as a follow-along strategy (see Table 4.1).

Control Groups

The use of an appropriate control group in follow-up studies is critical to the interpretation of the study results. That a particular sample of persons with learning disabilities is described as faring favorably or unfavorably on some dimension of adult adjustment is dependent on how well others are doing on the same dimension. For example, if a study found that 50% of young adults with LD were still living at home up to 5 years after high school, this would seem to be an unfavorable outcome. If, on the other hand, one had an appropriate comparison group of which 50% were also living at home up to 5 years after high school, then the LD outcome now appears more favorable. If a study reports an unemployment rate of 50% for a sample of adults with LD but the geographic area from which these adults were competing for jobs was economically depressed and 50% of all persons seeking employment were unable to locate a job, then this unemployment rate may not be an unfavorable outcome. Unfortunately, few follow-up studies have utilized a control group. Of the studies included in this review, only three included a control group (see Table 4.1).

Subject Selection

There are two important methodological considerations concerning the manner in which subjects for a study are selected. The first has to do with the way in which selection criteria are established; that is, does the

TABLE 4.1
Studies Included in Review

Study	Population descriptor	Follow-up/ follow-along	Control group	Type of study	Includes replication variables
Blalock (1981)	Young adult LD, no stated criteria $N = 38$	Follow-up	No	Descriptive	No
Chelser (1981)	LD adults belonging to ACLD $N = 562$	Follow-up	No	Descriptive	No
Cobb & Crump (1984)	School-identified adults with LD $N = 100$	Follow-up	No	Exploratory	Yes
deBettencourt et al. (1989)	School-identified adults with LD $n = 44$ (LD) $n = 64$ (NLD)	Follow-up	Yes	Descriptive	No
Fafard & Haubrich (1981)	School-identified LD adults $N = 21$	Follow-up	No	Descriptive	No
Frauenheim & Heckerl (1983)	Dyslexia identified in childhood $N = 11$	Follow-up	No	Descriptive	No
Hoffman et al. (1987)	Adult with LD identified by state vocational rehabilitation agencies $N = 381$	Follow-up	No	Descriptive	No
McCue et al. (1986)	Adults with LD, no information on source of evaluation $N = 100$	Follow-up	No	Descriptive	No
Rogan & Hartman (1990)	Adults with LD identified in childhood $N = 68$	Follow-up	No	Descriptive	No
Sitlington et al. (1989)	School-identified adults with LD $N = 1{,}012$	Follow-up	No	Descriptive	No
Wagner (1989)	School-identified adults with LD $N = 891$	Follow-along	No	Exploratory	No
White et al. (1980)	School-identified adults with LD $n = 47$ (LD) $n = 59$ (NLD)	Follow-up	Yes	Exploratory	No
Zigmond & Thornton (1985)	School-identified adults with LD $n = 60$ (LD) $n = 61$ (NLD)	Follow-up	Yes	Descriptive	No

subject really have a learning disability? There was wide variability among the studies in both the degree to which selection criteria were described and the specific criteria that were used. Several studies (Cobb & Crump, 1984; deBettencourt, Zigmond, & Thornton, 1989; Sitlington, Frank, & Cooper, 1989) reported that subjects had been identified as learning disabled by the schools but did not provide a description of the school criteria. Subjects in the Frauenheim and Heckerl (1983) study were simply described as being diagnosed "dyslexic." The subjects in the Hoffman et al. (1987) study had been found eligible for vocational rehabilitation services on the basis of a learning disability as defined by their state departments of vocational rehabilitation. Because the subjects came from three different states, the possibility exists that even within this sample different criteria were used. This wide variability of criteria makes comparing results across studies very difficult.

In addition, once selected, the subjects were not well described in many of the studies. Characteristics such as SES, IQ, initial severity of the disability, and age at the time of diagnosis have been found to affect adult outcomes (Horn, O'Donnell, & Vitulano, 1983), yet many studies do not include this information. The studies were analyzed to determine if they met the standards for subject description established by the Research Committee of the Council for Learning Disabilities (Smith et al., 1984). This committee recommended that the following information be provided about samples of subjects in learning disability research: the total number of subjects participating in the study, the number of male and female subjects, the age of the subjects, the racial composition of the sample, the subjects' socioeconomic status, the subjects' intellectual status, and the subjects' relevant achievement levels. Only one study met the minimum standard (see Table 4.1).

The second important consideration in subject selection concerns the purpose of the study. If the study is intended to provide a *description* of adult adjustment variables and their antecedents, then the sample must be constituted so that it is representative of the population to which the findings are intended to generalize. If the purpose of the study is to provide an *explanation* of adult adjustment variables and their relationships with their antecedents, then the sample must be sufficiently large to accommodate the number of variables included in the study (Halpern, 1990). Of the 13 studies included in this review, 10 were descriptive, and most of those provided little indication of how well their sample represented a larger population. One study (Blalock, 1981) specifically noted that the sample used was "a biased one and cannot be considered a representative sample of the learning disabled adult population" (p. 37). Of the three studies that included analyses of the relationships between variables, only one (Wagner, 1989) had a sample size sufficiently large to accommodate the number of variables explored (see Table 4.1).

Outcomes of Adults with Learning Disabilities

The following sections will discuss the results of the studies included in this review. Within each section is also a discussion of current social and/or economic changes and some of the implications of these changes for adolescents and adults with learning disabilities. The sections are organized around the major variables included in the studies.

One note of caution should be mentioned. By far the most information is available about the employment status of these adults, with less information about other dimensions of adult adjustment. Although employment status is an important dimension of adult adjustment, recent research has shown that success (or failure) in one dimension of adult life is only moderately related to success in other dimensions (Halpern, 1985). In fact, some persons with disabilities place more value on residential and personal/social adjustment than on vocational adjustment (Halpern, Nave, Close, & Nelson, 1986). To assume that employment is the only index of community adjustment may be detrimental not only to adults with learning disabilities but also to youth still in school who may be the recipients of transition programming unduly restricted to vocational training. Vocational outcomes are, however, much easier to quantify than social or even academic outcomes. It is much easier to count the number of persons employed, their hourly wage, the number of hours they work, and the types of jobs they hold than it is to quantify the degree of their personal satisfaction or their ability to function in a particular community environment. There is simply more information available about vocational variables than about variables concerning other areas of adult life. In addition, it is much easier to project into the future (e.g., what types of jobs might exist, what types of skills might be needed) in the vocational area.

Vocational Outcomes

Most of the studies reported that adults with LD were only somewhat successful in being able to get jobs, though the results were mixed. Overall employment rates ranged from a low of 36% (Hoffman et al., 1987) to 87% (Cobb & Crump, 1984), with most studies reporting rates above 50%. However, "employment" was typically defined as full- or part-time work, and in one case as working for pay for at least 10 hours per week (deBettencourt et al., 1989). In her national sample, Wagner (1989) found that only 38% of adults with LD were working full-time, which can be compared to another national study of noncollege high school graduates that reported an employment rate of 49% (William T. Grant Foundation, 1988). However, the Cobb and Crump figure reported above was the full-time employment rate for their sample (the LD unemployment rate of 13% was less than the county overall unemployment rate of 15%); and Rogan and Hartman (1990) reported that their college LD sample was employed full-time at a rate of 79% while the high school sample was employed at a rate of 69%.

Underemployment was also seen to be a problem. Most studies stated that the largest percentage of workers in their samples held low-level service, fast food, laborer, production, and helper occupations. Over 60% of the Sitlington et al. (1989) sample were in service or laborer positions, 37% of the Cobb and Crump (1984) sample held jobs in production, and the majority of workers in the Blalock (1981) sample were in fast food jobs. In a comparison of an LD sample with a non-learning-disabled (NLD) sample, White, Schumaker, Warner, Alley, and Deshler (1980) reported that the jobs held by the adults with LD had significantly less job status than the jobs held by the NLD adults. Given the degree of underemployment, it is not surprising that many adults with LD were not satisfied with their jobs (Chelser, 1982; White et al., 1980).

Data on earned income were difficult to interpret. Both Wagner (1989) and Sitlington et al. (1989) reported average hourly wages of a little over $4.60 for their LD samples, but neither study reported how this related to the average hourly wages of a similar-age NLD sample. Sixty-seven percent of the workers in the Cobb and Crump (1984) study earned $10,000 a year or less while 88% earned $15,000 or less, but, again, there was no comparison group. White et al. (1980) reported that the average yearly earnings of the LD and NLD samples in their study did not statistically differ. However, neither group had been out of high school for very long.

When these results are compared to statements in the rapidly growing literature about radical shifts in the types of jobs that are expected to be available over the next decade, the news may be both good and bad. On one hand, changing demographics in the labor pool may have a positive effect for young adults with learning disabilities. Currently, there is a shortage of entry-level workers, due to a very sharp decline in the number of workers age 16 to 24 entering the labor force. The proportion of workers in this age bracket dropped from 23% to 20% between 1972 and 1986 and is projected to drop to 16% by 2000 (Smith & Trist, 1988). Employers who recruit from this age group will be competing for a declining number of young people and will have to give individuals a chance who in the past might not have even been considered for employment (Carnevale, Gainer, & Meltzer, 1988). This may present the possibility for a larger percentage of young adults with learning disabilities to enter the workplace.

On the other hand, even if jobs for entry-level workers are plentiful, they may not provide a level of income that will allow workers to live independently. In the continuing transformation of the American workplace from a primarily goods-producing economy to a primarily service-producing and information-producing one, the fastest growing industries, by *rate*, will be in high technology, but the net addition of jobs in these industries will not be substantial. In addition, jobs created in high-tech fields will be open mostly to skilled workers. Therefore, growth in this area will not absorb much of the work force (Smith & Trist, 1988). Occupations that will provide the largest *net* addition of jobs will be primarily in the service sector. For example, currently, 22 of the top 25 employers in America are in the retail/service sector (Daggett, 1988), and retail trade will account for 22% of the job growth in the economy (3.7 million jobs) from now until the year 2000. Eating and drinking places will add more jobs (1.5 million) than any other industry in the economy over the same period (Department of Labor, 1989). But the jobs that will be added in the service sector will be predominantly low-skill, low-wage positions, such as retail salespersons, waiters and waitresses, janitors, orderlies, cashiers, clerical workers, secretaries, and guards (Smith & Trist, 1988). The number of jobs that will provide a middle class standard of living is shrinking.

Although it may seem paradoxical, the fastest declining occupations, in terms of total number of jobs, will also be low-skilled and semiskilled (Smith & Trist, 1988). Large numbers of low-skilled and semiskilled jobs will be lost in the manufacturing sector due to changing skill requirements and technology. Declining occupations will include machine operators, textile workers, assemblers and other handwork occupations, and several categories under helpers, laborers, and material movers (Smith & Trist, 1988). This may particularly hurt persons with learning disabilities who, as can be seen from this review, are frequently placed in production and laborer jobs.

These statistics point to radical shifts in the work force. No longer will many workers be able to earn the level of income from an unskilled job that would allow them to live independently. Medical benefits and health insurance will be more difficult to earn because many jobs will be part-time. The service sector will employ the majority of workers, yet the types of jobs adults with learning disabilities typically obtain in the service sector will be disappearing. Information management skills and technology-related skills will be increasingly essential to working. Opportunities for jobs that provide personal growth and a chance for promotion will not be as plentiful as in the past.

Reading, Writing, and Arithmetic Outcomes

Nearly all the studies investigating the reading and writing abilities of adults reported persisting problems in these areas. Frauenheim and Heckerl (1983) stated, "Patterns of skill weaknesses and cognitive abilities, as measured by academic and psychological tests, have remained remarkably consistent over a period of approximately seventeen years" (p. 345). Blalock (1981) reported that 50% of her sample complained of reading problems, particularly in the area of automaticity; that is, many in her sample were better at isolated skills tasks than in actual reading. Poor sight vocabulary, poor decoding skills, and slow oral reading rate were also mentioned as problem areas for many adults with learning disabilities (Frauenheim & Heckerl, 1983). Reading grade scores ranged from 2.6 (Frauenheim & Heckerl, 1983) to 15.0 (Blalock, 1981). McCue, Shelley, and Goldstein (1986) reported a reading grade score of 5.6 and a reading comprehension grade score of 4.9. Two studies with control groups (deBettencourt et al., 1989; Zigmond & Thornton, 1985) stated that the LD samples scored significantly lower on a reading test than did the NLD samples.

Spelling was also frequently mentioned as a serious problem in adulthood. Blalock (1981) stated that for her sample, spelling was the academic problem most frequently reported to be troublesome on the job. McCue et al. (1986) reported a mean grade score of 4.4 in spelling for their sample, while Frauenheim and Heckerl (1983) remarked that spelling remained the most severely impaired area of academic functioning for their sample.

In the area of arithmetic, nearly 50% of the adults in the Hoffman et al. (1987) study reported problems, primarily in the areas of banking and money. All of the subjects in the Frauenheim and Heckerl (1983) study acknowledged that they still had difficulty with multiplication tables. Blalock (1981) noted that the specific areas her adults scored lowest in were decimals, fractions, and percentages; they also had problems with estimating and explaining answers. McCue et al. (1986) reported a mean arithmetic grade score of 4.8 for their sample, and Frauenheim and Heckerl reported a mean arithmetic grade score of 4.7. As was the case in reading and spelling, the LD samples in the studies by deBettencourt et al. (1989) and Zigmond and Thornton (1985) scored significantly lower on measures of arithmetic than did the NLD samples.

The workplace demographic changes discussed earlier are disturbing, but they are not the whole story. At the same time that these shifts are occurring, changes in the skill requirements for jobs are also occurring. Although the impact of technology on job-specific skills is not yet clearly understood, it does seem apparent that the level of basic skills required both prior to employment and in a current job is increasing and expanding to include more abstract abilities. Narrow or fixed occupational skills will be increasingly inadequate (Smith & Trist, 1988). Employers want not only workers with a command of the traditional academic skills, but also workers who can use these skills to solve problems. Table 4.2 displays information about the types of skills employers

TABLE 4.2
Skills Employers Want[a]

1. The 3 Rs
    - Reading
        - Locating information
        - Solving problems
    - Writing
        - Analysis
        - Conceptualization
        - Synthesis
        - Distillation of information
        - Articulation
    - Math
        - Problem identification
        - Reasoning
        - Estimation
        - Problem Solving
2. Organizational effectiveness/leadership
3. Self-esteem/Goal setting–Motivation/Personal and career development
4. Interpersonal skills/Negotiation/Teamwork
5. Problem solving/Creative thinking
6. Listening and oral communication
    - Communication style (inflection, body language)
    - Following directions
    - Listening for content
7. Learning to learn
    - Ability to apply knowledge to new situations
    - Ability to be retrained

[a]Carnevale et al., 1988.

want and need today and will want and need through this decade. The three Rs are there, but the specific skills needed are not those typically taught in schools. In the area of reading, for example, instruction in schools is often geared toward increasing a student's ability to "follow directions or internalize data for future recall" (Smith & Trist, 1988, p. 10). Although these are important skills, reading on the job frequently requires analysis, summarization, and monitoring one's comprehension; active involvement in the reading task is important. Employers want employees who can use reading to locate information and use higher level thinking strategies to solve problems (Smith & Trist, 1988). In the area of writing, the successful employee will be the one who can analyze a problem, conceptualize a solution, and articulate that solution to another person. Workplace math skills include identifying a problem, reasoning, estimation, and problem solving.

The level of reading, writing, and arithmetic skills found in most of the studies reported on here is relatively low, but the literature concerning which academic skills are necessary in the workplace does not mention grade equivalents. Therefore, the implications of those low levels are unclear. Although sophisticated academic skills certainly would be helpful to an individual in the workplace, the key to success seems to be whether he or she can actually use academic skills to solve problems and communicate to others, rather than the absolute level of his or her skills. Teachers in classrooms for students with learning disabilities may wish to start concentrating on the application of academic skills in real life settings, or even classroom simulations, in order to better prepare students for the tasks they will encounter in adult contexts outside of the schools.

Graduation Rates and Participation in Postsecondary Education

Successful adjustment in postschool settings is strongly influenced by how well youth do in school. Graduation from high school has a significant positive relationship with participating in postsecondary education and training, employment status, and the degree to which a person engages in productive activities in general (Wagner, 1989). Therefore, the percentage of adults with LD who did not graduate from high school is deeply disturbing. Zigmond and Thornton (1985) reported that 54% of their sample dropped out of high school, versus 33% for the NLD control group. Other investigators reported somewhat lower, but still very distressing, figures: 42% (Cobb & Crump, 1984); 36% versus 12% in an NLD control group (deBettencourt et al., 1989); 36% (Wagner, 1989); and 26% versus 8.5% in an NLD control group (White et al., 1980).

Possibly due to the academic difficulties they experienced when they were in school, few adults with LD participate in postsecondary educational opportunities. Only 16.7% of Wagner's (1989) national sample were enrolled in any type of postsecondary education or training setting. Specifically, 9.6% were enrolled in a vocational or trade school, 6.9% were enrolled in a 2-year college, and 1.8% were enrolled in a 4-year college. Cobb and Crump (1984) reported that 69% of their sample had had no further education or training, and of the 31% who had, about one third had completed only one semester and one third had completed only two semesters. The young adults in the White et al. (1980) study reported significantly lower aspirations for future educational activities. On a brighter note, Sitlington et al. (1989) stated that nearly 20% of the high school graduates with LD in their statewide sample had been enrolled in community colleges, 5% in junior college, and 3.4% in a 4-year college; nearly 9% were in the military. Among the dropouts, 14% had enrolled in community colleges, 7% had participated in adult basic education classes, and over 5% were in apprenticeship programs.

One study reported substantially different results in the area of postsecondary education. Remarkably, 34% of the sample in the Rogan and Hartman (1990) investigation had completed 4 years of college or graduate work, and 39% had completed high school and "possibly some community or junior college work" (p. 92). These adults had participated in an earlier follow-up study (Rogan & Hartman, 1976) and had been enrolled in private schools for children with learning disabilities during their elementary and middle school years.

Social Adjustment

Of all of the areas of adjustment that were investigated in the studies reviewed, social adjustment got the least amount of attention. In the studies that did report social adjustment variables, the majority of adults with LD could be described as single (Chelser, 1982; Cobb & Crump, 1984; Rogan & Hartman, 1990; Sitlington et al., 1989; White et al., 1980) and living at home or with relatives (Chelser, 1982; Cobb & Crump, 1984; Fafard & Haubrich, 1981; Sitlington etal., 1989; White et al., 1980). Although many did participate in some leisure activities (Sitlington et al., 1989), adults with LD participated in significantly fewer recreational, fraternal, social, and community activities than NLD adults. In addition, they were significantly less satisfied with their family relationships and had fewer friends they could go places with or share activities with (White et al., 1980).

Areas of concern within the social domain that were mentioned in the reviewed literature include talking or acting out without thinking, shyness, dating, frustration, no self-confidence, and controlling emotions (Hoffman et al., 1987). In a national study of over 500 adults with LD, Chelser (1982) reported that the most frequently mentioned need for assistance was in social skill training and the fourth most frequent was overcoming dependence; academic areas such as reading and spelling ranked near the bottom of the top 10 concerns. Blalock (1981) commented that one of the most common complaints from her sample of adults concerned the amount of effort expended on hiding or avoiding the problems created by the learning disability.

These concerns about problems in social skills are significant because within the workplace social skills are very important; in fact, they may be one of the more important skills for successful adjustment (Carnevale et al., 1988). Table 4.2 lists interpersonal skills, listening, and oral communication as critical skills for employees to possess. Interpersonal skills important in the workplace include dealing with undesirable behavior in others, dealing with stress, dealing with ambiguity, interacting easily with others, and sharing responsibility (Carnevale et al., 1988). Communication skills such as understanding voice inflections and body language, adjusting to different communication styles, and resolving conflict are mentioned in the workplace literature as being important; critical listening skills include listening for content, listening to conversations, listening for long-term contexts, listening for emotional meaning, and listening to directions (Carnevale et al., 1988). That Chelser's (1982) respondents ranked social skill training as the area most needing assistance implies that the skills listed above as required in the workplace will not be areas of strength for many adults with learning disabilities and may prevent them from maintaining or advancing in employment.

Discussion

Though there were a few inconsistent (and even occasionally conflicting) results in the investigations reviewed, enough consistent findings were found that some generalizations can be made about adults with LD. First, it is clear that learning disabilities persist into adulthood. The majority of adults in these studies still demonstrated or reported substantial deficits in reading, spelling, and arithmetic. Second, the effects of the learning disabilities are frequently not the same as in school-age children. Learning disabilities cause academic difficulties for school-age children, but because the rate of participation in formal learning settings is very low for adults with learning disabilities, those disabilities do not typically cause academic difficulties for them. Instead, the learning disabilities more frequently cause problems in the vocational and social domains, as evidenced by the adults' high unemployment rates, underemployment, and general lack of satisfaction with their personal and vocational lives. Third, the number of adults with LD who have been able to achieve the level of independence and self-sufficiency necessary to "take their place in society" is disappointingly low. Although many adults with LD are enjoying satisfying and meaningful lives, many are not.

Returning to the basic criteria for adults mentioned in the beginning paragraph of this chapter (Clark & Kolstoe, 1990), the only criterion fully met was that there was no evidence that adults with learning disabilities behave in ways that are threatening or unacceptable. Only about 50% are able to live independently and the majority are not self-supporting. In the words of Edgar (1987),"[former] special education students do not appear to be partaking of the fruits of our society" (p. 556).

Unfortunately, future reviews of follow-up studies may report even more pessimistic results. Changes in skill requirements and the nature of work may combine to place adults with LD at an even greater disadvantage in adult contexts. The demands of adult life are changing rapidly but the schools' curricula are not. An analysis of Table 4.2. reveals few skills that are currently being included in most secondary curricula, yet these are the real adult demands young adults will encounter.

In the past it could be successfully argued that higher levels of basic skills would increase one's vocational chances. This may no longer be true. What is needed now and in the future is not simply more of the same basic academic skills that have been taught for 20 years: Adults are expected and will be expected to use these basic skills to solve problems and communicate with others; adults are expected and will be expected to listen to others, be able to negotiate, and work as team members. These are skills that will help students take their place in society. Special education teachers must begin to examine not only their own curriculum in light of the elements in Table 4.2, but also the curriculum of regular education to determine if, for any specific student, the knowledge and skills needed in the anticipated adult contexts are being provided.

I do not think the outcomes revealed in this review are the best that can be expected, or that anyone should be destined for a less-than-optimal adult status simply because he or she has a learning disability. I think it is possible to greatly increase the chances that more adults with learning disabilities will take meaningful places in society. But for that to happen, education professionals will have to begin paying as much attention to what young adults will need to do as is now spent on how they are doing. Students should be prepared for the environments in which they will find themselves, whether that be college, technical training, employment, or the home. Therefore, researchers must be diligent in providing current information about the demands adults will face both in the workplace and in everyday life, and teachers must be prepared to continually seek out this information and make the necessary adjustments in the curriculum. It is not enough to review the follow-up literature and feel disappointed that more adults with learning disabilities are not doing better. Significant work must be done to ensure that professionals spend the time students are in school preparing them to take their places in society.

5. *Learning Disabilities and Vocational Rehabilitation*

CAROL A. DOWDY, TOM E.C. SMITH, AND CARL H. NOWELL

Students with learning disabilities (LD) have been served in special education programs for many years. Although this was one of the latest disabilities recognized, it is currently the largest single disability group that receives special education services in public schools. The 12th Annual Report to Congress (U.S. Department of Education, 1990) noted that in 1988–1989, 1.9 million students classified as learning disabled received special education services. This was 47.7% of the total number of students receiving special education services.

Although the numbers of students in special education with learning disabilities have risen sharply over the past several years, adults with this disability still make up a small percentage of persons receiving services from vocational rehabilitation (VR) agencies. The number of clients with learning disabilities who were rehabilitated by vocational rehabilitation agencies increased from 1.3% to 4.9% between 1983 and 1988 (L. I. Mars, personal communication, April 9, 1990; Mars, 1986), but their number remains significantly smaller than the number of high school students with learning disabilities who are served in special education programs. In 1988–1989, 1.3 million students with learning disabilities,

---

Reprinted, with changes, from "Learning disabilities and vocational rehabilitation," by Carol A. Dowdy, Tom E. C. Smith, and Carl H. Nowell, *Journal of Learning Disabilities,* Vol. 25, 1992, pp. 442–447.

ages 12 to 21, received special education services (U.S. Department of Education, 1990).

Obviously, not all persons with learning disabilities need to be served by vocational rehabilitation agencies. However, the discrepancy between the number of adults who have learning disabilities and the number who receive vocational rehabilitation services suggests that some adults who are eligible for such services are not receiving them. Several reasons possibly explain the discrepancy between the number of teenagers with learning disabilities in special eduction programs and the number of adults with LD who receive vocational rehabilitation services. One of the most critical is the lack of information special education teachers possess about vocational rehabilitation services. Special education teachers, as well as young adults with learning disabilities, need to develop a better understanding of the vocational rehabilitation system in order to access services more efficiently. The purpose of this chapter is to present information that will explain how the vocational rehabilitation system deals with persons who have learning disabilities. The definition of LD used by the Rehabilitation Services Administration (RSA) will be presented, as well as diagnostic criteria and guidelines used for eligibility.

DEFINITION

Just as the field of special education has struggled to define learning disabilities, establish eligibility criteria, and provide appropriate services, the field of rehabilitation is currently faced with similar challenges (Szymanski, King, Parker, & Jenkins, 1989). Because of basic differences in the orientation of public school and VR programs, VR agencies have adopted their own definition and implemented separate diagnostic and eligibility criteria relating to providing services to persons with LD. Although the VR definitions and eligibility criteria better suit the needs of the adult service agency, the different approaches may have further limited the services provided to this group of individuals.

One of the original roadblocks to providing VR services to persons with LD was that the RSA system recognized only mental or physical disabilities. States began to initiate the development and implementation of services to individuals with LD only after the Rehabilitation Services Administration's 1981 policy directive making specific learning disabilities a medically recognized disability (Gerber, 1981; Miller, Mulkey, & Kopp, 1984; Rehabilitation Services Administration, 1981). In 1985, RSA distributed a program policy directive to the state VR agencies that contained a definition recommended for adoption (Rehabilitation Services Administration, 1985). That definition stated the following:

> A specific learning disability is a disorder in one or more of the central nervous system processes involved in perceiving, understanding, and/or using concepts through verbal (spoken or written) language or nonverbal means. This disorder manifests itself with a deficit in one or more of the following areas: attention, reasoning, processing memory, communication, reading, writing, spelling, calculation, coordination, social competence, and emotional maturity. (p. 2)

This definition is similar in many ways to the definitions of LD contained in the Education for All Handicapped Children Act of 1975 (P.L. 94-142; *Federal Register,* 1977) and the definition of LD recommended by the National Joint Committee for Learning Disabilities (NJCLD) (National Joint Committee for Learning Disabilities, 1981). All three definitions attempt to describe persons who have learning difficulties that are not explained by other disabilities.

Despite general similarities, the RSA definition differs from the other two in that it reflects the position that a learning disability is a lifelong (permanent) disability resulting from a central nervous system dysfunction as suggested in the definition recommended by the NJCLD for special education (National Joint Committee for Learning Disabilities, 1981). The definition of learning disabilities in P.L. 94-142 does not refer to the condition as a lifelong problem. The RSA definition's reference to processing deficits involved in perceiving, understanding, and using spoken or written language concepts is similar to the statement in the P.L. 94-142 definition (*Federal Register,* 1977). All three definitions contain a list of manifestations of learning disabilities; although most of these overlap, the RSA definition exclusively lists attention, memory, coordination, social competence, and emotional maturity. These specific manifestations are extremely important in that they are used by vocational rehabilitation agencies as criteria for eligibility.

The RSA definition does not include a clause excluding other primary handicapping conditions, as is in the NJCLD and P.L. 94-142 definitions, nor does it reference specific discrepancy criteria as found in the special education identification criteria issued in the *Federal Register* (1977). However, these two components of the definition and the identification criteria are inherent in the diagnostic criteria used by the majority of state vocational rehabilitation agencies.

Diagnosis

Most state vocational rehabilitation agencies require that a diagnosis of learning disabilities be made by a licensed physician or psychologist trained to identify persons with this condition. Because these professionals use the *Diagnostic and Statistical Manual–3rd Edition, Revised* (DSM-III-R; American Psychiatric Association, 1987) for diagnostic criteria, eligibility for vocational rehabilitation services is based on the DSM-III-R. The DSM-III-R does not include learning disabilities as a specific diagnostic category. The most logical categories used for persons with learning disabilities are Specific Delays in Developmental Disorders and Disruptive Behavior Disorders. These disorders generally begin in childhood or adolescence and persist in stable form (without remission or exacerbation) into adult life (American Psychiatric Association, 1987).

The Specific Developmental Disorders subclass in DSM-III-R includes disorders characterized by inadequate development of specific academic, language, speech, and motor skills. Part of the criteria requires that the inadequate development cannot be explained by demonstrable physical (including visual and hearing acuity) or neurological disorders, a pervasive developmental disorder, mental retardation, or deficient educational opportunities. Furthermore, the impairment must interfere significantly with school performance or activities of daily living. Achievement, measured by standardized, individually administered tests, must be markedly below expected levels, compared to the individual's intellectual capacity (measured by individually administered IQ tests).

Areas included in Specific Developmental Disorders are arithmetic, reading, expressive writing, expressive (oral) language, receptive language, articulation, and motor skills. Examples of specific skills are listed for each area. For example, the area of expressive writing includes spelling, grammar, punctuation, and paragraph organization.

The category Other Developmental Disorders is used as a diagnostic classification for additional developmental disorders that may be present but are not included in the Specific Developmental Disorder category. A final category that can be used for diagnosing individuals with learning disabilities is Disruptive Behavior Disorders. Under this category the two disorders applied to the LD population are Attention Deficit–Hyperactivity Disorder (ADHD) and Undifferentiated Attention Deficit Disorder (UADD).

ADHD essentially refers to varying degrees of inattention, impulsiveness, and hyperactivity that are developmentally inappropriate. The disorder typically is manifested in most environments; however, the behaviors may be absent in novel, strictly controlled, individualized, or reinforcing situations. Behaviors are typically the most prevalent in situations requiring sustained attention. When signs of hyperactivity and impulsiveness are not present, the diagnosis Undifferentiated Attention Deficit Disorder is usually made. However, the validity of this diagnostic category is raised in DSM-III-R.

Diagnosis and Referral

Most state vocational rehabilitation agencies will not automatically accept a school's label of learning disabilities as an official diagnosis because of the additional diagnostic categories (attention, motor skills, and articulation) available to state vocational rehabilitation agencies and the requirement that persons making the diagnosis be licensed professionals. Thus, even in cases where a student has been served as learning disabled in schools for several years, the diagnostic process is usually repeated. Teachers must therefore be aware that their former students will not automatically receive vocational rehabilitation services simply because they were in special education.

Any person can be referred to a state vocational rehabilitation agency for services. Referrals are frequently made by school special education programs, parents, and self-referrals. With the growing emphasis on the transition of students with learning disabilities from school to postschool environments, the likelihood increases that these students will be referred for vocational rehabilitation services. This fact alone makes it crucial that special education teachers understand how to access vocational rehabilitation services for their students. After referral, evaluation data are collected to determine if the individual is eligible for vocational rehabilitation services.

The evaluation process begins with an initial intake interview conducted by an appropriate vocational rehabilitation counselor. Some states have designated counselors who work only with persons with learning disabilities; however, general caseload counselors who work with persons with all disabilities are more common. The initial interview will focus on the individual's history, school records, and employment goals.

During the interview, the counselor establishes the applicant's interest in the rehabilitation process and commitment to work. Throughout the interview the counselor will be noting the individual's characteristic that may be a handicap to employment or a strength in a job setting. With the applicant's permission, the counselor arranges to obtain information from a variety of relevant sources, including medical, previous psychological or vocational testing, and school records. Each individual will generally be referred for a current medical exam and a diagnostic assessment.

This evaluation may include a comprehensive vocational assessment of career interests, functional limitations and capacities, as well as a test battery for diagnosis. For persons to receive appropriate vocational rehabilitation counseling and services, a thorough vocational evaluation is critical. Information obtained from the vocational evaluation enables vocational rehabilitation personnel to understand the person's strengths and weaknesses related to various jobs and necessary training. A comprehensive assessment and report from the persons conducting the evaluation is critical in providing the counselor with data to support eligibility for rehabilitation services (McCue, 1989; Vogel, 1989).

ELIGIBILITY

Understanding the concept of eligibility is the key to understanding the vocational rehabilitation process. It is important to note that, unlike public schools, vocational rehabilitation programs are not an entitlement program. The diagnosis of learning disabilities by a licensed professional does not automatically entitle one to vocational rehabilitation services (Abbott, 1987). In other words, a person may be diagnosed as having a disability but may not be eligible for vocational rehabilitation services. Specific criteria are established and each case may potentially be monitored to assure that the eligibility criteria established at the federal level by RSA have been met. General criteria include the following: (a) the presence of a physical or mental disability that constitutes or results in a substantial handicap to employment; and (b) a reasonable expectation that vocational rehabilitation services may benefit the individual in terms of employability.

Many vocational rehabilitation counselors tend to think of a learning disability as primarily an academic disability that does not necessarily result in a vocational handicap. If the diagnostic process used has been modeled after a school battery, the assessment may be limited to measures of academic deficits and intelligence. This limited view of learning disabilities will not provide counselors with information about the impact of the LD characteristics, which can impede vocational success (National Joint Committee on Learning Disabilities, 1987). For example, an individual with only a reading, math, or expressive language deficit may be employed in an occupation that bypasses the disability (Simpson & Umbach, 1989)—for example, a job in landscaping would not necessarily require academic skills. Therefore, a counselor would not be able to document that the disability meets the requirements for eligibility or constitutes a vocational handicap requiring vocational rehabilitation services in order for the individual to obtain employment. With proper training, vocational rehabilitation counselors learn that rarely does an individual with a learning disability have isolated academic skill deficits. More frequently, he or she manifests a variety of behaviors that will limit vocational success just as they have created difficulties in academic settings. In fact, a recent study showed that the problems and characteristics associated with learning disabilities persist, and even may worsen, into adulthood (Gerber et al., 1990). Characteristics frequently attributed to adults with learning disabilities include deficits in attention, reasoning, processing, memory, communication, coordination, social competence, and emotional maturity (Hawks et al., 1990; Johnson & Blalock, 1987; McCue, Shelly, & Goldstein, 1986; Newill, Goyette, & Fogarty, 1984; Patton & Polloway, 1982; Polloway, Smith, & Patton, 1984; Zwerlin, Smith, & Diffley, 1984).

Vocational rehabilitation counselors are faced with the challenge of observing and documenting these characteristics during a relatively brief intake interview in order to appropriately determine eligibility. This process is complicated by the fact that learning disabilities are not as obvious as some other handicapping conditions, such as a major physical disability that leaves a person immobile. Rather than displaying characteristics that reveal an obvious disability, persons with learning disabilities are more likely to display indirect characteristics, such as arriving late for an appointment, limited eye contact, responding to questions in short, simple sentences, and providing limited background information. An individual who displays these kinds of behaviors may appear to the counselor to be an unmotivated, uncooperative applicant, when in fact he or she could have limitations in time management, organization, social skills, oral language, and long-term memory. It would require multiple services to address these limitations (Kopp, Miller, & Mulkey, 1984).

Some aids have been developed to assist the vocational rehabilitation counselor in documenting the characteristics of learning disabilities. Comprehensive diagnostic batteries and vocational assessment can lead to a thorough investigation of the disability (Hawks et al., 1990; Hursh, 1984; McCue, 1989; Prickett, 1988). The LD Characteristics Checklist (Dowdy, 1990) and the Behavior Questionnaire and Rating Scale for the Learning Disabled (Koller, 1990) are also recommended as effective assessment tools.

RSA has alerted the state vocational rehabilitation agencies to the importance of identifying the behaviors characteristic of learning disabilities. In the previously referenced RSA policy directive to state vocational rehabilitation agencies (Rehabilitation Services Administration, 1985), it was emphasized that characteristics such as problems with attention, memory, and social interaction may have greater implications for vocational planning and employment than those associated with poor academic performance. Therefore, a primary consideration for vocational rehabilitation professionals is documenting the manifestations of learning disabilities that can cause vocational problems.

Severe Handicap Determination

Another important step in the vocational rehabilitation process is evaluating the individual to determine whether his or her specific learning disability constitutes a severe handicap. There has been resistance among some vocational rehabilitation counselors to coding an individual with learning disabilities as severely handicapped when the individual has no physical disabilities, has average to above-average intelligence, and manifests primarily academic deficiencies. Counselors are more likely to identify persons with paraplegia or quadriplegia as severely handicapped, even though a person with a learning disability may have a more difficult time experiencing job success than the person with the physical limitation. National data from RSA indicate that in 1988, only 50% of the rehabilitation clients with learning disabilities were determined to be severely handicapped, whereas approximately 70% of all other vocational rehabilitation clients were classified as severely handicapped (L. I. Mars, personal communication, April 9, 1990).

An individual with a severe handicap is defined in the 1986 Amendments to the Rehabilitation Act of 1973 (P.L. 99-506) as an individual with handicaps who has a severe physical or mental disability that seriously limits one or more functional capacities (mobility, communication, self-care, self-direction, work tolerance, work skills, or interpersonal skills) in terms of employability. Also, the vocational rehabilitation process must be expected to require multiple vocational rehabilitation services over an extended period of time.

In 1990 RSA appointed a task force to study this and other critical issues raised in the application of the vocational rehabilitation process to clients with learning disabilities. The result was a comprehensive guide that assists counselors in understanding and accessing the severe vocational limitations imposed by learning disability characteristics, such as attention, memory, and social skill deficits (Rehabilitation Services Administration, 1990). This effort was critical, because many state vocational rehabilitation agencies are under an order of selection that requires them to provide services to persons with handicaps on a priority basis or exclusively. As vocational rehabilitation counselors become more aware of the severe limitations imposed by learning disabilities, more persons with this disability will be classified as severely handicapped.

Vocational Rehabilitation Services

The focus of all services provided by VR agencies is on employment. These services are available to eligible individuals who are unemployed, at risk for losing their job, or underemployed. The comprehensive diagnostic assessment and intake process provides counselors with information about an applicant's functional limitations, learning style, and functional capacities. After the person is determined to be eligible for VR services, the counselor utilizes the vocationally pertinent information to develop an Individualized Written Rehabilitation Program (IWRP). Following agreement of the plan by the client, rehabilitation services begin.

Because IWRPs are individualized, there is no standard package of services for persons with learning disabilities. Counseling is at the core of the service program. Vocational rehabilitation counselors assist clients in career decisions and in identifying accommodations needed in postsecondary training sites and on the job. A key decision point is whether the client with a learning disability elects to go to college or some other form of postsecondary educational program. Many colleges and universities currently have programs specifically designed for students with learning disabilities. Vocational rehabilitation counselors should be able to help these students decide on an appropriate postsecondary education option. They also provide ongoing progress checks to monitor success and make adjustments as needed. Clients may be trained in a rehabilitation facility or receive partial or full support of college and/or technical school costs.

Many times counselors will enlist the support of professionals in other agencies, such as mental health or special student services on a college campus, in an advocacy role for their client. However, all of these services must ultimately focus on the client obtaining and maintaining employment.

Vocational rehabilitation services are not necessary for all adults with learning disabilities to reach their maximum vocational potential. However, when the need is present and eligibility can be supported, the vocational rehabilitation program can promote success in the life of the adult with a learning disability.

Too often, young adults with learning disabilities who are eligible for vocational rehabilitation services, and who could benefit from such services, are not receiving them. Although this could be the result of several factors, a primary reason is special education teachers' limited understanding of the vocational rehabilitation system. Limited understanding of special education services by vocational rehabilitation professionals also contributes to deficits in adult services.

For young adults with learning disabilities to receive vocational rehabilitation services at appropriate levels, rehabilitation counselors and special educators must begin working together to better understand each other's systems. Agreeing on a common definition, characteristics, and nomenclature would be an excellent beginning in the development of a service delivery system that is a coordinated, lifelong system, rather than the series of services currently provided by different agencies.

It is important for special education teachers and vocational rehabilitation counselors to continue to explore the vocational issues relating to individuals with learning disabilities and look for successful techniques in applying the education and rehabilitation process to such clients. It is just as important for adults with learning disabilities and their advocates to understand the vocational rehabilitation process and come to that agency as informed partners.

6. *Promoting Access, Accommodations, and Independence for College Students with Learning Disabilities*

LORING C. BRINCKERHOFF, STAN F. SHAW,
AND JOAN M. McGUIRE

Increasing numbers of students with learning disabilities (LD) are pursuing higher education as an option after high school (Astin, Green, Korn, Schalit, & Berg, 1988; U.S. Department of Education, 1987). To enhance understanding of the challenges associated with higher education for students with learning disabilities, consideration must be given to a number of issues relating to implementation of Section 504 of the Rehabilitation Act of 1973 in postsecondary settings. The purpose of this chapter is to identify several specific areas at the postsecondary level that may affect long-term outcomes for college students with learning disabilities. The points of discussion to be addressed surfaced on a recurring basis at numerous college campuses in the Northeast during the implementation of the Northeast Technical Assistance Center for Learning Disability College Programming (NETAC) grant sponsored by the U.S. Department of Education, Office of Special Education. Based on nearly 20 site visits

---

Reprinted, with changes, from "Promoting access, accommodations, and independence for college students with learning disabilities," by Loring C. Brickerhoff, Stan F. Shaw, and Joan M. McGuire, *Journal of Learning Disabilities,* Vol. 25, 1992, pp. 417–429.

to a variety of public and private, 2- and 4-year settings, LD service providers and higher education administrators requested more information and clarification on these critical issues than on any others (Brinckerhoff, Shaw, & McGuire, 1990).

This chapter will focus on four primary issues that will most likely affect the greatest number of students with learning disabilities as they plan to attend a postsecondary setting. Topics discussed include (a) How are high school and postsecondary settings different? (b) How are eligibility and access determined? (c) How are "reasonable accommodations" determined? and (d) How can the independence level of college students be fostered? Each of these issues will be discussed within the context of the student's transition from high school, where the Education for All Handicapped Children Act of 1975 (P.L. 94-142) is in effect, to college, where Section 504 of the Rehabilitation Act of 1973 applies. Suggestions for meeting challenges are offered based on prevailing practices on college campuses and discussions with numerous service providers in a wide variety of postsecondary settings.

Bridging the High School–College Gap

Before considering questions surrounding the concepts of eligibility and access, it is important to reflect on the differences between the demands in secondary and postsecondary settings. These differences will shed light on factors that bear heavily on outcomes for students who pursue higher education. Expectations in a postsecondary environment are both quantitatively and qualitatively different from demands at the high school level. College classroom instructional time is typically 12 to 15 hours per week (or perhaps less, for students with learning disabilities carrying a reduced course load), in contrast to 25 to 30 hours in high school (McGuire, 1988). This implies more emphasis in college on independent reading and study time, because learning is considered to be student-centered, not teacher-focused. Dexter (1982) suggested that college professors expect a higher level of academic proficiency than was acceptable in high school, and it is scholastic performance that determines student status in a college setting. Qualitatively, college, with its emphasis on student responsibility for decision making, is drastically different from high school. This freedom of choice is consistent with the tenet of academic freedom that is a long-established tradition in American higher education and that fosters the pursuit of inquiry and research among faculty (Gardner & Jewler, 1985). At the college level, students are expected to (a) balance personal freedom with the need to set personal goals; (b) work on semester projects; (c) glean information from numerous sources, including class notes, texts, and library reference materials; and (d) in general, function autonomously.

These differences between the setting demands of high school and college imply a need for the ability to use a broad array of learning and study strategies to achieve success. Yet, the literature addressing college-bound students with learning disabilities suggests a major area of concern regarding their level of preparedness. Dalke and Schmitt (1987) pointed out that individual guidance in a structured, extrinsically controlled, supportive setting such as high school may hamper the transition process to a college environment. Mangrum and Strichart (1988) stated that college students with learning disabilities frequently lack effective study habits and continue to exhibit deficits in basic skills. Carlson (1985) stressed that the emphasis at the secondary level should shift from subject-matter tutoring to instruction in enabling skills that will serve to lessen the impact of a learning disability on future learning. In essence, underpreparedness and limited awareness of postsecondary expectations may widen the gap between high school and college for many students with learning disabilities, and thereby diminish the potential positive effects of the guarantees for program accessibility under Section 504.

Determining Eligibility and Access

Section 504 as it applies to postsecondary institutions stipulates that "a recipient shall operate each program or activity . . . so that the program or activity, when viewed in its entirety, is readily accessible to handicapped persons" (Section 104.22[a]). Not only does this provision apply to physical facilities on campuses, but it also covers all aspects of student life, including admissions, recruitment to academic programs, and academic adjustments. For students with learning disabilities, each of these guarantees may play a critical role in their ultimate success or failure in higher education. In this section, issues of eligibility and access will be explored with consideration of the contrasts between protection under P.L. 94-142 (renamed the Individuals with Disabilities Act) and Section 504.

Prior to exploring some of the challenges at the postsecondary level, it is important to define the eligibility of persons with handicaps as a protected class under existing legislation. By virtue of P.L. 94-142, all children and youth with handicaps between the ages of 3 and 21 are guaranteed the availability of a free, appropriate public education (FAPE) in the least restrictive environment (LRE). Their entitlement is supported by the use of federal funds according to a payment formula that takes into account the national average expenditure per public school child and the number of students with handicaps receiving special education in each state (Ballard, Ramirez, & Zantal-Wiener, 1987). Under P.L. 94-142, two criteria must be met to establish eligibility: (a) A student must actually have one or more of the disabilities defined under the Act, and (b) such a student must require special education and related services. If these two conditions are met, a student is ensured a free, appropriate public education.

Section 504 refers only to nondiscrimination; it is not a funding statute (Rothstein, 1990). Eligibility for protection under Section 504 is determined by the following criteria:

1. If the person:
   a. has a physical or mental impairment that substantially limits one or more major life functions;
   b. has a history of such impairment; or
   c. is regarded as having such an impairment; and
2. If the person with a disability meets the academic and technical standards requisite to admission or participation in a college or university's programs or activities, then that student must be ensured equal educational opportunity, not a free, appropriate education.

Program accessibility is perhaps the most crucial term in Section 504, as it applies to all aspects of student life, including (a) admissions, (b) recruitment, (c) academic programs and adjustments, (d) treatment of students, and (e) nonacademic services (Sections 104.42 to 104.44; 104.47). Modifications to academic requirements, such as changing the length of time allowed to complete degree requirements or permitting alternative testing procedures, do not guarantee equal results or achievement for persons with or without handicaps. Such adjustments only afford an *equal opportunity* to achieve equal results (Biehl, 1978).

Determining a student's eligibility for protection under Section 504 becomes a complex issue for college personnel, in part because of limited judicial clarification of substantive issues. Rothstein (1986) pointed out that problems arise in determining whether a student actually has a specific learning disability. Although identification under the Individuals with Disabilities Act while in public schools is not a binding determination of LD, Rothstein speculated that such a determination most likely would carry considerable weight in justifying eligibility under Section 504. Although this may fall within the parameters of having a history of an impairment, the relevance of diagnostic data varies according to their recency. Information gathered at the elementary school level is of questionable value to determination of appropriate postsecondary accommodations. Given the heterogeneity of the LD population, blanket accommodations do little to build upon a student's strengths or compensate for specific weaknesses, or to ultimately equip the student to meet subsequent challenges after graduation in the world of work. In summary, there should always be a data-based connection between the student's learning strengths and weaknesses and his or her eligibility for *specific* types of accommodations.

Issues of eligibility as a protected class under Section 504 become even more complicated in cases where students have been diagnosed by private consultants or psychologists. Without consensus in the field regarding a definition or a validated theory for understanding learning disabilities, opportunities for unwarranted eligibility are rampant. This concern is not unique to postsecondary settings. Ysseldyke et al. (1983) investigated problems in assessment and decision making in elementary and secondary schools and concluded that identification often rests on inconsistent and indefensible criteria. Furthermore, Mellard (1990) suggested that the establishment of eligibility procedures at the postsecondary level should be tailored to individual postsecondary contexts. Does this mean that criteria will differ from campus to campus? Given the dearth of reliable and valid test instruments for diagnosing adults with learning disabilities (Carlton & Walkenshaw, 1991; Mangrum & Strichart, 1988), will postsecondary service providers face eligibility decisions without any agreement regarding appropriate documentation? How will the phrase "substantially limits one or more major life activities" be interpreted in justifying eligibility for those students who are tested and diagnosed for the first time during their college enrollment? Rothstein (1986) suggested that college and university personnel would be well advised to remain a breast of case law involving handicap discrimination claims, which will undoubtedly include issues such as these.

Application of the accessibility provision warrants consideration. The protection of students with learning disabilities against statutory discrimination in the admissions process may be a moot point in postsecondary settings that have open admissions policies. Community colleges and some junior colleges require only a high school diploma or General Education Development (GED) test to determine eligibility for admission (Scheiber & Talpers, 1987). In settings that use more comprehensive criteria to determine eligibility for admission, the question of ensuring equal educational access must be considered within the context of Section 504's stipulation that applicants must be "otherwise qualified" individuals with disabilities. Scott (1990) articulated a number of issues in the implementation of this construct, including the use of standardized admissions tests and the validity of traditional criteria, such as high school performance. Mangrum and Strichart (1988) described a variety of admissions policies and raised concerns about the validity of a standard policy that often uses data such as rank in class, scores on tests such as the SAT or ACT, and high school grade-point average, with no consideration as to whether the applicant is "otherwise qualified." Some postsecondary institutions have developed cooperative admissions procedures, which are based not only on standard criteria but also on supplementary information voluntarily submitted to further support an LD applicant's potential. LD service providers should consider planning a data base to gather longitudinal data on the characteristics of students with learning disabilities (e.g., high school rank, SAT/ACT, achievement tests, motivation and study skills, GPA, degree completion) who are successful. This information can be used to develop a profile of "typical students with learning disabilities" who have already been determined to be "otherwise qualified" as it relates to eligibility for admission. Although these approaches are only a beginning, they may serve as incentives for others to use for enhancing access.

Legal precedent regarding the definition of "otherwise qualified" has been established by the Supreme Court's ruling in *Southeastern Community College v. Davis* (1979). In that case, a nursing student with a hearing impairment was denied admission to a nursing program based on the advice of outside consultants, because she was dependent on lip reading and not able to understand normal spoken speech. The applicant sued the institution under Section 504. The court upheld the denial, ruling that the student's handicap did in fact prevent her from safely completing the program and performing in a nursing profession. The court concluded that "Section 504 imposes no requirement upon an educational institution to lower or to effect substantial modifications of standards to accommodate a handicapped person." Educational institutions may require reasonable physical qualifications for admission and are not required to eliminate requirements that are a necessary part of the curriculum (Heyward, 1990).

Open-admission policies or special admissions procedures that allow more flexibility in determining whether an applicant with a learning disability is qualified may have the potential for inadvertent negative results. Access, defined in Section 504 as including reasonable academic adjustments and use of auxiliary aids, may not be sufficient to overcome underpreparedness, skills deficits, and curricular deficiencies for students with learning disabilities who may have been in non-college-preparatory secondary programs. Although Section 504 speaks clearly to the fact that equal opportunity, not guaranteed outcomes, is the objective, it is important to bear in mind the financial, emotional, and psychological costs to students with learning disabilities if they are eligible for admission but are at risk for failure. Access should be addressed from this perspective: Does this student appear to have the potential to succeed in this setting with reasonable academic adjustments and auxiliary aids? Planned interventions at the secondary level may well be the key to future student success so that access means more than enrollment. McGuire and Shaw (1987) described a comprehensive process to help parents and professionals make reasoned judgments about the "match" between the student and the postsecondary setting.

Access to postsecondary settings by students with learning disabilities can be enhanced in several ways. High school staff need to establish linkages with postsecondary service providers and counselors so that college-bound students with learning disabilities can make a smooth transition from high school into an appropriate postsecondary setting. Evelo and Price (1991) described a model of interagency cooperation that focused on long-term planning. In this model, transition counseling services begin in high school and include objectives such as vocational assessment, personal goal setting, information gathering about postsecondary options, job shadowing and interviewing as they relate to career exploration, completion of financial aid forms, and application to colleges that are a suitable match given the students' strengths and weaknesses. Evelo and Price pointed out that once a student accesses college, continued monitoring by a postsecondary transition counselor should focus on objectives such as review of course selections, assistance in self-advocacy, arranging for appropriate accommodations, and ongoing goal setting. An adaptation of this model, developed by the LD Transition Project, a federally funded demonstration project at the University of Minnesota, could broaden opportunities for postsecondary access through collaborative efforts among consumers, high school personnel, and college service providers. Aune (1991) noted that students who participated in the LD Transition Project reported having, at the conclusion of the project, better study habits, more knowledge about postsecondary options, an ability to request the accommodations they needed, and an awareness of their learning disability including its strengths and weaknesses. Another approach to fostering successful transitions from high school to college is to develop a summer orientation program specifically for high school graduates with learning disabilities. The primary purpose of such a program is to systematically address some of the academic, social, and personal challenges that students with learning disabilities will face in college (Brinckerhoff & Eaton, 1991). Regardless of what programming option is used to smooth the transition from high school to college, disability self-awareness is pivotal in further operationalizing the provisions in Section 504 for program access via academic adjustments and auxiliary aids that are considered reasonable.

Determining Academic Adjustments

P.L. 94-142 stipulates that the local education agency (LEA) is responsible for identifying, assessing, and serving students with disabilities. In contrast, under Section 504, college students are viewed as being best equipped to initially identify themselves and assess their own individual educational needs. College students have the responsibility under Section 504 to notify the appropriate institutional representative or LD service provider of their learning disability and the types of accommodations that may be necessary. Self-identification may occur as part of the application process or at any point that academic adjustments are deemed necessary by the student. P.L. 94-142 mandates that the local education agency provide all the mandated services necessary for the child with a disability so that he or she can function in the least restrictive educational environment. The need for these services is determined by a multidisciplinary team, and an Individualized Education Program (IEP) is subsequently developed to document how the identified needs will be met. In the postsecondary setting, Section 504 views the student as the central figure in determining the educational program and services to be utilized. The student has the option of self-identifying and of requesting accommodations, auxiliary aids, and/or services that may be necessary to compensate for the learning disability. The student has the responsibility of providing documentation of the learning disability and working with the LD service provider to determine what academic adjustments will compensate for the learning disability. Scott (1991) stressed that once the accommodation is established, the student with a learning disability must also monitor his or her own academic performance.

P.L. 94-142 seems to encourage expectations and patterns of behavior that foster dependence in students with learning disabilities. The less prescriptive Section 504 puts much more responsibility on the student (Scott, 1991). As indicated in Table 6.1, P.L. 94-142 gives the LEA, parent, or placement team responsibility for most roles; at the postsecondary level that is not the case. P.L. 94-142 does encourage student participation in the placement team process, but years of parental and profes-

TABLE 6.1
Responsibilities Under P.L. 94-142 and Section 504 at Secondary and Postsecondary Levels

Issue	Responsibility at secondary level	Responsibility at postsecondary level
Identification	School	Student
Assessment	School	Student
Programming	School/parent	Student–institution
Advocacy	School/parent	Student
Decision making	Placement team	Student
Transition planning	Placement team	Student

sional control have not adequately prepared the student for that responsibility.

At the postsecondary level, once documentation of the learning disability is complete, it is the responsibility of the LD service provider or other institutional contact to respond to the student's request for services. The provision for services is required only if the student informs the institution of a handicapping condition and requests services (see *Salvador v. Bell,* 1986). Unlike P.L. 94-142, which spells out the responsibilities, time lines, and types of services to be offered, Section 504 has left it to the courts to determine an institution's response to service requests on a case-by-case basis. Some of these marker cases will be discussed in a later section of this chapter.

Under Section 504 of the Rehabilitation Act, institutions are required to respond by making modifications in academic requirements as necessary to ensure that such requirements do not discriminate or have the effect of discriminating against a qualified applicant with handicaps (Sec. 104.44 a). In a postsecondary setting, a variety of modifications should be made available to college students with disabilities to assist them in earning a degree. These "academic adjustments" may include adaptations in the manner in which specific courses are conducted, the use of auxiliary equipment, and modifications in academic requirements (Brinckerhoff, 1985). Specific examples include changes in the length of time permitted for completion of a degree, substitution of specific courses, administering an exam with additional time in a private room, or permitting a student to tape-record lectures. In addition, auxiliary aids must also be provided as necessary to ensure that a student with a disability is not "denied the benefits of, excluded from participation in, or otherwise subjected to discrimination in any educational program or activity" because of the absence of auxiliary aids (Section 104.44 d). Typically, auxiliary aids for students with learning disabilities include access to taped textbooks, readers, computers, lecture notes, or other effective methods for making oral information available in an alternative form. It is the responsibility of the institution to be sure that the appropriate aids are available at the proper time. It is suggested that the institution prepare a written statement on how it will provide and fund auxiliary aids and who will ultimately be responsible for coordinating them (Handicapped Requirements Handbook, 1985).

If the proposed accommodation does not pose an undue financial or administrative burden on the institution, or result in fundamental alterations in program requirements, then the institution must ultimately bear the costs of the accommodation. Scott (1990) developed a series of guidelines to assist service providers in the determination of what is reasonable concerning different methods of instruction, the use of auxiliary aids, and alternative methods of evaluation. If the institution considers the accommodation or auxiliary aid desired by the student with a disability to be excessive or beyond what is deemed necessary to promote equal access, then it need provide only the most basic accommodation to do the job. For example, if a student with a learning disability wants verbatim class notes from a lecture, but it is determined by the LD service provider that an equivalent level of access could be achieved with a tape recorder or by a student note taker, then the less costly accommodation may be provided. Heyward (1991) noted that this process is often a delicate "balancing act" of determining what is effective. If the institution makes a "good faith" effort to provide an accommodation that is effective, it does not necessarily have to provide the most costly or comprehensive accommodation requested by the student. However, the institution must also be prepared to defend its actions based on the documentation provided by the student. Rothstein (1990) pointed out that most accommodations require the institution to make an insignificant financial commitment. However, the most costly related expense for many college students with learning disabilities involves the costs associated with being formally diagnosed (Brinckerhoff, 1991). D'Amico (1989) stated that Section 504 does not require an institution to pay for a diagnostic evaluation to document a student's learning disability. However, if the institution disputes the evaluation material offered by the student, it may have to pay for a second or updated evaluation.

Conversely, in *Southeastern Community College v. Davis* (1979), the Supreme Court unanimously decided that an "otherwise qualified" person with handicaps is one who is able to meet all of a program's requirements *in spite of* the handicap. The intent of Section 504 is not to require postsecondary institutions to disregard program requirements for individuals with disabilities; it simply requires that decisions be based on actual abilities, rather than on the prejudicial assumption that people with handicaps are in all respects less capable than others (case brief 89-1607). The *Davis* case clarified that Section 504 does not require educational institutions to lower their standards or make "substantial modifications" to their programs to accommodate persons with disabilities (case brief 89-1607). Assuming that the cost of these accommodations is not unduly burdensome, and the accommodations do not require a fundamental alteration of any essential aspects of the program, postsecondary institutions are legally required to provide the services (Rothstein, 1990). If, however, the institution can demonstrate that academic requirements requested by the student infringe on a core program of instruction, or are directly related to licensing requirements, such actions may not be viewed as discriminatory.

Attaining an accommodation in college is a two-way street (Scott, 1991). It is the responsibility of the institution to provide the accommodation, and the responsibility of the student to make a timely request.

Scott suggested that there is a need to delineate the parameters of "reasonableness," and if the source of the academic difficulty is not disability related, the student is not entitled to the accommodation. At some point, the responsibility of the institution is limited. The LD service provider, the student, and the faculty member should work closely together to discuss the types of accommodations that may be necessary in a particular course. D'Amico (1989) observed that it is essential to recognize the individual nature of a learning disability for any student who requests services, and to develop a means of effectively meeting that individual need, rather than providing the same academic adjustment or auxiliary aid for every student who identifies as having a learning disability. He stressed that institutions may negotiate the types of auxiliary aids that are provided to a student "rather than accepting a laundry list as something that must be done or else."

Once the accommodation has been determined by the service provider, it is the student's responsibility to meet with the faculty member early in the semester to discuss his or her needs. King and Jarrow (1990) believe that the final determination of accommodation should be made by Disability Service staff and should not be open to reinterpretation by the faculty member. It is the service provider who is in the best position to determine what accommodations should be made to minimize the impact of the disability (King & Jarrow, 1990). King and Jarrow affirmed that "whether or not an accommodation is to be made is not negotiable. How an accommodation is to be made is negotiable" (p. 8). For example, the location in which a test is administered, changes in test format, and the amount of time allowed to complete an exam should be determined by the LD service provider and the student in conjunction with the faculty member. The appropriateness of the accommodation request should be based on the LD service provider's knowledge of the student's disability, the impact that the disability has on performance, and the effect that auxiliary aids may have on test-taking ability. It is the faculty member's role to insure that the proposed accommodations do not have the effect of "watering down" the curriculum or substantially altering standards.

On occasion, the student and the institution may not agree on what constitutes a "reasonable accommodation" in testing or in the classroom. The use of adaptive equipment such as tape recorders, calculators, or computers requires a great deal of time and effort on the student's part. The student may want a copy of the professor's notes, or a proofreader. Such accommodations may be excessive if they are too costly, infringe on the academic freedom of the instructor, or violate the integrity of the curriculum. Under Section 504, students with learning disabilities are entitled to "equivalent access" to the educational environment; however, theinstitution may determine that some accommodations requested by the student are not appropriate and propose alternative ones.

One final area of concern regarding accommodations concerns students becoming overly dependent on these accommodations. Despite the ramifications of the Americans with Disabilities Act (ADA), it is important to keep in mind that some of the accommodations offered in the postsecondary setting may not be transferable to the world of work. For example, few employers are comfortable giving their employees double-time to complete a job assignment. Thus, it is important to recommend accommodations that can be gradually reduced over the course of the students' careers, so that when they enter the work force they will be better prepared to compete with their nondisabled peers. The more "mainstream" the accommodations the students function with, and the more facility they develop in managing their own accommodations, the greater the likelihood that those students will be successful in translating their academic success into employment success (King & Jarrow, 1990).

The provision of academic adjustments, whether they be in the form of modified testing, reduced course load, course substitution, or use of auxiliary aids, provides an opportunity for student self-advocacy and the exchange of expertise between LD service providers and faculty. This type of a "team" collaborative approach, if implemented in a proactive fashion, has the potential for enhancing both knowledge and attitudes among all constituencies. Creative problem solving at the postsecondary level may be the forerunner of effective transition to employment.

Determining Reasonableness in the Classroom and the Courts

Recently, a number of test cases have surfaced that help to clarify the parameters of "reasonableness" as it applies to accommodations at the postsecondary level. Three significant cases will be reviewed, followed by a discussion of their potential impact on educational policy for college students with learning disabilities. The first case addresses the issue of test format modification for students with learning disabilities, the second case is concerned with providing for additional time on exams, and the final case focuses on the legality of charging college students with disabilities an additional fee for services.

Modifying the Test Format

The first case, *Wynne v. Tufts University School of Medicine* (1990), was heard in the First Circuit U.S. District Court of Appeals in April 1990. The case involved a first-year medical student who, after failing 8 out of

15 courses, was subsequently tested at university expense and found to be dyslexic. Mr. Wynne claimed that after he was identified as having a learning disability, the university unlawfully discriminated against him based on his handicap, in violation of Section 504, when it refused to modify testing methods to accommodate his learning disability. Mr. Wynne requested that he be given an alternative type of test, preferably an oral exam; this request was rejected by school administrators. He also sought (unsuccessfully) to take a reduced course load during his second attempt at the first-year program. Initially, a decision in Tufts's favor was issued by the District Court without a trial; later on, the case was appealed. The full bench of the Court of Appeals granted Tufts's request for a rehearing and permitted other institutions to participate as *amici curiae.* The Court was sharply divided on the issue of granting summary judgment on the claim involving discrimination based on handicap (disability).

The Tufts medical school did take some steps to address Wynne's difficulties. He received special tutoring in all subjects that he failed, the use of note takers in his classes, and assistance with a learning skills tutor to improve his study habits. In his second attempt in the first-year program, Wynne passed all but two of the subjects he had previously failed. He was permitted to retake those two examinations, passing one but failing biochemistry for the third time. Following the third failure, Wynne was dismissed from the medical school. He filed suit, basing his claim on the fact that because of his learning disability he was unable to demonstrate his knowledge of course content with a conventional multiple choice format. Specifically, he argued that a different format of the test would "give him meaningful access to the medical education . . ." (*Wynne,* 1990, p. 9). Tufts attempted to dismiss Wynne's claim by comparing it to the decision in the *Davis* case, pointing out that because Wynne was unable to meet an essential requirement for a Tufts medical degree (i.e., passing all of his courses), he was not otherwise qualified. It was the finding of the Court that insufficient evidence had been presented to support the university's assertion that "changing the testing method would result in a 'fundamental alteration' in the program" (p. 13). The Court concluded that the district court had erred in granting summary judgment for Tufts, and the present record demonstrated that "Tufts may not select the one technique that poses an insurmountable barrier to dyslexic students" (p. 16). The Court of Appeals remanded the case to the district court, where it is being appealed. Tufts University must present convincing proof that the testing method is an integral component of the medical curriculum. Professor Laura Rothstein, associate dean for student affairs at the University of Houston Law Center, recently commented on this case, noting that "there should be limits on what colleges are required to do for learning disabled students" (Jaschik, 1990, p. A17). She felt that it could be "terribly burdensome" to faculty members if courts required them to develop new tests for students with LD. Rothstein looks to the courts to provide additional clarification on this matter in the years ahead.

Providing Additional Time on Exams

The second case, *Campbell A. Dinsmore v. Charles C. Pugh and the Regents of the University of California* (1989), is a civil suit involving a mathematics professor at the University of California–Berkeley who refused to provide a student with dyslexia with additional time on an examination. When the student requested accommodations in testing, the professor rejected the request on the grounds that "there was no such thing as a learning disability" (W. Newmeyer, personal communication, December 10, 1990). Essentially, the professor maintained that the student was using the disability as a ruse for securing additional time on the examination. Additional negotiations with the professor proved to be unsatisfactory, resulting in the student filing suit against the professor, the regents of the University of California at Berkeley, and Does 1–10. The plaintiff stated that the Disabled Student's Program (DSP) and the university had attempted to rectify the problem but were "powerless" to change the professor's mind. The student demanded that the university develop a policy and procedures statement to address future situations wherein a faculty member might refuse to provide academic adjustments despite adequate documentation of the disability. The student was also seeking monetary damages against the math professor for not providing the accommodations requested and for the emotional distress in making the case public. The professor was directed by members of the UC–Berkeley administration to provide the student with additional time to take a final examination in class, but the professor ignored the directive and would not permit the examination to be administered with the accommodations. The professor contended that granting extra time was unfair to the other students in the course. He said, "There are fast students and slow students . . . I think all students should be tested equally" (Link, 1989, p. B-2).

The university promptly settled this case out of court and developed a comprehensive policy for accommodating the academic needs of students with disabilities, and the professor was required to pay monetary damages. The outcome of this case may assist other service providers who are confronted with similar situations, wherein faculty members believe they are in a position to dictate what they will and will not provide to students with disabilities. Campuses may want to take the lead from the case and develop their own policy statements that delineate the various roles and responsibilities of service providers in ensuring that students with disabilities receive appropriate accommodations in their instructional activities.

As a direct result of this suit, the administration and the academic senate at UC–Berkeley created an Academic Accommodations Policy Board. The Board has three primary functions: (a) advising the vice chancellor for undergraduate affairs about policies and procedures related to the provision of academic accommodations for students with disabilities, (b) developing mechanisms for increasing faculty understanding of disabilities and their accommodations in an academic setting, and (c) assisting the vice chancellor for undergraduate affairs in resolving any disagreements that might arise concerning particular academic accommodations (Academic Senate, 1990). The Board is composed of seven members, including three faculty members who are knowledgeable in the field of disabilities, three professional staff members from the Disabled Student's Program, and the campus Section 504 coordinator. It should be noted that the staff member who determined the accommodation in question for a particular student does not participate in the Board's review of the case. If an instructor has questions concerning the appropriateness of an accommodation that has been recommended by a DSP staff member, the professor should contact the DSP office immediately. If the instructor disagrees with the accommodation being recommended by the DSP staff person, he or she should seek review by contacting the campus 504 coordinator within 5 days of being notified of the accommodation. Under this policy, the instructor is obligated to provide the accommodation "until it is either set aside or modified by the campus 504 Coordinator or the Vice Chancellor of Undergraduate Affairs" (p. 3). The Section 504 coordinator will attempt to resolve the matter on an informal basis; however, if this effort is unsuccessful, the Section 504 coordinator will refer the instructor to the Academic Accommodations Policy Board, which will review the matter and advise the vice chancellor of undergraduate affairs of the final decision. Every effort is made to resolve disagreements as expeditiously as possible—generally, within 5 working days. It should be emphasized that it is the responsibility of all department chairs and deans to inform instructional staff concerning Section 504 and university policy regarding nondiscrimination on the basis of handicap.

Ensuring the Availability of Auxiliary Aids and Services

In the third case, *United States v. Board of Trustees of the University of Alabama* (1990), the Court ruled that the University of Alabama could not deny auxiliary aids to students with disabilities based on their ability to pay or their enrollment in nondegree programs. The case involved a variety of claims by students with different disabilities who felt the university violated their rights under Section 504. Complaints were filed by students with mobility impairments who were seeking access to campus transportation services and the swimming pool and by several deaf students at the University of Alabama at Birmingham who were required to request "all major or costly accommodations" in writing prior to the beginning of the school year. In addition, aids were only provided to students who were enrolled in degree-granting programs. Special students, such as postgraduates, temporary students, and students enrolled in nondegree programs, were not considered eligible for free aids or services. The District Court concluded that the financial-means test violated Section 504, which precludes such tests as criteria for providing auxiliary aids. On appeal, the 11th U.S. Circuit Court of Appeals affirmed the District Court's ruling that the University of Alabama must provide auxiliary aids to students with disabilities, regardless of financial need or enrollment status (Handicapped Requirements Handbook, 1990). This case may help to set precedent requiring institutions to accept responsibility for securing the funds necessary to provide essential services for students with disabilities regardless of their financial need or enrollment status.

Extending this case to students with learning disabilities, it can be assumed that students with learning disabilities areentitled to receive the same type of services that are available to all other students at no additional cost. D'Amico (1989) observed that if tutoring and counseling are available to nondisabled students without charge, the institution may not impose an additional fee on a student with a learning disability for the same services. It is permissible for the institution to charge an additional fee to students with learning disabilities if these services go beyond the generic campus support services available to all other students, for example, special courses that are offered exclusively to students with learning disabilities, such as specialized tutorial support or diagnostic testing. However, academic adjustments of a personal nature are not necessarily the responsibility of the institution. The hiring of attendants, individually prescribed devices, or readers for personal use are not covered under Section 504. Rothstein (1989) concurred, noting that colleges are probably not required to pay for readers for personal reading, tutoring programs, or other programs specifically for students with LD.

Each of these cases helps to sharpen the picture as to what constitutes "reasonableness" for college students with disabilities. When viewed together these cases suggest that colleges and universities are in a state of transition in their attempts to respond to the unique needs of college students with learning disabilities. Future cases will build on these foundations and should offer additional guidance in the form of institutional policies that will assist service providers who are now facing more complex issues, such as how to implement nonbiased identification procedures for non-English-speaking college students with learning disabilities, or how to ensure that college students with traumatic brain injuries are being fairly accommodated in their testing and course work.

Issues of Independence

A final area of concern for many college service providers centers around the issue of independence for students with learning disabilities. If the goal of postsecondary services for students with learning disabilities is to prepare them for adult life, then training for independence should become the focus of every activity. Although services for students with learning disabilities are being provided at increasing numbers of postsecondary institutions, there has been little discussion regarding the goal of these efforts (Valdes, Williamson, & Wagner, 1990). Is it to prepare students for the challenge of adult life or to help them to function in school so they can eventually graduate? Are these goals mutually exclusive? Many years of experience with programs for students with learning disabilities in *secondary schools* would suggest that they are. Outcome data for high school students with learning disabilities have been discouraging; recent studies (Bruck, 1987; Hasazi, Johnson, Hasazi, Gordon, & Hull, 1989; Zigmond & Thornton, 1985) consistently depict serious problems of unemployment and underemployment. The National Longitudinal Transition Study (Wagner, 1989) found that only 38% of students with learning disabilities who had been out of high school more than 1 year worked full time. It is now necessary for postsecondary service providers to reconsider their efforts in light of recent outcome data. Do current service delivery models encourage independence, or do they continue the same approaches that have proven ineffective in the typical secondary setting? For example, should the student receive a note-taker, instruction in taking notes at a class lecture, or assistance in using a tape recorder as a compensatory aid? Does the student need a waiver/substitution from a foreign language requirement? Should the student be encouraged to take a reduced course load or be trained in time management and organizational strategies? There are no absolute answers to these questions. However, it is recommended that, whenever feasible, the student be provided instruction in order to be weaned from accommodations and guided toward self-sufficiency.

Although Section 504 puts more responsibility on the shoulders of the student, there are many elements of professional behavior that continue to foster dependence. LD service providers and other professionals must evaluate decisions regarding the provision of services in terms of the degree to which they will foster responsibility and self-determination in the student. Table 6.2 presents alternative sets of professional behavior, one leading to dependence and the other encouraging independence. It is possible for competent professionals to defend some of the behaviors in the "dependence" column as appropriate for some students in specific situations. The intent of the juxtaposition of behaviors in each column, however, is to operationalize a mind-set. In the dependence column the professional functions as "helper and expert" to rescue the passive student. In the "independence" column, the professional functions as "facilitator" to empower the student to become a successful decision maker and problem solver.

Postsecondary Programming

Programming for students with learning disabilities in postsecondary settings is a complex process (Brinckerhoff, 1991; Vogel, 1982). Service provision at the postsecondary level should prioritize service delivery options that promote student independence by providing learning strategy instruction and self-advocacy training within a setting that can be tailored to meet the unique needs of the student. The following section will highlight some techniques for fostering student independence in college for students with learning disabilities.

One of the reasons that high school students with learning disabilities are having trouble succeeding after graduation is that secondary school programs have, for the most part, implemented a tutorial model whereby students receive instruction in the content in which they are having difficulty in regular classes (Spector, Decker, & Shaw, 1991). The goal is to help these students succeed in school, feel better about themselves because they receive better grades, and eventually graduate from school. The reality is that other than assisting students to pass some classes and fit into systems, content tutoring offers few long-term benefits (Okolo & Sitlington, 1986). Ellis (1990), commenting on the tutorial approach, said that "many teachers appear to remediate, placate and suffocate students while intending to be supportive and empathetic" (p. 61).

The type of instruction that should be encouraged in college is training in learning strategies, including study skills, memory techniques, test-taking strategies, time management, note taking, and organizational strategies. Although the goal of virtually all instruction should be to develop academic self-sufficiency, the student's current courses, syllabi, textbooks, and tests are used as the content to teach these skills. This is best exemplified by the work of Byron and Owen (1990), who developed

TABLE 6.2
Service Provider Behaviors That Foster Dependence or Independence

Dependence	Independence
1. Allows student to interrupt or "barge in" to get immediate response to perceived need	1. Uses such occurrences to teach or practice appropriate social skills
2. Takes responsibility for the products and grades of a seemingly sincere and hard-working student	2. Maintains focus on helping student learn without taking responsibility for student success or failure
3. Advocates for untimed tests in all subjects	3. Encourages extended time on certain tests in specified courses based upon specific assessment data
4. Helps a student write a paper	4. Provides instruction on how to write a paper
5. Edits and corrects a student's paper	5. Teaches the student how to proofread a paper and/or teaches the use of appropriate computer software
6. Explains the student's disability and needed accommodations to a professor	6. Role-plays discussion with a professor so the student can self-advocate
7. Sends a list of students with learning disabilities to all faculty	7. Discusses with student when, if, and how to disclose a learning disability
8. Mails a letter to faculty requesting test modifications or accommodations	8. Gives a letter to the student that indicates provider's availability to support the student's request for test modifications or accommodations
9. Tells the student that a certain credit load, course, or major is inappropriate or unacceptable	9. Helps a student determine the pros and cons of a particular decision and allows the student to experience the consequences (positive or negative) of that decision
10. Organizes the student and controls his or her environment to ensure success	10. Encourages the student to assess needs, identify problems, and develop compensatory strategies
11. Attempts to meet all student instructional, counseling, advising, and personal needs using resources of LD services	11. Helps student identify and access other campus and community resources

Note. From *Programming to Help Postsecondary Students with Learning Disabilities Become Independent* (Cassette Recording 247-F39) by S. F. Shaw, N. Bieber, and J. Byron, 1990, San Diego, CA: Convention Recorders.

a metacognitive training course that is taught in conjunction with an introductory psychology class. However, tutoring subject matter solely to teach the student course content is not an appropriate long-term strategy. Carlson (1985) made the best argument for learning strategy instruction instead of content tutoring by emphasizing that an effective program is one in which instruction will serve to diminish the impact of the presenting handicap on future learning or enable the individual to function more adequately.

Another critical component of service delivery is training in self-advocacy. It is clearly quicker and easier for a service provider to make a telephone call or write a note explaining a student's disability, request an accommodation, or make arrangements for modified testing. It is preferred, however, that the service provider share the diagnostic data with the student, help the student understand and learn to explain his or her disability, and model and practice approaches for the student to identify and request the necessary accommodations. The passage of the Americans with Disabilities Act, with its regulations regarding the provision of modifications by employers, makes student self-advocacy an even more critical life skill. A U.S. Department of Labor report, "Workplace Basics: The Skills Employers Want" (Carnevale, Gainer, Metzer, & Holland, 1988), specified that in addition to basic academic skills and knowing how to learn, critical workplace skills include self-esteem and motivation, critical thinking and problem solving, interpersonal and communication skills, and goal setting. Given that many adults with learning disabilities evidence documented deficiencies in these areas (Adelman & Vogel, 1990; Greenspan, Apthorp, & Williams, 1991; Hoffman et al., 1987; Johnson & Blalock, 1987), training in these skills is a necessary part of any postsecondary program. A recent study has documented that skills taught in postsecondary settings do transfer. In a follow-up program of college graduates, Adelman and Vogel (1990) noted that compensatory strategies learned in a postsecondary support program were later applied to work settings. They concluded that developing self-understanding of one's learning disability and the use of effective learning strategies were important for success in the adult world.

If the development of independence is to become a reality, there should also be a process to move the student to a less restrictive or more independent environment. The idea of a formal process has a number of advantages. Typical support services that provide accommodations will require the same accommodations at the same level of intensity (hours per week) over the 2, 4, 5, or more years until the student leaves the college setting. A model program for promoting independence in postsecondary settings for students with learning disabilities is presented in Figure 6.1.

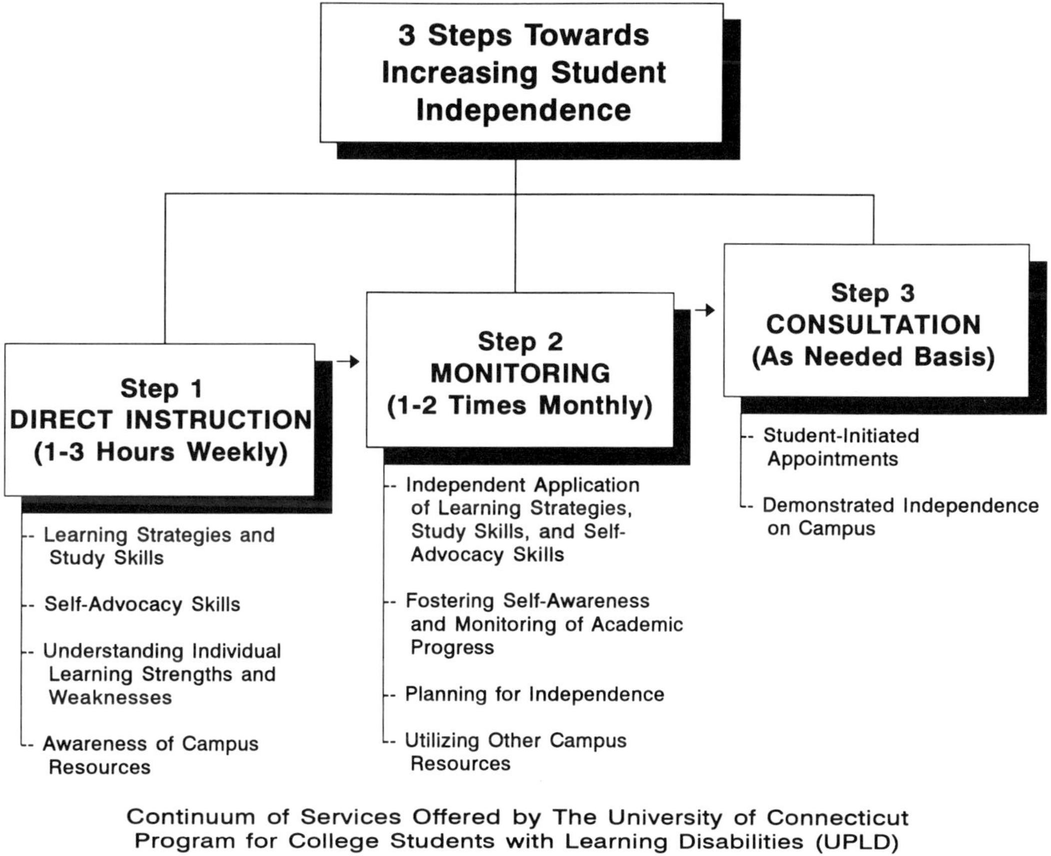

Figure 6.1 Three steps toward increasing student independence. *Note.* From *Continuum of services* (UPLD Tech. Rep.) by A. V. Litt and J. M. McGuire, 1989, Storrs: A. J. Pappanikou Center on Special Education and Rehabilitation, The University of Connecticut. Adapted by permission.

Litt and McGuire (1989) described a three-stage process of program services ranging from direct instruction (2 to 4 hours weekly) to monitoring student progress (one to two meetings per month) to consultation (on an as-needed basis). This continuum of services sets up both an expectation of and a process for moving toward independence. It allows for more intensive instructional support during the initial semesters, with the expectation that reduced levels of support will be realized as the student becomes more self-sufficient. In these times of limited or reduced resources, this approach may have fiscal as well as educational benefits. In addition, a written process gives the service provider time to help the student set goals and timelines for steps toward independence. McGuire (1990) gathered data that demonstrate that students with learning disabilities in a very competitive university setting continue to maintain average or above-average performance (mean grade-point average > 2.0) as they progress through this continuum to the consultation stage, where any support services needed are by student request. Similarly, at the secondary level, programming to achieve student independence has proven to be effective (Phillips, 1990; Spector et al., 1991).

Summary

At a time when postsecondary education and future employability are becoming increasingly intertwined (Education, 1990), the goal of pursuing college course work is being realized by more students with learning disabilities. Yet, there are subtle nuances in interpreting issues of eligibility, access to higher education, and guidelines for determining reasonable accommodations that professionals must begin to address prior to students' high school graduation if education is to serve as a bridge to employment. With the development of strong linkages between high school personnel and postsecondary service providers, students with learning disabilities will become better prepared for independence in the classroom as well as the workplace.

7. Assessing Students with Learning Disabilities in Postsecondary Settings

MELISSA BEHRENS-BLAKE AND BRIAN BRYANT

The employment forecast for adolescents and adults with learning disabilities (LD) has been depicted as grim (Chelser, 1982). Some progress has been made toward providing persons with LD an opportunity to find and maintain useful employment and to work in positions that are commensurate with their abilities (Sitlington & Frank, 1990). This change is due in large part to the postsecondary training opportunities resulting from the passage of several laws, including the Education for all Handicapped Children Act of 1975 (P.L. 94-142); the amendments to this law, which was retitled the Individuals with Disabilities Education Act in 1990; the Vocational Rehabilitation Act of 1973; and, most recently, the Americans with Disabilities Act of 1990.

Passage of the Vocational Rehabilitation Act (specifically Section 504, Subpart A) allowed persons with disabilities greater access to institutions of higher learning (i.e., colleges, universities, vocational institutes, and other educational settings accepting federal funds). For most students with LD, however, the legislation was of little immediate benefit, because few of these students had the academic preparation needed to succeed at the postsecondary level (Prater & Minner, 1986). P.L. 94-142 rectified this shortcoming to some extent because it mandated that appropriate special education services be provided to students with disabilities. Subsequent educational services have made it possible for students with special needs to continue their education at the postsecondary level (Gerber & Leiff, 1985). In particular, transition programs at the secondary level have worked to focus academic preparation on career planning and have enabled students to take advantage of the "equal access" laws for entering postsecondary training programs.

Although currently there are increasing numbers of students with LD who are enrolled in postsecondary education and training programs, two groups of adults with LD have yet to benefit fully from legislation enacted on their behalf. The first group is composed of those individuals who attended grade school prior to 1978 and who are now attending institutions of higher learning. These "nontraditional" students are entering advanced educational settings at an increasing rate, primarily taking advantage of available vocational and community college educational opportunities. Many of these students have learning disabilities without knowing it. Some struggled in grade school but were able to do well enough to graduate (Cooper, 1987); others dropped out of school, choosing instead to enter the work force. Many of the people in this latter category went on to receive a diploma through adult education classes or through testing for the GED.

The second group consists of students who attended grade school in 1978 or later, but who were never identified as having learning disabilities. These students are also entering postsecondary programs and they, like many of their older colleagues with LD, are experiencing difficulties in their new surroundings. An increasing number of them are finding their way into offices for students with disabilities at postsecondary institutions seeking assistance with their learning problems.

Another postsecondary-level group consists of adults with learning disabilities who are involved with employment training through such programs as Vocational Rehabilitation and the Job Training Partnership Act. Programs such as these offer persons with LD employment training and concurrent remedial instruction in deficient academic areas.

Regardless of the setting, assessment plays a critical role in program planning. This chapter provides a description of the assessment process, particularly as it relates to adults with LD who are attending college. We first discuss several issues pertaining to assessment in general. It is the purpose of this section to examine adult assessment by: (a) presenting an overview of general assessment techniques, (b) examining the reasons for testing adults, (c) discussing the types of adult assessment scenarios, and (d) describing several instruments that are available to assist diagnosticians in the assessment process.

General Assessment Techniques

Assessments employ techniques that are either standardized or nonstandardized. The qualities of standardized instruments and the value of nonstandardized techniques are discussed in the following paragraphs.

Standardized Procedures

For an assessment instrument to be considered standardized, it must possess three specific properties (Hammill, 1987): It must be reliable, it must yield valid results, and it must have a specified frame of reference.

Reliability. In assessment, the term *reliability* is synonymous with *consistency.* To be useful, assessment devices must provide consistent results. Instruments that provide inconsistent results are clinically worthless, because examiners cannot trust their findings.

Hammill, Brown, and Bryant (1992) suggested that test authors provide, at minimum, evidence of internal consistency or stability reliability. *Internal consistency reliability* estimates the degree to which a particular scale's test items are related to one another. *Stability reliability* refers to the extent to which test results remain constant (i.e., stable) over time.

For the most part, studies exploring the reliability of tests report their findings using a statistic called the *reliability coefficient,* a version of the common correlation coefficient. Tests with reliability coefficients below .80 (after the spurious influence of age is controlled) should not be used for screening and diagnosis.

Validity. Instruments that yield valid results are those that measure what they are intended to measure. Consumers of assessment devices should examine their instruments for content, criterion-related, and construct validity (Salvia & Ysseldyke, 1991). Hammill et al. (1992) discussed in detail how this evaluation is made. In general, standardized instruments should be composed of items that have been selected empirically; should demonstrate relationships to other scales that measure similar or related constructs (e.g., tests of reading should correlate with other tests of reading, as well as with tests of other achievement areas such as math and writing, or measures of general cognitive functioning); and should demonstrate the ability to differentiate between groups of people who perform well and those who perform poorly in the construct being assessed. Tests that exhibit such evidence can be considered properly standardized. Instruments that do not provide valid results should not be used at all.

Specified Frame of Reference. For a test to be considered standardized, it must have a specified frame of reference. Tests that are norm-referenced yield scores that are used to identify relative standing of a person's performance when compared to a peer group. In this way, it is possible to identify where a person performs along a continuum from well above average to well below average. For a norm-referenced scale to be considered sufficiently standardized, it must yield standard scores or percentiles and have a normative group that was tested within the past 15 years, and the test group must comprise a normative sample that is large (i.e., consists of at least 750 people, preferably 1,000 people) and representative (i.e., matches national demographic figures regarding gender, race, ethnicity, urban–rural residence, etc.). Table 7.1 presents population data regarding several demographic variables in the United States according to the 1990 U.S. Census.

The results of criterion-referenced measures are examined in terms of mastery. *Mastery* is defined as a preset level of performance that indicates competence. For example, if 10 math problems of a specific type are presented, mastery may be set at 90%, which means that a student must get 9 of 10 items correct to demonstrate competence in the math content being assessed. This frame of reference is important when attempting to identify individual strengths and weaknesses and when evaluating the effectiveness of a remedial or intervention program.

Some procedures do not compare performance to either a specified group or to mastery levels. Instead, these procedures examine strategies that are employed during problem solving. One example of a nonreferenced procedure is miscue analysis in reading (see Wiederholt & Bryant, 1987). Here, a person's reading performance is categorized according to classifications that attempt to determine the types of syntactic, semantic, and graphic/phonemic cues a person is using as he or she reads aloud.

To summarize, standardized assessment procedures are those that empirically demonstrate consistent, valid results and that are either norm-referenced, criterion-referenced, or nonreferenced. The degree to which the procedures conform to standards of technical adequacy determines where the procedures fall along a continuum ranging from highly standardized to poorly standardized.

Nonstandardized Procedures

In numerous instances in assessment, examiners need to deviate from standardized procedures in order to gain clinically useful information. When an examiner uses instruments that are nonstandardized, such deviation should occur *after* formal assessment takes place. That is, performance probes can be used after the administration of a test or subtest, so that assessments will yield maximum benefit. Bryant, Patton, and Dunn (1991) provided an example of a nonstandardized probing technique that can be applied to the Math Calculation subtest of their Scholastic Abilities Test for Adults. The standardized procedure is employed to establish a score that is based on the number of calculation problems that are answered correctly. Nonstandardized procedures can then be employed to conduct an error analysis.

The examiner can evaluate the examinee's calculations for miscues (e.g., evidence of errors in calculation or a misunderstanding of the algorithm). If the examiner thinks the individual made a careless mistake on certain problems, items similar to the missed items can be created and given to the examinee to solve. The examiner can also have the examinee explain the procedures used when solving the problem, thus providing information about where procedural breakdowns occur. An effective way to determine why examinees calculate as they do is to role play. That is, items similar to the ones missed on the subtest are created, and the examinee plays the role of the instructor. The examinee demonstrates verbally and graphically the procedures that are involved when solving the problem. In so doing, the examinee provides clues as to where procedural errors occur (Bryant et al., 1991, pp. 23–24).

Reasons for Assessing Adults

Psychological assessment of adults has been undertaken for many decades. An examination of the table of contents of the text *Testing Adults: A Reference Guide for Special Psychodiagnostic Assessment* (Swiercinsky, 1985) provides evidence of the scope of assessment in adulthood. Topics include anxiety and depression, psychopathology, hysterical conversion/psychosomatic disorder and physical disease, posttraumatic stress disorder, sexual dysfunction, and family treatment. Although adults with learning disabilities do not necessarily require testing in all of these areas, there is no reason to suggest that adults with LD are immune to disorders that affect the general public.

It is not our purpose to describe all of the specific areas that can be assessed in adults with suspected or known learning disabilities, although those working with adults with LD should be aware of the types of cognitive, affective, and academic disorders that their clients may have. Rather, this section provides information regarding the assessment process in general, particularly as it relates to screening, diagnosis, and identification of strengths and weaknesses.

Screening

Screening is a process of identifying persons who exhibit *warning signs* that may be indicative of disabling conditions (McLoughlin & Lewis, 1981). In most schools, this process involves surveying all children in a school and identifying those children who are at risk (Hammill, 1987). A similar process occurs with certain adult vocational training programs.

TABLE 7.1
Demographic Characteristics of the U.S. Population[a]

Characteristics	Percentage of U.S. school-aged population	Percentage of U.S. population
Gender		
Male	51.2	48.8
Female	48.8	51.2
Race		
Caucasioid	80.1	84.1
Negroid	15.7	12.4
Mongoloid	4.2	3.5
Ethnicity		
Anglo/European	70.4	75.8
African American	14.1	11.9
Hispanic	10.6	7.9
Oriental/Pacific Islander	3.3	2.9
Native American/Eskimo/Aleut	1.1	0.8
All others	0.5	0.7
Principal language spoken in the home[b]		
English	90.4	88.6
Spanish	6.2	5.0
French	0.5	0.8
German	0.4	0.9
Italian	0.3	0.9
Chinese dialects	0.2	0.3
Polish	0.1	0.5
Greek	0.1	0.2
Philippine dialects	0.1	0.3
Portuguese	0.1	0.2
Japanese	0.1	0.2
Korean	0.1	0.1
Vietnamese	0.1	0.1
All others	1.3	1.9
Geographic region of residence		
Northeast	18.7	20.2
North central	24.4	23.9
South	35.5	35.0
West	21.4	20.9
Domicile		
Urban and suburban		77.5
Rural		22.5
Educational attainment of individuals 25–54 years of age[c]		
Completed 0–8 grades		5.9
Completed 1–3 years of high school		9.8
Graduated high school		40.3

Table continues

TABLE 7.1 (cont.)

Characteristics	Percentage of U.S. school-aged population	Percentage of U.S. population
Attended college or technical school		19.8
Graduated college		18.9
Completed postgraduate training		5.3
Employment status of individuals in the work force[c]		
Unemployed		5.4
Resident armed forces		1.4
Managerial and professional services		23.7
Technical, sales, and administrative support		28.8
Service occupations		12.4
Precision production, craft, and repair		11.1
Operators, fabricators, and laborers		14.4
Farming, forestry, and fishing		2.8
Family income[c]		
Under $5,000		4.4
$5,000–$9,999		7.3
$10,000–$14,999		9.1
$15,000–$24,999		18.7
$25,000–$34,999		17.5
$35,000–$49,999		20.2
$50,000 and over		22.8

Note. From Hammill et al. (1992). Copyright © 1992 by PRO-ED, Inc. Reprinted by permission.
[a]Unless otherwise noted, all figures are based on the 1990 census projections reported by the U.S. Bureau of the Census in *Statistical Abstract of the United States 1990.*
[b]Based on 1985 census projections.
[c]Based on 1988 census projections.

For some Job Training Partnership Act programs, for example, a reading test is often administered to incoming clients to determine their reading level. This process screens for persons who require remedial reading assistance prior to participating in vocational training.

For most postsecondary educational institutions, screening begins with self-referral. That is, adults who believe that they have a learning disability seek the services of a private psychologist or a person associated with an office for persons with disabilities. By gaining information about a person's developmental and educational history (see sample surveys in the appendices), one can determine if a comprehensive LD evaluation will be necessary. This information can be gleaned either through informal interviews or the use of screening instruments that examine a person's performance in one or more of the following areas: listening, speaking, reasoning, reading, writing, and mathematics (Hammill, Leigh, McNutt, & Larsen, 1989).

Diagnosis

Webster's New World Dictionary (Guralnik, 1984) defined *diagnosis* as "the act of deciding the nature of a disease, situation, problem, etc. by examination and analysis" (p. 171). For diagnosing learning disabilities, professionals must decide, first of all, what "learning disabilities" is in adults; only then may they identify the disorder. Hammill (1987) reviewed the various definitions of learning disabilities that have been offered over the years. Examination of the various definitions indicates that LD is a condition of academic underachievement that is caused by dysfunction of the central nervous system (CNS). By noting the terminology employed in the literature that deals with CNS-related learning disorders (e.g., dyslexia, dyscalculia, dysphasia, dysgraphia) one could reword the earlier diagnosis definition to state that learning disability diagnosis is *the act of deciding the nature of an academic dys-ease by examining the cause of the underachievement.* Later sections of this chapter describe in detail methods used to diagnose LD in adults, particularly those who attend colleges or universities.

Identifying Strengths and Weaknesses

An important reason for testing adults is to identify individual strengths and weaknesses. Mangrum and Strichart (1988) identified seven areas that are of interest when examining persons with LD: cognition, language, perceptual motor functioning, academics, work and study habits, social competence, and personality. Examining strengths and weaknesses across and within these areas can be of value when designing a training program.

For example, if a trainee has a writing deficiency, yet has strengths in reading and listening, arrangements can be made to have another person take notes for the trainee during lectures. The notes can then be studied in depth later. Without a knowledge of strengths and weaknesses, accommodations will not be made and the trainee will not benefit sufficiently from instruction.

Adult Assessment Scenarios

Assessment of learning disabilities takes place in a variety of settings. Later in this chapter, we discuss in detail assessments as they pertain to colleges and universities. In this section, we overview briefly the assessments that take place in adult basic education and vocational rehabilitation along with assessments that occur as a part of research efforts.

Adult Basic Education

With the dropout rate increasing steadily, more and more young people are entering the work force and returning to school later in life to receive their high school diploma. Formal high school coursework is presented within an Adult Basic Education (ABE) scenario. ABE also offers literacy programs (i.e., remedial instruction in reading, writing, and mathematics) for those with basic skill deficiencies.

In many adult basic education programs, assessments are conducted in basic skill areas for screening purposes. Throughout subsequent remedial programs, assessments are conducted to document progress and to determine whether the students are mastering the content being taught.

Vocational Rehabilitation

In 1981, the Rehabilitation Services Administration broadened its eligibility guidelines to provide services to persons with learning disabilities. Since that time, the number of persons with LD receiving rehabilitation services has increased steadily (see Dowdy, Smith, & Nowell, Chapter 5 of this book). Swiercinsky and Fisk (1985) identified six reasons why persons seek vocational rehabilitation assistance:

1. To find appropriate employment;
2. For assistance in learning marketable job skills;
3. To receive financial aid for returning to school or entering job training programs;
4. For guidance in locating additional sources of help with physical or mental problems that interfere with the capacity to find and maintain employment;
5. For assistance in making career choices; and
6. For obtaining diagnoses regarding the disability to establish eligibility for public financial aid when one cannot reasonably return to competitive work. (p. 188)

Although the types of testing done with vocational rehabilitation clients depend upon the specific needs of the individual, typically assessments examine physical status; cognitive functioning; academic achievement; vocational interest, aptitude, and awareness; learning styles; neuropsychology; language; and personality (Anastasi, 1988; Dowdy et al.,

Chapter 5 of this book; McLoughlin & Lewis, 1981; Swiercinsky & Fisk, 1985). Such testing is usually accomplished only after the client's school, employment, and medical records are examined.

Research

Concurrent with the influx of adults into postsecondary training programs is the increased interest in research using adult subjects (Gerber & Mellard, 1985). Assessment instruments are critical features in good research.

Not only are standardized tests used in gauging the effectiveness of research efforts with standard group designs: Some single-subject designs employ direct daily measurement procedures (D. D. Smith, 1989). With these procedures, applied behavioral analysis measurement principles are employed to monitor progress on a daily basis.

Assessment Instruments

Inspection of such publications as *The Eleventh Mental Measurements Yearbook* (Kramer, 1989) and Sweetland's and Keyser's (1990) *Tests: A Comprehensive Reference for Assessments in Psychology, Education, and Business* shows that a myriad of assessment instruments have been created for use with adults. Until fairly recently, however, there has been a dearth of individually administered tests available for use with adults that assess a wide variety of academic areas and are technically sound (Ross, 1987). In addition to new instruments for adult assessment that are being published, several tests that currently have norms through adolescence are in the process of adding norms for adults (N. Pearson, 1992, personal communication). Also, it is possible to examine tests that are standardized with older adolescents (ages 16–18 years) to determine their appropriateness for use with young adults (ages 18–30) (Bryant & Rivera, 1992). With a little work, users of these tests can check the scales for reliability and validity and can examine the test's current norms in light of older individuals' performance.

Table 7.2 provides an overview of standardized tests that are currently available for use with older adolescents and adults (i.e., those ages 16 and up). The table depicts each test and what it measures, the ages with which the scale can be used, and the purpose for administering the scale.

Postsecondary Education Programs for Students with LD

The need for postsecondary services for students with learning disabilities continues to increase (Bursuck, Rose, Cowen, & Yahaya, 1989; Decker, Polloway, & Decker, 1985; Hoy & Gregg, 1986a; McGuire, Norlander, & Shaw, 1990; Scott, 1991). The incidence of learning disabilities among college students has increased tenfold since 1978 (Learning Disability Update, 1986) and continues to rise. A 1985 national survey indicated that 1.1% of the total freshman population have learning disabilities (Hippolitus, 1987) and this percentage continues to climb (Report on Educational Research, 1990). With this drastic increase in student population as well as new attention focused on civil rights issues, the development of postsecondary support programs for students with learning disabilities is receiving serious consideration. Twenty years ago, professionals within the field of special education focused their efforts on children who demonstrated significant difficulties in their ability to learn within the conventional public school setting. These children have grown and are seeking appropriate services within institutions of higher education. As this population has aged, relevant publications and research have increased dramatically.

Transition issues (Dalke & Schmitt, 1987; Evelo & Price, 1991; Halpern, 1985; Haring, Lovett, & Smith, 1990; Siperstein, 1988; Sitlington & Frank, 1990) and outcome studies (Adelman & Vogel, 1990; Greenspan, Apthorp, & Williams, 1991; Herzog & Falk, 1991; Rogan & Hartman, 1990; Spekman, Goldberg, & Herman, 1992) emphasize that adults with learning disabilities have become a unique population with differing needs and characteristics (Adelman & Vogel, 1991; Buchanan & Wolf, 1986; Garnett & La Porta, 1984; Gerber et al., 1990; Hoffman et al., 1987; Johnson & Blalock, 1987; Polloway, Smith, & Patton, 1984).

On university and college campuses across the nation, the arrival of students with learning disabilities is in step with the increasing proportion of minorities, individuals with disabilities, and older students. Although they are not marked by any outwardly visible sign of their disability, these students may pose the greatest challenge to higher education's ability to accept and adapt to diversity of any population accommodated thus far (Longo, 1988). In many settings, students with learning disabilities were preceded by high-risk students whose needs required the establishment of programs termed as basic skills, remedial, or developmental. This has proven to be confusing for faculty and administrators who lack backgrounds in special education. As a result, the question inevitably arises: "Do students with learning disabilities really belong here?"

TABLE 7.2
Tests Available for Use with Older Adolescents and Adults

Test	Ages for intended use	Measurement areas	Purpose
Wechsler Adult Intelligence Scale–Revised (Wechsler, 1981)	16 years to adult	general intelligence	cognitive strengths and weaknesses
Woodcock-Johnson Psycho-Educational Battery–Revised (Woodcock & Johnson, 1989)	15 years to adult	general intelligence and academic achievement	cognitive and academic strengths and weaknesses
Detroit Tests of Learning Aptitude–Adult (Hammill & Bryant, 1992)	16 years to adult	general mental abilities	mental processing strengths and weaknesses
Scholastic Abilities Test for Adults (Bryant et al., 1991)	16 years to adult	general intelligence and academic achievement	cognitive and academic strengths and weaknesses
Nelson-Denny Reading Test (Brown et al., 1981)	Grade 9 to adult	reading	vocabulary, comprehension, and rate
Diagnostic Spelling Potential Test (Arena, 1982)	7 years to adult	spelling	general spelling
Wide Range Achievement Test–Revised (Jastak & Wilkinson, 1984)	5 years to adult	reading, spelling, arithmetic	general achievement
Gray Oral Reading Tests–Third Edition (Wiederholt & Bryant, 1992)	6 to 18 years	reading	oral reading miscues, comprehension, and rate
Test of Written Language–2 (Hammill & Larsen, 1988)	Grades 2 to 12	writing	contrived and spontaneous writing
General Aptitude Test Battery (U.S. Employment Service, 1983)	adolescent, adult	vocational aptitude	vocational planning

Table continues

TABLE 7.2 (cont.)

Test	Ages for intended use	Measurement areas	Purpose
Occupational Aptitude Survey and Interest Schedule–Second Edition (Parker, 1991)	adolescent, young adult	vocational aptitude and interest	vocational planning
Minnesota Multiphasic Personality Inventory–Revised (Hathaway & McKinley, 1991)	adolescent, adult	personality	emotional disorders
Test of Adolescent Language–2 (Hammill, Brown, Larsen, & Wiederholt, 1988)	Grades 7 to 12	receptive and expressive language	language disorders
Goldman-Fristoe-Woodcock Auditory Skills Test Battery (Goldman, Fristoe, & Woodcock, 1976)	child through adult	auditory perception	receptive disorders
Luria-Nebraska Neuropsychological Battery (Golden, Hammeke, & Purisch, 1980)	15 years to adult	cognitive processing	central nervous system dysfunction

Now that colleges and universities are faced with the task of educating students who have learning disabilities, academic performance of students becomes a pressing concern for admissions officers, academic support personnel, and career counselors in higher education (Wilczenski & Gillespie-Silver, 1992). Mangrum and Strichart (1984) outlined several factors that have led to the development of programs for students with learning disabilities. These factors can be summarized as follows: (a) Colleges and universities feel they have a social mission to serve various groups with disabilities; (b) declining enrollments are offset by tuition received from students with learning disabilities; and (c) compliance with state and federal law is now increasingly enforced (Parks, Antonoff, Drake, Skiba, & Soberman, 1987). As a result, institutions of higher education have reached the point where the question changes from "Should we include these students?" to "How should we provide effective services for them?"

Development of Diagnostic Services

The foundation for service delivery to students in postsecondary settings lies in the Section 504 phrase "otherwise qualified." Who is an otherwise qualified student with a disability? Unfortunately, the vague terminology of Section 504 makes the answer to this question difficult with regard to specific learning disabilities. As Vogel (1982) pointed out, there was no universally accepted definition of learning disabilities, most specifically regarding the adult population, among professionals in the early 1980s; the situation remains the same well into the 1990s. Even more difficult than defining the term *learning disability* is distinguishing between *qualified* and *unqualified* college students with learning disabilities. As postsecondary programs emerge, it is imperative that specific diagnostic services be geared to make this distinction. Clearly, there is a need to establish eligibility criteria at the postsecondary level that can be tailored to individual postsecondary contexts (Mellard, 1990). What may be appropriate at a 4-year university setting may not be necessary or even helpful in the context of a vocational institution. The depth of diagnostic services may depend on additional support services available to the student.

Surveys indicate that diagnostic services provided by individual institutions vary greatly. Often, "diagnostic services" are limited to the review of previous diagnostic reports as used in relation to admission requirements. Although diagnostic service programs were not included in a nationwide survey conducted by Bursuck et al.(1989), it was noted that diagnostic testing conducted on campus (rather than through the professional community or public school setting) was rated as the most important service goal by 25% of respondents. Beirne-Smith and Deck (1989) stated that one of the most disturbing outcomes of their survey was the disclosure of failure of over one fourth of the LD centers to provide any type of assessment. Parks et al. (1987) stated that it is difficult to understand how individual programs and services can be planned and implemented without evaluative information. McCue (1989) emphasized that assessment for learning disabilities should not be limited to educational achievement. It is necessary that further comprehensive assessment include examination of processing difficulties related to disorders of the central nervous system and how they affect all aspects of behavior.

In the area of diagnostic services, it is evident that there is little consensus concerning appropriate measures for identifying adults with learning disabilities (Blackburn & Iovacchini, 1982; Cordoni, 1982; Hoy & Gregg, 1986b). There is also a lack of consistency in admissions criteria across programs designed for students with learning disabilities. In a review of support programs conducted by Nelson and Lignugaris-Kraft (1989), it was noted that support services were offered to students in some colleges based only on their own request or following student and parent interviews. Other programs described in the review required complete neuropsychological or psychoeducational evaluations that based findings on a significant discrepancy between aptitude and achievement. Still other programs served only those students who were previously diagnosed with learning disabilities according to the eligibility criteria found in public schools. It was also noted that some programs admitted students based on the fact that they demonstrated academic difficulties and were considered "low achievers." In fact, admission to one program was based on a high-average IQ, evaluations from former teachers, a personal interview, and a 100-word statement by applicants indicating why they had applied to the program for support services (Bireley & Manley, 1980). Often, the original diagnosis in public schools was attained at the elementary school level and had been reviewed by brief "re-evaluations"; in some instances, students had been out of high school for more than 3 years and their records had been purged. A position paper presented by the National Joint Committee on Learning Disabilities (1985) stressed that "learning disabilities are both persistent and pervasive throughout an individual's life. The manifestations of the learning disability can be expected to change throughout the lifespan of the individual" (p. 172). It is evident that students and professionals need to understand a previously diagnosed learning disability from the adult perspective; attaining this perspective may require additional evaluation.

Qualifications of Personnel at the Postsecondary Level

Norlander, Shaw, and McGuire (1990) pointed out that professionals specifically trained in special education have been responsible for the development and implementation of support programs for students with learning disabilities at the elementary and secondary levels. However, special education involvement has not held true at the postsecondary level. Professionals in related fields such as counseling, school psychology, rehabilitation, and social work have often been given the role of coordinating services for students with learning disabilities (Shaw, Norlander, & McGuire, 1987). Most often, programs at the postsecondary level are coordinated by a director of disabled student services who is responsible for all services provided to students with various disabilities (including students with hearing, visual, and/or physical impairments). Very few of these directors have special education backgrounds.

Counseling and academic services typically are described as including personal or social counseling, academic or program counseling, and career or vocational counseling. Strichart and Mangrum (1985) suggested that specialists in learning disabilities should provide both individual and group counseling for academic stress. Although it was reported that 97% of the schools surveyed provided counseling services (Bursuck et al., 1989), only one third of these services used counselors trained in the area of learning disabilities. A similar finding was reported for tutors. Results indicated that 80% of the institutions were doing one-to-one tutoring; however, only 32% of the tutors were trained in the area of learning disabilities. These data need to be interpreted cautiously, because it is likely that many respondents to these surveys described counseling and academic services offered to all students rather than specialized services for students with learning disabilities.

Norlander et al. (1990) emphasized that if postsecondary preparation is to be effective and if institutions of higher education are to hire appropriate personnel, an effort must be made to develop the qualifications and competencies of those hired. In an attempt to identify needed competencies for both administrative and direct services personnel, they developed a survey to tap both present and desired levels of competence (Norlander et al., 1990). This survey was very carefully designed, and a thorough discussion of the findings indicated assessment skills were seen as necessary competencies. This need was also suggested by Johnston (1984) and Mellard and Deshler (1984). The National Joint Committee on Learning Disabilities (1985) further stated that "program selection and choice of intervention strategies must be based on the results of a comprehensive and integrated assessment of the individual" (p. 2).

For students with learning disabilities to be eligible for special accommodations, they must present documentation of their learning disability. Most institutions expect students to bring documentation with them during the application process. Because of the variation in diagnostic procedures, differences in eligibility criteria, and disagreement in the interpretation of test results, there are valid concerns regarding the acceptance of some eligibility statements.

In order to maintain a consistent level of service delivery to students identified as demonstrating learning disabilities, some postsecondary institutions are choosing to provide their own diagnostic services. In a recent survey conducted by Carlton and Walkenshaw (1991), 35 college programs that provide support services for students with learning disabilities and offer a diagnostic component described the type of services available within their institutions. Approximately 25% of the campuses appeared to be making diagnostic decisions using a team of three or more individuals; 25% used a team consisting of two members and 40%

reported using a single person to make diagnostic decisions. The educational backgrounds of those participating in diagnosis varied significantly and included individuals from psychology, speech–language pathology, rehabilitation counseling, counseling psychology, school psychology, neuropathology, special education, reading, and learning disabilities. Approximately 48% of the evaluators had educational training at the master's level and 46% were at the doctoral level or working on a doctorate. Another 6% of those conducting diagnostic evaluations had no formal training beyond the bachelor's level.

Although diagnostic services are not clearly mandated by Section 504 or the ADA, access to support services within most institutions is based on qualification through the diagnostic process. Adelman and Taylor (1991) emphasized that we are now in an "age of accountability"; therefore, evaluation will be increasingly mandated by legislation and government regulations. This need for accountability (especially as enforced by the ADA) may encourage institutions to develop on-site diagnostic services. Although the cost of these services is substantial, the resulting consistency in the quality of diagnostic information assures the institution that students receiving specialized support have met clear eligibility criteria. An evaluation conducted by a licensed school psychologist or educational diagnostician will assure that the student receives consistent diagnostic service while also creating a standard that protects the institution.

Assessment for Accommodation

Vocational rehabilitation assessment for individuals with specific learning disabilities serves two major functions: (a) providing information that enables an individual to make a diagnostic determination, and (b) providing information about a client's strengths and weaknesses in order to develop and implement a vocational rehabilitation plan (McCue, 1989). At the college or university level, the provision of a "rehabilitation plan" must evolve into the provision of a plan that enables the student, with the assistance of support service providers, to develop a realistic approach to accommodation. Qualitatively, college, with its emphasis on student responsibility for decision making, is drastically different from high school (Brinckerhoff, Shaw & McGuire, Chapter 6 of this book). The responsibility for accommodation has been shifted from the school staff to the student; it is now the student who needs a clear understanding of the specific procedures for services, an understanding of his or her own strengths and weaknesses, and an ability to describe his or her specific need for reasonable accommodation. Again, much of this information is based on the documentation of the student's learning profile as well as the recommendations made following a diagnostic evaluation.

As an adult, the student will and should play an active role in the diagnostic process. Development of rapport with the evaluator is a key issue, because these students are in a position to reveal aspects of their lives that they have worked hard to overcome or keep secret. A large part of the evaluator's job is to observe processing as well as any compensatory strategies the student employs. These behaviors should be documented using standardized procedures and should be discussed later in some detail with the student in order to gain clarification of the observations. Much attention will be given to the examination of normative data and patterns of scores. However, equally important is the examination of the cognitive functions these scores summarize, the manner in which the student attained these scores (Porch, 1971), the preserved functions the scores reflect, and the way in which these scores relate to the student's daily life and academic program (Milberg, Hebben, & Kaplan, 1986). Mercer (1987) emphasized that assessment is the collection of data for the overall purpose of improving the student's educational program and that it is important to recognize sources of data that offer instructionally relevant information. Teachers and other school personnel are cited as rich resources of viable information. Postsecondary students, especially those who are being evaluated for the first time and do not have a background in special education services, often bring to the diagnostic process unique insights. These insights are invaluable and should be encouraged in order to obtain the most accurate profile of the individual's learning style. With this consideration in mind, the adult student becomes a key member of the diagnostic team.

An individual who has been identified as demonstrating a learning disability leaves the high school setting where his or her support system is readily available and enters a world where self-advocacy skills are critical (Roffman, Herzog, & Wershba-Gershon, 1994). Interaction with students suggests that in many instances it is evident that these individuals continue to lack a full understanding of their own strengths and weaknesses. Often students who have been identified as having a learning disability since childhood demonstrate less insight into their own difficulties than those adults who were not identified until reaching the college level.

As a result of inclusion in the diagnostic process, students are placed in a position to maximize their own understanding of their individual learning styles. The goal of the diagnostician is to present this information to the individual so that he or she becomes comfortable in explaining his or her own strengths and weaknesses to others. This is crucial for the student when interacting with faculty and other support staff (e.g., tutors, counselors, and academic advisors). Few colleges and universities have specialized programs for students with learning disabilities beyond the "basic 504 services." Often, tutoring is based on content subject matter rather than focusing on a strategy approach. This may present problems for students unless their individual learning styles and strategies are fully understood. Without the assistance of a specialized tutoring program, the responsibility for explaining special needs falls solely on the student. The learning strategies approach as described by Alley and Deshler (1979) and Lenz (1992) has proven applicable to college students with learning disabilities (Gajar, Murphy, & Hunt, 1982) and has been incorporated into programs that combine content-based learning with the development of individual strategies (Denton, Seybert, & Franklin, 1988). Carlson (1985) stressed that although content-area tutoring may meet the legal obligations of the school, ethical standards may be better served through strategy development. The goal, especially in the postsecondary setting, is to decrease the student's dependence upon the tutor by developing the independence of the student as an effective learner and self-advocate.

Adult Assessment Practices: An Example

Organizational Structure and Program Description

Over the past several years, The University of New Mexico (UNM) has made a concerted effort to meet the diverse needs of students with varying disabilities. Meeting the needs of students with learning disabilities has presented some unique challenges. For example, college officials can provide support for a student only if the student has been identified as having a disability; yet there is a legal prohibition against requiring information about disabilities as part of any admissions decision. As a result, university records reflect information about only those students who voluntarily report disabling conditions. Although many students will report such information, some students with disabilities may be reluctant to do so. In talking with students at the university who have been identified as having learning disabilities, some have related that they are embarrassed to reveal this. Others have stated that they fear that their disclosure might appear on school records or affect the manner in which they are assessed in their academic programs. It has become very evident at the University of New Mexico, as well as at other institutions across the country (Carlton & Walkenshaw, 1991), that there are many students who have never been properly identified as having learning disabilities. These students are unaware of specific diagnostic conditions other than general difficulties in academic achievement. As a result, there are no firm figures available regarding the prevalence of learning disabilities among postsecondary students.

The student population at the University of New Mexico is approximately 26,000. It is estimated that there are now between 700 and 800 students with known disabilities enrolled in academic programs, and this figure represents more than double the number of students with disabilities enrolled 5 years ago. Of the identified students with disabilities currently being served through Disabled Student Services, approximately 53% have learning disabilities; 20% have visual impairments; 13% have mobility impairments; 9% have hearing impairments; and 5% fall into the category of "other," which includes various medical or emotional impairments (these numbers were supplied by UNM's Office of Disabled Student Services). UNM follows the national trend in that students with learning disabilities are the fastest growing single group of college students with disabilities receiving support services (King, 1987).

It has been suggested that assessment and identification are critical educational components of university programs designed for students with learning disabilities (Levinson, 1986). In order to meet the growing needs of these students, the University of New Mexico established the Educational Diagnostic Unit (EDU) in June of 1987. Since its establishment, the goal of the unit has been to provide educational diagnostic services to UNM students who are experiencing significant academic problems due to undefined or previously diagnosed difficulties in their learning styles. Complete diagnostic evaluations focus on identifying specific learning disabilities through testing intellectual expectancy, academic achievement, and cognitive processing. Full funding for the unit is provided by the university, and it receives no additional federal or grant monies at this time. The diagnostic staff includes two full-time certified educational diagnosticians as well as support personnel in academic advisement and counseling. The EDU is one component of a network of services available for students with disabilities attending the university (see Figure 7.1). The EDU is located within University College, which houses incoming freshmen, sophomores, and other students who are undecided as to their academic major. Although physically located within University College, the EDU serves all students, including those in graduate programs. The EDU routinely interacts with the departments of Special Education and Communicative Disorders and works regularly with Disabled Student Services and Learning Support Services (described in detail later in this chapter; see also Note at end of chapter). All divisions operate on a year-round basis.

Since its establishment, the EDU has completed comprehensive evaluations on 510 students referred for testing. Of the total population of students seen for evaluation, 75% had never been tested for a learning disability prior to entering the university. Of the students who had been previously diagnosed as having learning disabilities, only 66% had received special education services in elementary or secondary school.

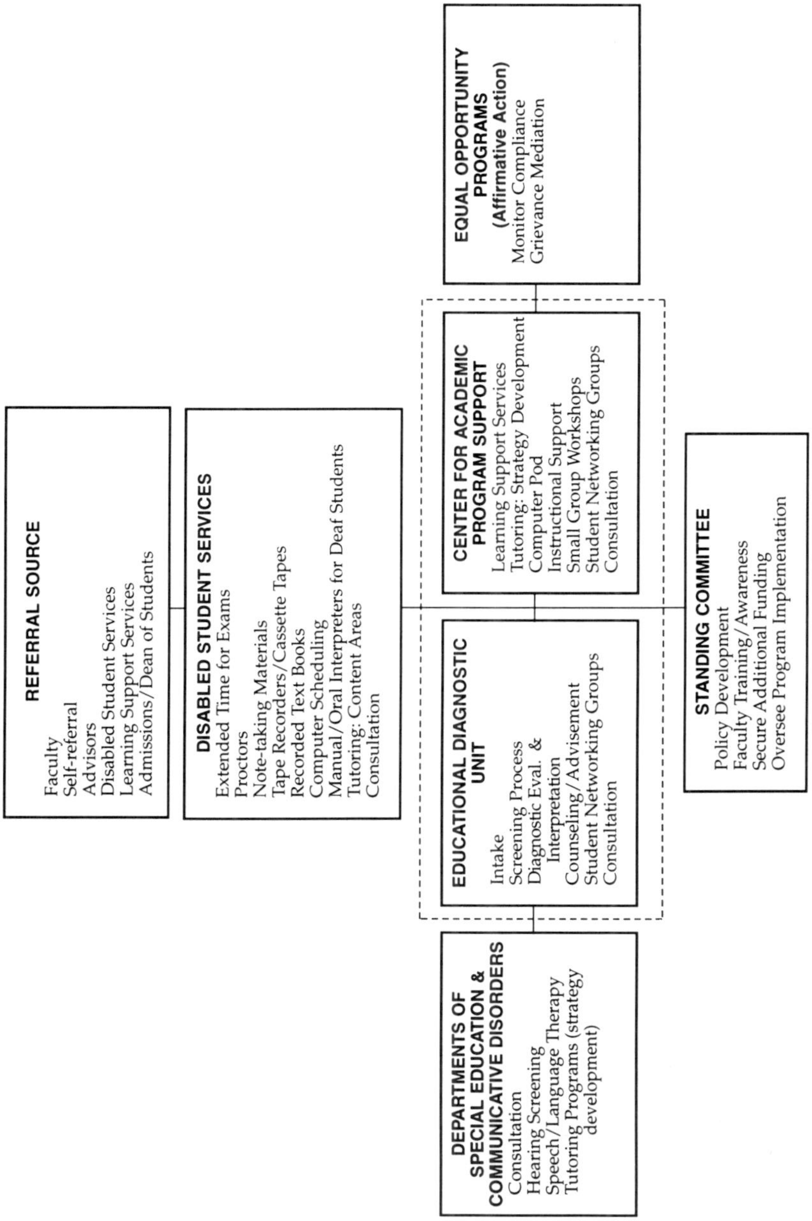

Figure 7.1 Service delivery network at the University of New Mexico.

The two reasons most frequently cited for a failure to receive services were (a) the family chose not to place the student, and (b) the student was attending a private or parochial school that did not offer special education services.

The average age of students seeking diagnostic services at UNM is 27, which also reflects the average age of the university's general student population. It should be noted that the average age of students seeking diagnostic services has lowered over the past 2 academic years. As transition programs in the community improve and as the support services at UNM gain wider recognition, another shift in the average age of the students served may occur.

Referrals for diagnostic testing following enrollment at the University come from several sources (see Table 7.3). Most referrals to the EDU coming from Disabled Student Services involve individuals who have been diagnosed in the past but who have no documentation or have documentation that is old or does not clearly meet eligibility criteria. Other referrals are of individuals who have been identified for the first time as having a disability. As inservice training and publications for faculty, advisors, and counselors have become increasingly available, referrals have risen. Similarly, as student groups have become more active in raising awareness regarding disabilities and as more students have been through the evaluation process, self- and peer-referrals have also increased.

Because of the structure of UNM's network model, students with learning disabilities currently receive primary services from two service delivery network programs that work closely with the EDU. The first, Disabled Student Services, provides students with basic Section 504 ser-

TABLE 7.3
Referral Sources for Educational Diagnostic Services

Referral source	Percentage LD (n = 355)	Percentage NLD (n = 155)
Faculty	27	27
Self	19	25
Academic advisors	12	12
Disabled Student Services	13	8
Counselors	10	8
Learning Support Services	9	9
Peers	7	9
Parents	1	1
Physicians	1	1

Note. LD = with learning disabilities; NLD = nonlearning disabled.

vices, which include arrangements for extended time on exams (scheduling of rooms, proctors, and computers); note-taking materials (NCR or no-carbon-required paper and/or tape recorders and tapes); textbooks on tape (ordered from Recordings for the Blind); content area tutoring; and resource counseling.

Second, the Center for Academic Program Support offers content area tutorial assistance to all undergraduate students. In 1989, the Center added a specialized program designed to serve students who have a documented learning disability. This program (Learning Support Services, or LSS) offers one-to-one tutoring that focuses on general learning strategies rather than specific content areas and is implemented in conjunction with content-area tutoring. Examples of specific learning strategies include the development of listening skills; memory; general reading, writing, and spelling strategies; communication skills; time management and study skills; note-taking; test-taking; and organizational and social interaction skills. A 2-hour-credit course has been developed through LSS for students with learning disabilities and focuses on the acquisition of independent learning skills and skills necessary for successful classroom study. This basic course is a prerequisite for a sequence of two additional courses that students with learning disabilities are encouraged to take. The first of these courses teaches information management and focuses on use of library tools and research strategies. The second course focuses on applying previously learned skills in the development of a research paper that covers individualized research topics.

LSS and the EDU also have provided support groups specifically designed for students with learning disabilities. The primary focus of these groups has been to give students an opportunity to discuss their specific needs and concerns with peers who are experiencing similar difficulties. Professionals in the areas of diagnostics, counseling, and academic strategy development promote discussions and assist the students in offering one another helpful hints related to survival on campus.

The Process: Who Should Be Tested

The EDU is designed to work primarily with students suspected of having a learning disability, those previously diagnosed as having a learning disability, or those students demonstrating learning difficulties as a result of traumatic injury or other medical conditions (e.g., epilepsy or stroke). Although differential diagnosis does occur within the classification of learning disability, diagnostic evaluations designed for use with other related populations are utilized to provide information concerning specific strengths and weaknesses, as well as recommendations for appropriate accommodation.

Initiation of the Evaluation Process

Following a formal referral, or upon self-referral, the student initiates the diagnostic process by picking up a Case History Form and a Characteristics Checklist (see Appendices A and B) from the EDU. These forms are accompanied by a cover letter that explains the diagnostic process and encourages the student to return the forms as soon as possible. The EDU has established a thorough evaluation procedure that requires a 2- to 3-hour screening session followed by approximately 6 to 9 hours of diagnostic testing. Because there is always a waiting list of approximately 30 to 40 students seeking services, screening groups have recently been implemented. When the student returns the Case History Form, he or she is scheduled for screening and intake procedures. Instruments used in screening include:

- Case History Form
- Characteristics Checklist
- Written Language Sample (nonstandardized)
- Nelson-Denny Reading Test (Brown, Bennett, & Hanna, 1981)
- Diagnostic Spelling Potential Test (Arena, 1982)
- Math Worksheet (Woodcock-Johnson Psycho-Educational Battery–Revised; Woodcock & Johnson, 1989)
- Raven Standard Progressive Matrices (optional; Raven, 1958)
- Scholastic Abilities Test for Adults (Bryant, Patton, & Dunn, 1991)

Following screening, each student is assigned to one of the two diagnosticians on staff. Usually assignment is made on an alternating basis (one student to Diagnostician 1; one to Diagnostician 2). However, students sometimes request a diagnostician based on whether or not they feel more comfortable working closely with a man or a woman. UNM has a large Native American population. As noted by Chamberlain and Medeiros-Landurand (1991), it is important to realize that "assessment is a subjective process that is highly influenced by the socio-political, cultural, and linguistic context" (p. 112). Due to the significant impact of cultural and linguistic variables on the assessment process, it is crucial that all educators involved in the assessment of this diverse population recognize the extent to which these variables operate to affect test results and the interpretation of those results. The EDU seeks assistance from American Indian Student Services if a translator is required or for assistance in test interpretation. Similar arrangements are made through the

International Center and various foreign language departments when assessing students who come from different backgrounds. At this time, the EDU has one diagnostician who is fluent in Spanish. If a student's primary language is Spanish and it is the language with which he or she is most comfortable, that diagnostician will be assigned to the student.

Most often, screening occurs before the diagnostician completes the intake procedure. This procedure includes a thorough review of the Case History Form and Characteristics Checklist with the student as well as discussion pertaining to the student's current concerns and academic needs. Screening results are also reviewed aduring the intake procedure.

The Case History Form (see Appendix A) is extensive and requests information from the student concerning current educational status; educational history; family, developmental, and medical history; and current health status. Specific questions concerning personal and social factors are also included. Students are asked to identify their own strengths and weaknesses as well as their educational expectations and goals. Information concerning the student's attitudes toward family, school, faculty, and peers is sought in relation to how academic performance is affected. Employment information is requested as is other demographic data. Table 7.4 is based on these demographic data and presents a general profile of all students who have completed the diagnostic process.

The Characteristics Checklist (adapted from Mangrum & Strichart, 1984, pp. 32-37; see Appendix B) is completed by the student and provides valuable information concerning the student's perceptions of his or her learning difficulties. An important screening instrument, it affords the diagnostician an opportunity to note which items the student perceives as significantly affecting academic performance. A student who focuses on the characteristics listed under "Work and Study Habits" often should be referred to other service units. The Center for Academic Program Support, for instance, offers coursework specifically designed for the development of academic strategies, time management, and organizational skills, and an academic advisor can help the student develop realistic goals and an appropriate courseload. Students who focus their attention on the characteristics listed under "Social" or "Affective" may need additional assistance through a personal counselor or mental health team member. In reviewing the data collected from 510 completed evaluations, we found that the average number of characteristics checked by students was 26 (range = 3 to 76). Although formal research has not been conducted in this area, preliminary inspection of the data indicates that a bell-shaped curve exists, with the students most in need of support services falling at either end of the continuum. The students who check very few characteristics (yet for whom diagnostic testing indicates significant learning difficulties) seem to be least likely to use the support ser-

TABLE 7.4
Demographic Profile: Students Who Have Completed Full Diagnostic Evaluation

	LD (*n* = 355)	NLD (*n* = 155)
Men	56%	41%
Women	44%	59%
Average age	27 yrs	27 yrs
Right hand dominant	86%	88%
Left hand dominant	14%	12%
Ethnicity		
Native American	3%	3%
African American	6%	6%
Asian	0%	0%
Hispanic	20%	17%
White	70%	74%
Educational history		
Previously diagnosed as LD	31%	14%
Of those previously diagnosed: Percentage who received special education services in elementary and/or secondary settings	22%	7%
Out-of-state high schools	38%	46%
Graduate equivalency diplomas	9%	10%
University graduate students	12%	11%
Employment as student		
Full-time	17%	15%
Part-time	42%	48%
Not employed	41%	37%

Note. LD = with learning disabilities; NLD = nonlearning disabled.

vices offered. Self-advocacy and self-awareness seem to be underdeveloped in these students, and there is a concern among researchers and providers that these students may “fall through the cracks.” Students who check many characteristics may be overwhelmed by the transition to a university setting and in need of additional counseling or mental health intervention.

The Written Language Sample has proven to be a key screening instrument. This nonstandardized measure is not scored in any formalized manner. Students write for no more than 1 hour about their perceptions regarding their learning difficulties. Use of a pen is required so that organizational difficulties, self-corrections, and misspellings are clearly evident. Although writing style, organization, spelling, punctuation, and syntax are obvious diagnostic indicators, the content usually provides the most valuable data. Often the student will include additional information that was not shared in discussion or on the Case History Form. As noted by Johnson and Blalock (1987) and Rogers (1991), the content of the writings of individuals with learning disabilities often reveals that a learning disability affects more than academic work and is never limited to a single area of achievement such as spelling or reading. Written language samples often reveal the frustration and feelings of isolation and lowered self-esteem these individuals have endured. The written language samples of individuals referred for diagnostic testing at UNM provide a key to screening and are often the springboard for the intake interview.

Due to the backlog of students awaiting completion of the diagnostic process, temporary memos that qualify the student for provisional services can be written if the screening and intake procedures indicate the need for immediate intervention. The memo is written by the diagnostician who is working with the student. It is important for the diagnostician to make sure that the student understands that these services are provisional pending the outcome of the full diagnostic evaluation. It is also important that the diagnostician makes sure that the student understands the process for obtaining these services (e.g., how to arrange for extended time for an exam through Disabled Student Services). As a result of the screening process, intake interview, and a collaborated decision for provisional services, rapport between the student and diagnostician can be established prior to the diagnostic testing sessions.

Diagnostic Evaluation

The general philosophy of the EDU is that diagnostic evaluation at the postsecondary level should be very different in approach than what is normally provided in the public school setting. It must be taken into consideration that the individual who is seeking evaluation is an adult and should play an active role in the process. It is also important to consider the types of support services available and the role that the student must play in obtaining this support. Services vary widely among postsecondary settings, and it is unrealistic for a student to expect a comprehensive special education program to be provided at the university or college level.

Many students who previously have not been diagnosed as having a disability enter the diagnostic process with a great deal of anxiety and frustration. A student who has done well enough to be admitted to a university or 4-year college program is most likely very bright and has been able to compensate for academic weaknesses. However, at this level of education a point may be reached where program requirements make it impossible to avoid, or compensate for, particular areas of difficulty. Diagnostic services are often seen as a way to provide an explanation for, or even more importantly, a validation of their academic problems through a documentation procedure. The diagnostician frequently hears such comments as

> Even though I'm working as hard as I can, I'm still not doing well in my classes . . . am I just dumb?
>
> When I was a child, I was told I was just lazy . . . . Maybe I am.
>
> I could do okay on my exams, but I run out of time.
>
> Why can't I remember what I read?
>
> I know what I want to say, but it just doesn't come out.

Because 75% of the referrals at UNM are of students who previously have never been tested for learning disabilities, insight provided during diagnostic procedures concerning self-assessment and the compensation strategies a student employs is of great interest. Each diagnostic procedure becomes a learning experience for the diagnostician as well as for the individual who is being evaluated. Additional time must be allowed so that observations related to specific strategies and compensatory behaviors can be noted and verified. Adult students frequently will stop the testing to ask what a specific task is measuring. At the appropriate time, this should be discussed so that the individual understands the process and leaves the evaluation knowing that he or she has contributed to the procedure.

The core diagnostic appointments for each individual are scheduled over 3 days (each appointment lasts $2^1/_2$ to 3 hours), preferably within a 1-week period. It is during these appointments that the diagnostic battery is administered and observations of student behaviors are noted. The interpretive session is then scheduled for the following week. The diagnostic battery for each student includes the complete administration of the following tests:

- Wechsler Adult Intelligence Scale–Revised (WAIS-R; Wechsler, 1981)
- Woodcock-Johnson Psycho-Educational Battery–Revised (WJ-R: Achievement; Woodcock & Johnson, 1989) or Scholastic Abilities Test for Adults (SATA; Bryant et al., 1991)
- Woodcock-Johnson Psychoeducational Battery–Revised (WJ-R: Cog. Processing)
- Bender Visual–Motor Gestalt Test (Bender, 1938)
- Wechsler Memory Scale–Revised (WMS-R—if warranted; Wechsler, 1987)

Although there is little consensus on appropriate measures for identifying adults with learning disabilities, these tests and others administered during the screening session were chosen as the best diagnostic measures available for the adult population (Bracken, Prasse, & Breene, 1984; Cuenin, 1990; Cummings, 1985; Dalke, 1988; Estabrook, 1983; Gregg & Hoy, 1985; Gregory, 1987; Hoy & Gregg, 1986b; Johnson, 1987; Kaufman, 1985, 1990; Salvia & Salvia, 1985; Slate, Frost, & Cross, 1990, 1991). Although alternate measures (i.e., The Stanford-Binet Intelligence Scale, Fourth Edition) may be required in some circumstances, the battery of tests listed above is most often relied upon. Frequently, informal evaluation by methods such as the observation and documentation of processing and compensatory behaviors, error analysis and patterns of scores, and expressive language abilities becomes as important as standardized testing in diagnostic decision making.

After all administered tests have been scored, the diagnostician prepares a memo ("To whom it may concern") for students qualifying for LD support services or a summary report for those who do not. The memos are to be provided to faculty who work with the student. Students who do qualify for support services are provided with a resource packet consisting of copies of the memo, the *Handbook for Students with Disabilities,* a LSS flyer, and a description of services offered by Disabled Student Services. A cover letter included in the packet explains that the interpretive session will be followed by a complete diagnostic report. This letter encourages the student to make a follow-up appointment if he or she has questions concerning the full diagnostic report. Diagnostic reports are only released to the student or to the appropriate support service, with the consent of the student.

Confidentiality

In general, the issue of confidentiality continues to challenge student affairs professionals in university settings (Stone & Lucas, 1990). As stated in the American College Personnel Association's Statement of Ethical Principles and Standards (1990), protection of confidentiality refers to a general standard of conduct that requires student affairs professionals to

> 1.11 Inform students of the nature and/or limits of confidentiality. They will share information about the students only in accordance with institutional policies and applicable laws, when given their permission, or when required to prevent personal harm to themselves or others. (p. 13)

As related to eligibility for learning disabilities support services, confidentiality issues at the postsecondary level differ from those in earlier levels in that the postsecondary students are seeking diagnostic services based on a referral or their own desire for information. The youngest students tested are usually 18 years old and thus do not need parental consent to initiate the evaluation process. Once the evaluation process is completed, information concerning the diagnostic findings is disclosed to faculty or other university staff at the student's discretion. A high level of confidentiality is stressed within the EDU, where diagnostic information is shared with other parties such as parents, faculty, and tutors only when the request is accompanied by a release from the student. Parents and spouses are not included in the process unless invited by the student. The students themselves are solely responsible for providing information concerning their learning disability to faculty members. In addition to a detailed diagnostic report, the EDU provides the student with a brief memo (mentioned previously) that may be presented to faculty. The memo validates the student's qualification for services as an individual with a learning disability and outlines several basic adaptations that the student may need in class.

Students are not placed in a special setting following diagnostic testing. Although support services are offered, they are not mandatory. Students are encouraged to make their own decisions concerning accommodations, and these decisions are based on the information and recommendations provided in the extensive diagnostic report.

The diagnostic report provides the student's test scores and an interpretation of what the scores mean. Referral and disclosure to support programs following the diagnostic evaluation is not automatic. Often a student may not be ready to pursue support services and seems to go through a "cycle of acceptance" when dealing with the concept of being identified as an adult with learning disabilities. Occasionally students return to the EDU for referral to support services several semesters later, when they are ready to disclose their difficulties outside of the diagnostic setting. It is important that students feel comfortable with the diagnostician as well as the process, so that they will return for additional information and clarification as needed.

Eligibility Criteria for Learning Disabilities

Wood (1991) provided a review of the most common methods for determining severe discrepancies between intellectual ability and achievement or academic performance in the identification of students with learning disabilities. In that review, Wood discussed discrepancy formulas (Dangel & Ensminger, 1988) and the multiple regression discrepancy method (Evans, 1990). Wood stressed that a consonance between definitions and identification criteria must be achieved in order to reduce the variance that occurs with classification. However, Mellard (1990) recognized that eligibility procedures appropriate at one postsecondary setting may not fit another. Keogh (1983) addressed this specifically by emphasizing that if the purpose of classification is to provide educational services, perhaps the term *learning disabilities* (suggested by Mann, Davis, Boyer, Metz, & Wolford, 1983) should be used to cover all "mildly" handicapped students. Keogh proposed that learning support programs be established to provide services, not to solve the scientific riddle of learning disabilities, and that the goal of advocacy and delivery of services should be stressed. Although this goal may be the most relevant aspect of diagnostic services for the student, concerns such as professional accountability and research issues should not be ignored. Vogel (1987) stated that in all cases colleges and universities need to develop systematic procedures that corroborate the diagnosis or provide differential diagnosis. The goal of diagnostic procedures should always be to determine whether academic difficulties are caused by the learning disability or some other factor.

The University of New Mexico's EDU has patterned its eligibility criteria on those utilized by the public schools in New Mexico. A discrepancy formula is employed that compares standard scores across the areas of intelligence or expectancy, academic achievement, and cognitive processing. Review of the assessment data will generally indicate average to superior intelligence with a significant deficit in at least one academic area as well as in at least one of the specific learning processes. Discrepancies may exist between verbal and performance scores on a measure of overall intelligence; however, this does not always occur.

Eligibility must be based on the following specific criteria (adapted from a UNM handout):

I. Exclusion of the following as *primary* disabilities or conditions:
   A). Mental retardation
   B). Visual impairment
   C). Deafness or hearing impairment
   D). Physical impairments
   E). Emotional disorders
   F). Poor educational background or lack of opportunity to learn
   G). Cultural differences or lack of experience with the English language

II. Significant discrepancy calculated relative to expectancy, where
   A). *Expectancy* is defined as a standard score (or intelligence quotient) obtained on an intelligence test. Where a significant difference is calculated between verbal and performance scores, the verbal, performance, or full scale score (whichever

best represents the individual's level of intelligence as documented) may be used. A .01 confidence level is used in the determination of significant difference (Sattler, 1988, p. 848).

B). *Significant discrepancy* is defined as a negative difference of 20 standard score points (Gregg & Hoy, 1985) between the standard score on an intelligence test and the standard score obtained in an academic area as well as in a specific area of processing ability. This discrepancy in scores must be documented in terms reported in the technical manual of the individual test instrument.

III. Evidence of a significant academic deficiency relative to expectancy as well as a significant discrepancy in at least one area of cognitive processing

A). Based on expectancy, a statistically significant discrepancy shall be calculated (as defined previously) in one or more of the following academic areas as measured by standardized tests:
1. Reading (basic reading skills and/or reading comprehension)
2. Written Language (basic writing skills and/or written expression)
3. Mathematics (basic math skills and/or mathematical reasoning)

B). In addition to the discrepancy measured between expectancy and in a minimum of one academic area, a statistically significant discrepancy must also be found in at least one area of cognitive processing abilities. These abilities as measured by standardized tests include the following:
1. Visual Processing (i.e., visual–perceptual speed, visual–spatial abilities, visual–motor integration, and visual memory).
2. Auditory Processing (i.e., auditory sequencing ability, auditory discrimination, auditory attention skills, and auditory memory).
3. Verbal Processing (i.e., word retrieval abilities and verbal fluency).
4. Fluid Reasoning Ability (i.e., the ability to approach problem solving in a logical and sequential manner; the ability to shift cognitive strategies as the specific task requires).

These criteria were developed in order to assist the EDU in differentiating students with learning disabilities from those who demonstrate academic difficulties related to other causes. The inclusion of the cognitive processing component is felt to be crucial in assisting the diagnostician in making a differential diagnosis. This area serves as the key to providing an explanation for the student concerning individual strengths and weaknesses. A profile concerning cognitive processing also contributes essential information for future strategy development.

The Student's Perspective

The number of students who were previously undiagnosed and have now been found to demonstrate learning disabilities is very high. When asked about how this new information made them feel, most indicated that it was a relief and that it helped to know there was something different about them that could be documented. The following quotes are taken from students' nonstandardized Written Language Samples. A 28-year-old man in his fifth year of school recently stated:

> I thought I was just dumb. My parents constantly told me that I wasn't dumb, but that I was just lazy. They said I never tried, so I never got good grades. What they didn't seem to understand was that I was trying. I tried so hard that sometimes I just gave up. I knew that I just wasn't smart enough. Now at least I know that I am smart and have been all along. I just learn differently and now I need to understand that and go on.

In an attempt to obtain insight into students' perceptions of identification, several students were asked to write about the diagnostic process. The following passage was written by a student who was diagnosed in 1988, soon after the establishment of the Educational Diagnostic Unit. She has recently completed a bachelor's degree and has been accepted into a graduate program.

> I am 34-year-old female who was diagnosed as having some fairly pronounced learning disabilities at the age of 30. The diagnostic process itself was a positive experience for me particularly since it came at a time when I had assumed that I would need to drop out of college for the third time in 13 years due to a lack of ability and a perceived lack of motivation and self-control. Dropping out of school was not something I wanted to do since I am also a high school dropout and did not need yet another failure to lower my already weakened self-esteem.
>
> When I turned 30 I decided to give college yet another try. My two prior college experiences resulted in the completion of about seven semesters and 50 credit hours. There was never a semester that I completed the original amount of hours registered for and most semesters I received at least an F or incomplete. As I mentioned above, I truly believed that my lack of success was due to immaturity and a weak will. I think I adopted this attitude because although I was failing some classes and not completing others, I was also earning A's in a respectable number of classes.
>
> Through a number of experiences that in retrospect appear to be truly cosmic in nature, it was suggested that I seek out academic counseling

> and/or diagnostic services. To me the idea that I be tested for learning disabilities was a gift. The prospect that somehow the problems I had encountered over such a long period of time might be attributed to something that I didn't necessarily have control over was nothing short of a miracle.
>
> The actual testing process was fairly palatable since the diagnostician was able to administer the tests in three half-day sessions. Then the payoff came when the results confirmed the original suspicions and some definite deficiencies were identified. The results and their ramifications were explained to me in great detail and with much insight and sensitivity on the behalf of the diagnostician. I found this to be very helpful in making further decisions about how to approach my academic career; what type of classes to take, study strategies, and most importantly how much time I needed to allocate to strengthen my retention skills.

The content of most of the responses received was very similar to this and related that the diagnostic process was a valuable experience. A few students indicated that, although the testing was helpful, they still had difficulties in disclosing this information and had experienced periods of feeling both good and bad about their abilities. One student jokingly responded to the request for a written essay by stating, "How could you even ask? You guys know how much I *hate* to write . . . you're the ones who tested me!"

Note

Due to a reorganization of services at UNM, the EDU has been moved to the Center for Academic Support — Learning Support Services. It is no longer a separate service unit.

APPENDIX A: DIAGNOSTIC EVALUATION–CASE HISTORY

Name: ______________________ Date: ______________________

Soc. Sec. #: ______________________ Address: ______________________

Date of birth: ______________________ ______________________

Age: ______________________ Zip code: ______________________

Sex: ______________________ Phone (Home): ______________________

Educational level: ______________________ (Work): ______________________

College major: ______________________ Marital status: __________ Race: _____

Referral Source: ____
(Name) (Title)

Reason for referral: ____

Number of semesters completed at UNM: ______________________

Other colleges/universities or technical schools attended since high school: __________

____

____

EDUCATIONAL HISTORY

Schools Attended: (elementary to present)

School Name	City/State	Date (from–to)

Special School Programs Attended		*Grade Levels or Dates*
Special education placement	________	______________________
Speech/language therapy	________	______________________
Occupational therapy	________	______________________
Physical therapy	________	______________________

Tutoring	________	______________________________
Psychological or counseling	________	______________________________
Retention (repeated a grade)	________	______________________________
Acceleration (honors, moved	________	______________________________
ahead, etc.)	________	______________________________

Were you ever tested for eligibility in special education (i.e., learning disabilities) prior to enrollment in college?

_____ Yes _____ No _____ Don't know

If yes, when and at what school or agency? ________________________________

If services were received through a special education program, what was the primary classification? Learning Disabled ___; Communication Disordered ___; Behaviorally Disordered ___; Hearing Impaired ___; Visually Impaired ___; Physically Impaired ___; Mentally Impaired ___; Gifted ___.

Grades achieved in high school (approximate GPA): ____________________________

Was your attendance regular during high school?: ______________________________

If not, what was the most frequent reason for your absences?

_____ illness _____ taking care of siblings
_____ work _____ moving
_____ lack of interest _____ other (explain below)

____

____

Did you drop out of school between kindergarten and 12th grade? ________________

If yes, what grade were you in when you dropped out? __________________

For what reasons? ____

____

If you did not graduate from high school, when did you pass the GED? ____________

____

As far as you can recall, when did you first start having difficulties in school? ________

____

Are you currently receiving services from other campus or community program(s), for example: DVR, VA, Disabled Student Services, Student Mental Health, etc.?
___ yes ___ no

If yes, please list below: ____

____

____

How many hours are you currently taking at UNM? ____________________________

Are you required to take a certain number of hours? ___________________________

If so, why? ____

List your current courses. Please describe the specific difficulties, if any, that you are experiencing in each:

Course	*Difficulties*
______________________	______________________
______________________	______________________
______________________	______________________
______________________	______________________
______________________	______________________
______________________	______________________

In what classes have you done well? ______________________________

____

____

Indicate your *weakest* general areas:

_____ Reading comprehension
_____ Reading rate
_____ Writing skills: _____ Organizing thoughts when writing; _____ Punctuation;
_____ Spelling; _____ Handwriting
_____ Expressing yourself orally
_____ Math
_____ Maintaining attention/concentration
_____ Organizing time, study methods, problem solving, etc.

On the average, how many total hours per day do you spend studying?

_____ 0–2 hrs _____ 2–4 hrs _____ more

Is your attendance regular since you've been at UNM? ______________________

To what do you attribute your problems in school? (Check all that apply):

_____ Learning disability
_____ Home environment
_____ Emotional problems
_____ Economic disadvantages
_____ Poor teaching
_____ Limited ability
_____ Cultural differences
_____ Motor handicap
_____ Tasks too difficult
_____ Lack of interest
_____ Poor attendance
_____ Work schedule

Has anyone in your family had learning problems in school?

_____ No one _____ Father _____ Mother _____ Brother(s) _____ Sister(s)
_____ Don't know

Explain: ____

____

What do you consider to be your primary language? ______________________

Which language was most often spoken in your home when you were a child? _______

Which is language is most often spoken in your home now? ____________________

Do you consider yourself to be bilingual? _____ yes _____ no

FAMILY HISTORY

Father's name: ______________________ Occupation: ________________

Mother's name: ______________________ Occupation: ________________

Were both parents in the home throughout your childhood? ________________

If not, explain: ____

List your brothers and sisters and their ages: ____________________________

____

Are you currently living in your parents' home?_____ If so, list others living in the home at this time: ____

Are there any events such as deaths, accidents, divorce, or family separations that may have caused problems for you as a student in the past or that might be affecting you now? (explain briefly): ____

____

____

If you are married, please provide:

Husband's/wife's name ___________ Occupation: ________________

Do you have any children? _________ If so, what are their ages? __________

DEVELOPMENTAL/HEALTH HISTORY

Did your mother have any serious health problems during her pregnancy or delivery with you? If so, please explain these difficulties:

____

____

____

Did your overall development seem to be within normal limits in the following areas?

Motor (walking, running, etc.)	Yes _____	No _____
Speech (pronunciation, stuttering)	Yes _____	No _____
Language development	Yes _____	No _____
Academic performance	Yes _____	No _____

If you have marked any of the above as "no," please describe the specific concerns briefly:

____

____

____

Which hand do you use when you write? _____ Right _____ Left

Do you have vision problems? _____ Yes _____ No

If yes, describe: ____

What was the date of your last eye exam? ____

Do you wear glasses or contact lenses? _____ Yes _____ No

If yes, indicate which: ____

Do you wear them on a regular basis? ____

Do you have problems with hearing? _____ Yes _____ No

If yes, describe: ____

What was the date of your last hearing exam? ____

Do you use a hearing device (e.g., a hearing aid)? _____ Yes _____ No

Do you have a history of recurrent ear infections? _____ Yes _____ No

Do you have allergies? _____ Yes _____ No

If yes, how do they influence your class work? ____

____

Have you ever had any serious injuries or illness? _____ Yes _____ No

If yes, specify when and describe: ____

____

Have you ever been hospitalized for a head injury? _____ Yes _____ No

If yes, specify when and describe: ____

____

To which hospital were you admitted? ____

Did you lose consciousness? _____ Yes _____ No For how long? ____________

Have you ever had seizures? _____ Yes _____ No

If yes, specify when and describe: ____

____

Are you currently on any medication? _____ Yes _____ No

If yes, please give name and dosage:

Name of medication ____________________________ Dosage ________________

Name of medication ____________________________ Dosage ________________

Do you take over-the-counter medication? _____ Yes _____ No

If yes, describe: ____

____

How much do you use? ____

How frequently? ____

Do you use drugs or alcohol? _____ Yes _____ No

If yes, which? ____________________

How much do you use? ____________________

How frequently (daily, weekly, etc.)? ____________________

Have you ever been hospitalized for emotional problems? _____ Yes _____ No

If yes, specify when and describe: ____________________

____

Are you participating in individual or group counseling? _____ Yes _____ No

If yes, how often do you attend sessions? ____________________

SOCIAL AND PERSONAL FACTORS

What do you feel are your strong points? ____________________

____

____

What do you feel are your weak points? ____________________

____

____

What educational expectations do you have at this time? ____________________

____

How would you describe your attitude toward school? ____________________

____

How would you describe your relationships with your professors/instructors? __________

____

How would you describe your relationships with your peers? ____________________

____

What type of job do you expect to obtain after graduation? ____________________

____

Do you plan to go to graduate school? ____________________

List some of your outside interests: ____________________

____

Do you currently have a job? _____ If so, please include place of employment, address, and work schedule:

____

____

What questions would you like answered as a result of this evaluation?

____

____

____

Additional comments: ____________________________

____

____

____

____

____

____

____

APPENDIX B: STUDENT REFERRAL INFORMATION

Center for Academic Program Support
Learning Support Services

Name of Student: ______________________________

Social Security Number: ______________________________

Phone Number: (Days) ______________ (Evenings) ______________

How did you find out about our services? ______________________________

____

Instructions: As you read through the following characteristics, check only those that are clearly evident to you (that you notice occurring repeatedly in your life). When you check a characteristic, you should be able to say "This really fits me." Be careful not to check the ones that you notice only occasionally. *Everyone* experiences most of these at some time. **Only check the ones that you feel interfere with your overall ability to learn.**

COGNITIVE

_____ Difficulty putting events and ideas in order
_____ Difficulty understanding abstract concepts
_____ Difficulty in distinguishing important from unimportant information
_____ Little awareness of cause-and-effect relationships
_____ Memory (inability to remember what you've heard)
_____ Poor visual memory (inability to remember what you've seen or read)
_____ Difficulty staying on task
_____ Difficulty in organizing ideas and information
_____ Difficulty in applying skills from one task or situation to another

LANGUAGE

Spoken Language

_____ Difficulty understanding what others say
_____ Use of poor grammar
_____ Limited range of vocabulary
_____ Difficulty retrieving the appropriate word for a situation
_____ Inappropriate use of words or using a word where it doesn't belong

Written Language

_____ Imprecise and unclear expression (trouble getting your ideas across on paper)
_____ Grammar errors (trouble with tense agreement, etc.)
_____ Poor organization of thoughts
_____ Incorrect use of punctuation
_____ Seldom use phrases or sentences with long or difficult words
_____ Compositions usually too short for purpose

PERCEPTUAL–MOTOR

_____ Reversals of letters and numerals
_____ Difficulty perceiving spatial attributes (i.e., trouble reading a map)

_____ Difficulty dealing with three-dimensional figures and/or shapes
_____ Difficulty hearing differences in similar-sounding words

READING

_____ Difficulty sounding words out
_____ Poor ability to understand what was read
_____ Poor ability to determine main ideas
_____ Slow rate of reading
_____ Difficulty remembering what was read

SPELLING

_____ Transposition of letters when spelling words (such as writing "saw" for "was" or "fo" for "of")
_____ Omits letters when spelling words
_____ Phonetically spell most words (such as writing "guvernmint" for "government")
_____ General avoidance of writing words that are difficult to spell

HANDWRITING

_____ Awkward and uncomfortable style of handwriting
_____ Slow rate of writing
_____ Poorly formed or not easily read letters
_____ Writing that is overly large or small
_____ Difficulty keeping writing within the margins or on the line

MATHEMATICS

_____ Poor computational skills (adding, subtracting, etc.)
_____ Incomplete memorization of multiplication tables
_____ Poor mathematical reasoning (i.e., word problems)
_____ Difficulty recalling the sequence of an operational process or formula
_____ Failure to understand and retain terms related to math concepts

WORK AND STUDY HABITS

_____ Poor organization and budgeting of time
_____ Difficulty completing work when due
_____ Difficulty getting work started
_____ Difficulty staying with a task
_____ Difficulty establishing short- and long-term goals
_____ Inability to identify the basic requirements of a task
_____ Difficulty bringing together information from various sources
_____ Difficulty using the dictionary or other reference tools
_____ Notes that are typically incomplete, inaccurate, or lacking important facts
_____ Difficulty outlining important information in a text
_____ Excessive test anxiety

SOCIAL

_____ Difficulty establishing good relationships with others
_____ Difficulty working effectively with others

_____ Poor family relationships
_____ Problems saying what is thought or felt
_____ Misunderstanding humor and sarcasm
_____ Difficulty engaging in "small talk"
_____ Few hobbies and interests
_____ Difficulty relating to authority figures such as professors and advisors

SELF-AWARENESS

_____ Low sense of self-worth
_____ Lack of self-confidence
_____ Overdependence on others
_____ Overly sensitive to criticism by others
_____ Frustrated easily
_____ Tendency to think negatively about outcomes of your own efforts
_____ Unclear values about life
_____ Tendency to respond immediately without thought about the outcome
_____ Low degree of motivation
_____ Excessive anxiety about things
_____ Defensiveness in interacting with others

Additional comments (list any questions or concerns that you might have that you feel have not been covered):

____

____

____

____

____

____

____

____

Note. Checklist adapted from Mangrum and Strichart (1984).

8. The Success of College Students with Learning Disabilities: Factors Related to Educational Attainment

SUSAN A. VOGEL AND PAMELA B. ADELMAN

In the decade of the 1980s we witnessed a rapid increase in the number of students with learning disabilities (LD) attending colleges and universities (Astin, Green, Korn, Schalit, & Berg, 1988; Decker, Polloway, & Decker, 1985; Shaw & Norlander, 1986). According to the American Council on Education's freshman norms for 1988 (Astin et al., 1988), 6% of all full-time/first-time college freshmen reported having at least one disability. This percentage is more than twice the number of freshmen with disabilities of a decade ago. Moreover, 1% of the total number of freshmen with disabilities self-identified as LD; however, this is a minimal estimate of the total number of college freshmen with LD, because a large number of university students with LD transfer from one postsecondary institution to another. Many others take a part-time load and, by design, transfers and part-time students were excluded from Astin et al.'s data.

The U.S. Department of Education (1987) reported that 10.5% of all postsecondary students in the nation are disabled, that is, approxi-

Reprinted, with changes, from "The success of college students with learning disabilities: Factors related to educational attainment," by Susan A. Vogel and Pamela B. Adelman, *Journal of Learning Disabilities,* Vol. 25, 1992, pp. 430–441.

mately 1.3 million out of a total of 12.5 million students, including those enrolled in community colleges, professional schools, and doctoral programs. Of the 1.3 million disabled students, 12.2% (approximately 160,000) reported having a learning disability. Moreover, this significant increase in the last 10 years in the number of students with learning disabilities attending colleges and universities is accompanied by a commensurate concern among service providers regarding the academic failure rate of these students. In a survey of 911 high school graduates with learning disabilities, Sitlington and Frank (1990) found that 1 year after graduation only 6.5% of the 50% who had enrolled in some type of postsecondary setting were still in school.

Even with greater numbers of students with LD enrolling in postsecondary institutions and the growing concern for their academic success, very few institutions are systematically monitoring these students' academic performance or graduation and attrition rates. What little information we have indicates that there is some reason to be concerned about degree completion by students with learning disabilities.

Bursuck, Rose, Cowen, and Yahaya (1989) sent a survey to the 336 members of the LD Special Interest Group of the Association on Handicapped Student Service Programs in Postsecondary Education (AHSSPPE). Members of this organization are directors or coordinators of services for students with handicaps in community colleges and public and private colleges and universities. Out of a total of 197 respondents, only 20 (10%) responded to the question regarding the percentage of students who graduated or completed a course of study. The average graduation or completion rate for those who responded was 30%. However, the authors did not describe the degree earned (2-year or 4-year) or separate those who reported graduation rate versus completion of a course of study, nor did they provide comparison group data, making interpretation of this information difficult. Nonetheless, a 30% graduation or completion rate, compared to approximately a 50% national graduation rate as reported by the National Association of Independent Colleges and Universities ("Years in College," 1990), is a matter of some concern.

To date, only Vogel and Adelman (1990) have addressed the question of educational attainment in a systematic way. They compared a group of 110 students with learning disabilities (the LD group) to a random, stratified sample (the RSS group) of 153 students attending the same college. The groups were matched on gender and year and semester of entrance to the college. They were then compared on high school preparation and performance, ACT composite, college grade point average (GPA) at the end of each semester and at exit, graduation and academic failure rate, and time to complete the bachelor's degree. The present study is a sequel to the 1990 one and was undertaken in an effort to clarify some unexpected findings. Below we present an overview of these earlier findings so that the reader can better understand the purpose of the present study.

Vogel and Adelman (1990) predicted that students with learning disabilities enter college with significantly poorer high school preparation, as reflected in the number of courses in the core curriculum (i.e., English, social studies, math, and science) for college-bound students completed with a grade of C or better. The high school variables of greatest interest were those four found to be the most highly correlated with college exit GPA and included the number of regular (rather than developmental or remedial) English and math high school courses completed with a grade of C or better ($r = .40$, $p < .000$, and $r = .26$, $p < .012$, respectively) and the total number of D and failing grades received ($r = -.25$, $p < .016$, and $r = -.40$, $p < .000$, respectively). Not surprisingly, these four variables differentiated between the groups at the $p < .008$ level, with the total number of D grades contributing the most.

In an effort to understand better why the number of D grades was a more sensitive discriminator than the number of F grades, the number of Ds earned in core, noncore, and elective courses was tallied. It was found that the number of D grades in noncore and elective courses was more discriminating than the number of Ds in regular core curriculum courses. After examining the specific courses in which the students received Ds, Vogel and Adelman (1990) found that a very high proportion were in physical education. Because it is customary to give a C or better grade in physical education classes for attendance, following dress code, positive attitude, and good sportsmanship, this finding was thought to reflect noncompliance with school regulations and a poor attitude rather than athletic skill, balance, coordination, endurance, speed, or strength. Other possible reasons for the poor grades in physical education may be related to the students' learning disability, that is, memory deficits (e.g., causing students to forget to bring appropriate gym shoes, uniform, towel) or poor social-interpersonal skills (e.g., causing the teacher to misinterpret their behavior as poor sportsmanship).

The LD group scored significantly more poorly than the RSS group on all four ACT subtests and the composite. However, a different pattern emerged in comparing the LD and RSS college graduate subgroups. The LD graduates scored significantly more poorly only on the English and Social Studies subtests, perhaps because they required the most reading and the students with LD still had deficits in reading comprehension. However, these deficits did not preclude college graduation. The correlation of ACT subtest scores and college exit GPA indicated that the ACT English, Social Studies, and Science subtests are not good predictors of college success for students with learning disabilities. Namely, for the LD group, there was a significant correlation with college exit GPA for only the ACT Math subtest. These findings confirmed the importance of examining the ACT subtest scores and other supplementary information rather than relying solely on the composite score.

Because LD applicants scored significantly more poorly than non-LD college applicants on the ACT, even when they used modified examination procedures, Vogel and Adelman (1990) raised the question about the predictive power of the ACT for individuals with learning disabilities. This question has relevance for college counselors, high school guidance counselors and academic advisors, LD advocates, individuals with LD and their parents, and college admissions officers.

For this LD population, the ACT was found to be an accurate predictor of college success, but not as powerful a predictor asfor the non-LD population. The ACT accounted for 31% of the variance in graduation status for students with LD, compared to 39% in the RSS. These findings indicated that the ACT subtest and composite scores do have relevance and predictive power. However, Vogel and Adelman (1990) recommended that ACT information be supplemented by a careful analysis of the high school transcript and other relevant information, such as recent results from the Wechsler Adult Intelligence Scales–Revised (WAIS-R), academic achievement levels, previous psychoeducational reports, case history information, letters of recommendation, and interviews.

Vogel and Adelman (1990) also reported that the GPAs of students with learning disabilities were significantly lower than for the RSS group at the end of each year of study and when they exited from college (graduated, transferred, failed, or dropped out). Their transcripts had significantly more D and P (pass) grades than did the RSS group. The latter is to expected in the LD sample because many highly recommended college developmental courses are offered only Pass/Fail. Surprisingly, no differences between groups were found on number of withdrawals (W), incompletes, and F grades, perhaps because of the special academic advising available to the students with LD, including assistance in monitoring of drop/add deadlines and frequent communication between the students with LD and their advisors.

Given that the students with LD performed significantly more poorly in high school, scored lower on all ACT subtests and the composite, and had lower GPAs at the end of each year of study in college and at exit, it was expected that significantly fewer students with LD would graduate and a larger number would have been dismissed as a result of academic failure. In addition, it was predicted that the graduates with learning disabilities would have taken a lighter course load and longer to graduate than the RSS graduates. Of special interest were the findings that in spite of poorer academic preparation for college, the students with learning disabilities graduated at about the same rate (37%) as their nondisabled peers (39%) and within the same time frame (6½ years). Moreover, the academic failure rate for the two groups was almost identical (LD 17% and NLD 18%).

These findings were interpreted in light of the sample and setting characteristics. Namely, when students with learning disabilities self-identified and were carefully screened at admission, were highly motivated to succeed in college, and used comprehensive, highly coordinated support services, including special academic advisors, they were almost identical to the general college population on this specific campus in graduation and failure rate and time to complete their degree.

The surprising and puzzling findings that the LD and RSS students graduated within the same time frame and carried approximately the same number of credit hours per semester (10.5) contradicted observational data and the present widespread academic advising recommendation for students with learning disabilities to take a part-time load. Based on the finding that the RSS students were significantly older than the students in the LD group, we speculated that the demographics of the student body had contributed in some way to the findings regarding course load and time taken to complete degree.

Because this is a small, suburban college whose mission included responding to individual needs, college officials encouraged the development of comprehensive LD support services (Vogel & Adelman, 1993). Many traditional-age students with learning disabilities from different states and Canada were attracted to the college because they wanted to avail themselves of the comprehensive, highly coordinated LD support services. In the 1970s and early 1980s the college expanded its mission and became responsive to the needs of other nontraditional students, namely, students who were employed part-time or full-time and/or had childcare responsibilities. A childcare center was provided, and evening and weekend classes were offered. We hypothesized that many of the RSS students had to carry a part-time load and therefore took longer than 4 years to graduate.

Vogel and Adelman (1990) cautioned that the two major findings regarding the similarity between the two groups on graduation and academic failure rate, though encouraging, may not generalize to other LD samples in different college settings. However, it could be tentatively said that though the students with learning disabilities entered with significantly poorer high school preparation and performance and ACT scores than the randomly selected students, they were achieving similar success rates.

Based on the previous findings, the present study was designed to (a) determine the educational attainment of students with learning disabilities as compared to their peers matched on gender and ACT composite scores, (b) determine the importance of ACT performance in predicting college success for students with LD and their matched peers, (c) determine if students with LD are similar to their peers in course load per semester and length of time taken to complete their bachelor's degree, and (d) delineate further the effect of LD support services on academic success and failure in the group of students with LD by comparing them with the group equated on ACT composite score at entrance to college.

We hypothesized that (a) there would be no significant differences between the groups on high school preparation and performance and year-in-college at entrance, (b) the college performance of students with learning disabilities would be superior to the ACT-matched group, (c) the students with learning disabilities would graduate at a significantly higher rate and fail at a lower rate than their ACT-matched peers, and (d) the students with learning disabilities would take a significantly lighter load and take longer to complete their degree than the ACT-matched group.

Method

Subject Selection Criteria

All students attended the college for at least one semester between 1980 and 1988. English was the primary language of all students and all were accepted as degree candidates. Women outnumbered men two to one in both groups, because this school had been a women's college until 1982. Men presently constitute 25% of the total student population. The college has 17% minority students and, like other suburban samples, fewer students (8%) in the LD samples were minorities. Ethnicity and socioeconomic status are not readily available on the matched sample; however, the group is thought to resemble the general college population.

We identified 62 students who had taken the ACT out of the total pool of 110 students with learning disabilities. In this setting, only traditional-age (TA) applicants (those between the ages of 18 and 25) who have not completed an associate's degree are required to provide ACT test results. This subset of 62 students with learning disabilities (the LD group) was compared to a matched sample (the MS group) of 58 students matched on gender and ACT composite score.

Because the groups were matched on ACT composite (either exact match or ±1 point), we wanted to verify that, in fact, the procedures used were effective in matching the groups. The mean ACT composite score for the LD group was 12.57 as compared to the MS group mean of 13.45. (See Vogel & Adelman, 1990, for a national overview of the ACT performance among students with learning disabilities and those without.) Not unexpectedly, the mean for the MS group was slightly (though not significantly) higher, perhaps because exact matches were unavailable for the four students with learning disabilities who received the lowest ACT composite scores. However, the difference in ACT composite means was not significant, $F(1,116) = 1.52$, $p < .05$, confirming the effectiveness of the matching procedures.

No match was available for the four students with learning disabilities who received the lowest ACT composite scores. These 4 students, along with 10 others, composed a subgroup within the LD sample whose ACT composite scores were between 7 and 9 or below. It was hoped that a qualitative analysis of high school and college performance and educational attainment in the LD and MS subgroups scoring between 7 and 9 would provide important insight into the predictive power of the ACT and other types of information that students provide at admissions.

All students took three screening tests that are used college-wide. The screening tests consisted of a timed reading comprehension test (Stanford Diagnostic Reading Test–Blue Level, Subtest 1, Reading Comprehension; Karlsen, Madden, & Gardner, 1977), a writing sample on an assigned topic scored holistically by four English professors (see Vogel & Moran, 1982), and a measure of knowledge of sentence structure (Sentence Structure Test from the Descriptive Tests of Language Skills of the College Board; Educational Testing Service, 1977). These screening instruments provided an indication of present functioning levels, as well as the relative standing of applicants as compared to the general college population.

The MS Group

None of the MS students had requested or been referred for evaluation because of a suspected learning disability in spite ofthe high level of awareness regarding learning disabilities among the admissions officers, faculty, and student body on this campus. The MS group had significantly better reading and written language abilities than the LD group, as measured by the three college-wide screening tests (see Table 8.1).

The LD Group

The mean Verbal, Performance, and Full Scale IQ were at average and quite even (100, 102, and 101, respectively). Similarities and Com-

TABLE 8.1
Raw Scores on Reading and Written Language Measures

Group (*n*)	$\overline{X}$	*SD*	Range	*t*
Reading Comprehension				
MS (40)	41.10	9.57	18–55	–3.41**
LD (62)	33.84	11.07	9–56	
Sentence Structure				
MS (51)	23.35	5.41	10–31	–3.54**
LD (61)	19.64	5.61	9–33	
Essay Total Score[a]				
MS (48)	9.55	1.30	7.00–13.50	2.94*
LD (47)	10.43	1.60	7.25–16.00	

Note. MS = matched sample; LD = learning disabilities.
[a]The lower the score, the better.
*$p < .01$. **$p < .001$.

prehension were the two highest mean scaled scores ($\overline{X}$ of approximately 11.00), and Arithmetic and Information the two lowest ($\overline{X}$ = 8.00). Though performance across different measures of academic achievement was not comparable, grade equivalents are reported in Table 8.2. They were used as an indication of academic achievement, because the standard score scales varied widely among the measures.

Academic achievement abilities ranged from a high of 12.4 grade equivalent on silent reading vocabulary as measured by the Stanford Diagnostic Reading Test (SDRT)–Blue Level to a low of 7.7 grade equivalent on spelling recall as measured by the Wide Range Achievement Test–Revised (WRAT-R; Jastak & Wilkinson, 1984). Because many adults with learning disabilities report that they are hindered by slow reading rate, we expected the mean score on the Fast Reading subtest of the SDRT to be lower than the other reading measures (see Note). Much to our surprise, Phonetic Analysis, a measure of phonological segmentation abilities and word attack skills, was the next to the lowest ($\overline{X}$ = 8.0 grade equivalent), as reflected also in spelling recall, confirming the chronicity of phonological coding disabilities, incomplete mastery of word attack skills, and spelling disabilities in adults with learning disabilities (see Table 8.2).

Diagnosis of LD was verified for students previously identified by examining past psychoeducational evaluations completed by a qualified psychologist, current WAIS or WAIS-R test results, academic achievement, LD specialists' reports, and/or recent IEPs. One or more of the above was available for 94% of the students in the LD group; that is, 94% had been previously diagnosed and self-identified in the application process, while 6% were diagnosed for the first time after acceptance to college.

TABLE 8.2
Academic Achievement Profile of Group with LD

	Mean grade equivalent
Reading Vocabulary	12.4
Reading Comprehension (untimed)	10.6
Math Applied Problems	9.8
Math Calculation	9.6
Reading Comprehension (timed)	9.1
Fast Reading	9.0
Phonetic Analysis	8.0
Spelling Recall	7.7

Because early intervention and extensive remediation may diminish aptitude–achievement discrepancies and/or underachievement in some adults with learning disabilities, and because there is a considerable number of non-LD college students who also have significant intelligence–achievement discrepancies (Gajar, Salvia, Gajria, & Salvia, 1989), significant aptitude–achievement discrepancy was not used as one of the criteria for establishing the diagnosis of LD. Rather, early history of learning problems was considered essential in establishing the diagnosis of LD. Therefore, applicants and their families (if appropriate and available) provided extensive background information regarding birth, developmental, medical, and educational history, prior intervention, and incidence and type of learning difficulties in family members. In addition, prior to acceptance, self-identified students visited the campus and were interviewed by an admissions officer, the director of the LD program, and dean of students (Vogel & Adelman, 1993).

In this study, the groups were compared on age, high school preparation and performance, year-in-college at entrance, college performance, graduation and academic failure rate, course load, and time taken to complete the bachelor's degree.

Results

Age

Not surprisingly, there was no significant difference on age ($\overline{X} = 20$ for both groups). The ranges in age for the LD and MS groups were 17.42 to 26.83 and 17.08 to 31.08, respectively. Although students older than 25 were not required to provide ACT test results, some did. The earlier finding that both LD and RSS graduates took 6½ years to complete their degrees had been attributed to the significant difference in age and responsibilities. This study provided the opportunity to reexamine this interpretation and the effect of learning disabilities on time needed for degree completion for two groups of similar age.

Academic Preparation for College

One major source of information reflecting academic preparation for college is high school course work and performance. The groups were compared on the number of courses taken in the core curriculum (English, social studies, math, and science), electives, developmental courses completed with a grade of C or better, the number of D and failing grades, and high school GPA. (For an in-depth description of the high school transcript analysis guidelines, see Vogel & Adelman, 1990.) Whereas both groups had taken developmental English and math courses, only the LD group had taken developmental science and social studies courses. The only significant difference on high school transcript analyses was that students with learning disabilities took significantly more developmental math courses than those in the MS group. This finding may reflect the 2:1 ratio of women to men in the sample and may indicate that mathematics is often a significant area of weakness when learning disabilities occur in women (Vogel, 1990; see Table 8.3).

Because colleges with competitive admissions rely heavily on college admissions test scores and high school performance, we examined the correlation of high school and ACT performance with college exit GPA. College exit GPA was selected rather than the more frequently reported correlation with college freshman GPA in predictive studies for the following reasons:

1. Exit GPA is typically based on longer than 1 year of college work and encompasses a more representative course of studies than freshman year courses.
2. Some of the students in the two samples were transfers. Transfer credits are commonly accepted as a "package" and, therefore, freshman GPA is unavailable.
3. Exit GPA is available for all subjects.
4. Exit GPA correlated very highly with both freshman and senior year GPA for the total group and graduate subgroups.

The correlation between the ACT composite and college exit GPA for the students with LD was almost zero ($r = .04$) and for the MS group

TABLE 8.3
High School Preparation and Performance for Group with LD and Matched Sample (MS)

Variable		(*n*)	$\overline{X}$	*SD*	Range	*F*	*p*
Regular English Courses	MS	(38)	5.50	2.14	0–8		
	LD	(48)	5.94	3.96	1–16	.59	*ns*
Regular Social Studies Courses	MS	(37)	3.87	1.89	0–8		
	LD	(47)	4.02	2.16	1–8	.12	*ns*
Regular Science Courses	MS	(34)	2.53	1.60	0–6		
	LD	(45)	3.16	1.64	1–8	2.89	*ns*
Regular Math Courses	MS	(37)	2.89	1.98	0–8		
	LD	(40)	3.40	1.92	1–8	1.31	*ns*
Ds in Regular Courses	MS	(37)	6.65	3.67	0–13		
	LD	(42)	6.36	4.53	1–18	.10	*ns*
E/Fs in Regular Courses	MS	(28)	1.64	1.93	0–6		
	LD	(22)	2.05	1.43	1–5	.67	*ns*
Foreign Language GPA	MS	(15)	1.72	.79	.33–3.25		
	LD	(25)	1.82	.96	.00–4.00	.11	*ns*
Ds in Electives	MS	(34)	2.41	2.63	0–13		
	LD	(35)	3.17	2.48	1–10	1.53	*ns*
Fs in Electives	MS	(28)	0.68	1.31	0–6		
	LD	(21)	1.24	.44	1–2	3.54	*ns*
Total Ds	MS	(37)	9.89	6.29	0–26		
	LD	(44)	9.75	6.74	1–16	.01	*ns*
Total E/Fs	MS	(29)	2.38	2.53	0–9		
	LD	(33)	2.30	1.72	1–7	.02	*ns*
High School GPA	MS	(19)	2.36	0.64	1.13–3.30		
	LD	(24)	2.50	0.50	1.14–3.28	.62	*ns*
Developmental English Courses	MS	(18)	1.72	2.14	0–8		
	LD	(20)	2.85	2.64	1–12	2.06	*ns*
Developmental Social Studies Courses	MS	(11)	0	—	—		
	LD	(2)	1.50	0.89	1–2	—	
Developmental Science Courses	MS	(11)	0	—	—		
	LD	(3)	1.67	0.58	1–2	—	
Developmental Math Courses	MS	(14)	1.21	1.48	0–4		
	LD	(22)	2.41	1.50	1–6	5.49	.03
Ds in Developmental Courses	MS	(8)	1.00	1.31	0–4		
	LD	(9)	2.44	3.97	1–13	.96	*ns*
E/Fs in Developmental Courses	MS	(4)	.25	.50	0–1		
	LD	(2)	1.50	.71	1–2	6.67	*ns*

was also very low ($r = .20$). The best predictor of college exit GPA for the LD group was the number of regular high school English courses completed with a grade of C or better ($r = .46$, $p < .001$). This was not the case for the MS students, for whom the correlation was .02. For both the LD and MS groups, high school GPA was significantly, albeit not highly, correlated with college performance ($r = .41$ and $r = .48$, $ps < .05$, respectively).

Year-in-School at College Entrance

Eighty-seven percent of the LD group and 98% of the MS group were freshmen at entrance to the college ($z = -1.323$, $p < .01$). Eight percent of the LD group and 2% of the MS group were sophomores ($z = 1.58$, $p < .05$), and 5% of the LD group and none of the MS group were juniors ($z = 1.70$, $p < .05$). However, when the graduates and nongraduates (i.e., academic failures) were compared on year-in-school at college entrance, some interesting similarities emerged. First, the LD and MS graduates no longer differed significantly in prior college experience ($z = -.73$, $p < .05$). In both groups, as the percentage of freshmen decreased, the number of transfers increased. Second, all of the LD and MS students who were dismissed due to academic failure entered as freshmen (see Table 8.4).

College Performance

Table 8.5 presents data regarding academic performance in college. The groups were compared on GPA at the end of each academic year and at exit from the college, on the number of credit hours at exit from the college, and on the number of D, F, incomplete, passing (P), and withdrawal (W) grades. There were no significant differences on GPA at the end of freshman, sophomore, junior, or senior year. However, the mean GPA of students with learning disabilities was slightly higher ($p < .059$) than that of the MS group ($\overline{X}$ GPA = 2.43, compared to 2.18) at exit from the college. Not surprisingly, students with LD received significantly fewer failing grades than the MS group.

The groups also differed on the number of passing grades received, with the LD group taking significantly more courses pass/fail (P/F) ($p < .0001$). The latter is to be expected, because students with learning disabilities are required to take several developmental English courses that are only offered on a P/F basis.

Graduation and Academic Failure Rate

Given that the two groups did not differ significantly on age at entrance or college preparation as reflected in high school and ACT

TABLE 8.4
Summary of Year-in-School at College Entrance for Grads (G) and Nongrads (NG) in the Group with LD and Matched Sample (MS)

Year in School	LD (*n* = 23) Grads		MS (*n* = 12) Grads		LD (*n* = 9) Non-Grads		MS (*n* = 24) Non-Grads	
	n	%	*n*	%	*n*	%	*n*	%
Freshman	19	82.6	11	91.7	9	100	24	100
Sophomore	1	4.3	1	8.3	0	—	0	—
Junior	3	13.0	0	—	0	—	0	—
Senior	0	—	0	—	0	—	0	—

TABLE 8.5
College Performance for Group with LD and Matched Sample (MS)

Variable		(*n*)	$\overline{X}$	*SD*	Range	*F*	*p*
Freshman GPA	MS	(42)	2.29	(.63)	1.39–3.48		
	LD	(40)	2.51	(.44)	1.67–3.70	3.17	*ns*
Sophomore GPA	MS	(24)	2.50	(.57)	1.65–3.50		
	LD	(30)	2.60	(.54)	1.64–4.00	.49	*ns*
Junior GPA	MS	(16)	2.70	(.48)	1.79–3.50		
	LD	(19)	2.75	(.42)	2.00–3.76	.10	*ns*
Senior GPA	MS	(12)	2.88	(.40)	2.29–3.50		
	LD	(17)	2.87	(.36)	2.31–3.71	.00	*ns*
Exit GPA	MS	(58)	2.18	(.83)	0–3.62		
	LD	(62)	2.43	(.60)	.83–3.83	3.65	.059
Exit Hours	MS	(58)	58.41	(43.08)	0–148		
	LD	(62)	62.00	(42.10)	8–132	.21	*ns*
W Grades	MS	(58)	.79	(1.45)	0–9		
	LD	(62)	.76	(1.18)	0–6	.02	*ns*
Incomplete Grades	MS	(58)	.09	(.43)	0–3		
	LD	(62)	.10	(.43)	0–3	.02	*ns*
F Grades	MS	(58)	1.24	(1.56)	0–7		
	LD	(62)	.63	(1.06)	0–5	6.40	.013
D Grades	MS	(58)	1.83	(2.01)	0–11		
	LD	(62)	1.27	(1.50)	0–7	2.95	*ns*
P Grades	MS	(58)	1.79	(2.75)	0–17		
	LD	(62)	4.50	(3.16)	0–14	24.94	.000

performance, and that the students with learning disabilities were enrolled in the support services program, we predicted that a significantly larger percentage of students with learning disabilities would graduate and fewer would fail. However, only one of these predictions was confirmed. When the number of LD and MS students graduating between 1980 and 1988 was compared, it was found that 33% of the students with learning disabilities had graduated as compared to 25.5% of the MS students (a nonsignificant difference). However, almost three times more MS students (51%) failed academically compared to the LD group (18%), $\chi^2(1) = 11.23$, $p < .001$.

Course Load and Time Taken to Complete Degree

A course load and time study was also conducted to determine if the students with learning disabilities took longer than the matched sample to complete their degrees. When the two groups were compared, the students with learning disabilities more often took a significantly ($p < .002$) lighter course load (10.02 credit hours compared to 12.60 for the LD and MS groups). As would be expected, the students with learning disabilities took almost 1 year longer than the MS group (6 years rather than 5) to complete their undergraduate degree (see Table 8.6). Though a nonsignificant difference, 1 year in a 21-year-old's life can feel like a very long time.

Discussion

One of the questions that inevitably comes to mind in any study utilizing a contrast group in which some of the students' ACT scores are

TABLE 8.6
Credit Hour Load and Time Taken to Complete Undergraduate Degree for Group with LD and Matched-Sample (MS) Graduates

Variable		(*n*)	$\overline{X}$	*SD*	Range	*F*	*p*
Years of Study	MS	(12)	4.99	(0.71)	4.5– 6.0		
	LD	(15)	5.87	(1.54)	4.5–10.5	3.29	*ns*
$\overline{X}$ Credits Earned	MS	(12)	12.46	(1.99)	9.50–15.88		
Per Semester	LD	(15)	9.97	(1.78)	5.48–11.90	11.76	.002
$\overline{X}$ Credits Attempted	MS	(12)	12.60	(1.99)	9.50–15.88		
Per Semester	LD	(15)	10.02	(1.80)	5.48–12.10	12.48	.002

below average is: Are one or more students in the comparison group unidentified students with learning disabilities? Based on these students' reading and written language abilities, we know that the MS group had significantly better reading and written language skills than the LD group. Yet to be determined is how the MS group compares to a random sample of students on this campus. In addition, future research should explore the reasons for some of the MS students receiving low ACT composite scores. However, at the present time we cannot rule out the possibility that among the MS students who scored a 7, 8, or 9 ACT composite, one or more may have an unidentified learning disability. A qualitative analysis comparing the subgroups on high school preparation and performance and college performance may provide some insight into this question.

One of the hallmark characteristics of adults with learning disabilities is written language deficits (Johnson & Blalock, 1987; Vogel, 1985; Vogel & Moran, 1982). Therefore, the finding that the students with learning disabilities scored significantly poorer on the essay writing task was not surprising. Even when students with learning disabilities are able to "play it safe" (e.g., avoid overly complex sentence structure and words that are difficult for them to spell, omit punctuation marks, and produce shorter essays), the quality of their writing is distinguishable from that of their MS peers. When the essays were evaluated analytically in the four areas of mechanics, organization, development, and style, the students with learning disabilities were significantly poorer on mechanics ($p < .05$) and style ($p < .002$) as compared to the MS students' writing. These findings confirm those of earlier studies by Vogel and Moran (1982) and Gregg (1982).

The findings regarding high school preparation and performance are not at all surprising and indicate that these two groups were very similar on academic preparation for college. Based on the correlation between the number of D and F high school grades and college exit GPA, it seems the fewer the number of Ds (rather than Fs) on the high school transcript of a student with LD, the higher that student's college exit GPA is likely to be. For the MS group, neither the number of D nor the number of F grades was significantly correlated with college exit GPA. We can only speculate that high school teachers use D letter grades differentially for students with LD and MS students. For example, a D grade may indicate good effort but inadequate mastery for students with LD. Alternatively, it may indicate that teachers have a desire to assist students with LD in graduating and give them a passing grade instead of failing them.

We can only speculate as to the significance of prior college experience on educational attainment for students with learning disabilities. For example, we were often told that students with learning disabilities who entered this specific setting as transfers chose the institution because they wanted to receive LD support services. Perhaps the institutions they attended previously did not provide appropriate LD support services. Indeed, finding the right college has been thought to be more difficult for students with LD (Cowen, 1985; Vogel, 1987; Vogel & Adelman, 1993), resulting in their transferring from one institution to another in an attempt to find the setting in which they can succeed (Vogel, 1986). The striking finding that 100% of the students in both groups who failed academically entered the college without any prior college experience seems to confirm that having the chance to experience firsthand the demands of college life, to compete in an academically competitive environment, and, in the case of students with LD, to recognize the effect of their learning disability and utilize accommodations and services contributed to their success.

Many factors influence students' decisions to utilize or not utilize support services. A student may not recognize the need to utilize them or, having recognized the need, may not know how to access the available support services. Self-understanding, prior experience and reality testing, level of acceptance and denial, availability and quality of intervention, developmental life stage motivation, and goals are some of the complex factors that enter into the decision to acknowledge one's learning disability and seek out support services (Adelman & Vogel, 1991).

Transfer students with or without LD may have a higher level of persistence, as indicated by their seeking out of another college to complete their degree. Faas (1987) and Gerber, Ginsberg, and Reiff (1990) identified persistence as the outward manifestation of a high level of motivation in the groups of successful adults with LD that they studied. Likewise, reapplying to college indicates that they are still invested in the learning process and that they have more clearly defined educational goals. Goal-setting behavior was also identified by Gerber et al. as characteristic of successful adults with learning disabilities.

Alternatively, it is possible that prior college experience allowed these students to develop more effective coping strategies and study skills and, in the case of students with LD, self-knowledge, insight, willingness to acknowledge their learning disability, and the desire and readiness to seek out needed services and/or accommodations. Confirmation of these speculations must await further research.

The seemingly contradictory finding of lower GPA at exit in spite of better reading and writing abilities of the MS group ascompared to the LD group is thought to relate to the academic advisement available to the students with LD. In this setting, LD specialists act as academic advisors for students with learning disabilities in their first year or until they declare a major. These specialists closely monitor academic performance and assist students in monitoring deadlines for taking a course pass/fail or dropping a course so that no record is retained, rather than risking receiving a failing grade. The effect of this advisement system on GPA was confirmed by the finding that students with learning disabilities received significantly fewer failing grades ($\overline{X}$ = .63, compared to 1.25).

Another one of the major advisement tasks of the LD specialists is to assist students in determining the right course load and identifying instructors who are sensitive to the needs of students with disabilities. The right course load is one that is a balanced array of courses taken in the correct sequence within a specific department or across the curriculum (Faas, 1987; Vogel & Adelman, 1990). Advisors also have the responsibility of reviewing end-of-semester grades, reevaluating the courses that were selected during preregistration, monitoring warning signals of academic difficulty, and adjusting students' schedules.

Having a group of highly trained academic advisors who maintain close contact with their advisees benefits all students, but especially benefits high-risk students with or without a learning disability. Initially, weekly meetings, or even more frequent ones in the first 2 weeks of each semester, may be necessary to fine-tune the schedule. When difficulties arise on assignments or quizzes, problem solving can begin promptly. Because of the integral relationship among academic advising, instruction in basic skills, and course support, there should also be close communication among the LD specialist, advisor, faculty, teaching assistants, and/or tutors.

One of the striking findings of the present study is that all of the students in the LD and MS groups who failed were considered to be freshmen (either first-time college freshmen or transferred in with less than 24 credit hours). We speculated that perhaps some may have attended other colleges but been unsuccessful. It seems apparent that transfer students in general, but especially those with learning disabilities, benefit from trying out one or more colleges and acquire increased maturity and motivation to complete their degree. Perhaps they perceive the college that accepts them as transfer students as giving them a much desired second or third chance.

Alternatively, perhaps transfer students represent a subset of the total population of college students with learning disabilities. Within this subset could be the group who succeeded in community college courses, while many of those who were unsuccessful did not pursue a postsecondary degree further. In order to address this question, students with learning disabilities who enter as freshmen could be compared to those who enter college as transfers. However, given these findings, college admissions personnel should perhaps consider transfer students with learning disabilities as having a better chance of success than students having no prior college experience, if other indicators of success are present.

Because previous college experience seems to significantly enhance students' chances of academic success, students with LD should be encouraged to visit college campuses, talk to college students with LD, and experience firsthand the demands of college courses by participating in special transition programs (Dalke, 1993; Dalke & Schmitt, 1987). In such programs, they can experience the contrast between high school and college life with regard to frequency of exams, availability of instructors, and frequency of feedback, and can develop effective coping strategies and improved study skills. Similarly, if students decide to work for a year or more between high school and college, they should be encouraged to study part-time in order to experience college and do the reality testing that allows individuals to assess their goals and motivation for college while exploring career options.

Based on this study, we recommend that admissions officers weigh high school preparation and performance (as reflected in high school courses, grades, and GPA) significantly more heavily than admission test scores. Of the 14 students in the LD group who scored 9 or below on the ACT, 6 have already graduated (3 from this specific Midwestern college and 3 from other colleges and universities). One even graduated magna cum laude. It appears that for some individuals with LD, extremely low entrance exam scores are not reliable indicators of future academic progress. Vogel and Adelman (1990) pointed out that the graduates differed significantly from the academic failures on motivation and attitude toward the teaching/learning process. Poor motivation and negative attitudes, along with concomitant factors such as substance abuse, denial of one's learning disability, and unrealistic expectations, appear to be more predictive of poor academic performance than ACT performance. The two best predictors of college success in the present study as indicated by the correlation analysis were high school preparation and overall GPA.

If the number and distribution of regular core curriculum courses that the student successfully completed resembles that of non-LD applicants, it is a good predictor of success in college. On the other hand, many Ds in noncore required or elective courses may indicate a motivation or attitude problem. Careful examination of high school transcripts and interviews can provide useful information regarding special talents and/or interests as well as risk-taking behavior. An occasional C grade in areas of weakness should be expected, along with As and Bs in the areas of strength and advanced placement or honors classes—a not uncommon pattern in gifted students with learning disabilities applying to highly selective colleges and universities (Shaywitz & Shaw, 1988).

The findings regarding graduation and attrition rate seem to indicate that the support services and advising available to the students with learning disabilities were effective in reducing the risk of failure and in helping the students with learning disabilities overcome, compensate for, or bypass their academic and basic skills deficits. Another factor that may have contributed to the almost 3:1 discrepancy in failure rate between the two groups was the advisors' practice of counseling unmotivated students with learning disabilities or those who were experiencing significant academic difficulties even with consistent effort and support to consider options other than a 4-year college. Some of them, in fact, did withdraw from college and continue their education in other, less demanding settings. In a follow-up study, Adelman and Vogel (1990) reported that some of the students who had been dismissed or were counseled out of the college prior to dismissal enrolled later in community colleges and/or were involved in informal education.

The results regarding time taken to complete a bachelor's degree contradicted those of the earlier study by Vogel and Adelman (1990), in which the graduates with LD and RSS took the same amount of time to complete a bachelor's degree ($6\frac{1}{2}$ years). This contrast seems to relate to the difference in age of the present two samples (20) as compared to the older LD ($\overline{X} = 21$) and RSS ($\overline{X} = 23$) groups. We postulated that the LD and RSS groups both took a part-time load but for different reasons. This second study confirms that students with learning disabilities took a lighter course load compared to their peers; this practice was confirmed only when comparing the two matched groups who were younger and did not differ on age.

In the college counseling process, students and parents (if appropriate) should be told that students with learning disabilities often take longer than 4 years to complete their undergraduate degree and that they are not the only ones to do so. There is no longer the traditional lock-step progression from high school to completion of a bachelor's degree in 4 years. Taking courses during summers can also be beneficial in that it allows the student to take a lighter load during fall and spring semesters and continue to practice newly acquired skills and study strategies, while progressing toward the goal of degree completion. Summers have also been utilized effectively to concentrate all of one's efforts on the most challenging required course, especially if it involves the student's areas of weakness. The important message is that there is no point in rushing toward failure.

It is important to keep in mind certain limitations of this study. These findings cannot be generalized to all college students with learning disabilities but, rather, are specific to this subgroup within the total population of adults with learning disabilities. First, this subset represents only those who are collegeable; second, all students had taken the ACT and had a mean age of 20; third, this group had to meet specific college and program admissions criteria to be accepted to this competitive college (vs. an open-admission or highly selective college); fourth, the 2:1 ratio of women to men may have influenced the type and severity of LD and outcomes in unknown ways; and, last, the students with LD requested and received comprehensive LD support services not readily available in the majority of postsecondary institutions. Therefore, because of the specific selection criteria, admissions requirements, gender ratio, and intervention at this specific institution, we cannot assume that these findings will generalize to other settings and other subgroups of students with LD.

Summary

In this study, a group of college students with learning disabilities who (a) self-referred at admissions; (b) were screened for high school preparation and performance, intellectual ability, type and severity of LD, and motivation and attitude toward the teaching–learning process; and (c) used LD support services, including special academic advising, were compared to a group of peers matched on gender and ACT composite score. No significant differences were found on age or high school preparation and performance (except in the number of developmental math courses taken by the group with LD), although the MS group had significantly better reading and writing abilities at entrance. The two most highly correlated variables with college exit GPA for students with LD were the number of regular high school English courses completed with a grade of C or better and high school GPA. For the MS group, the most highly correlated variable was high school GPA.

College exit GPA was slightly higher for the group with LD, as was graduation rate, but not significantly higher. However, students with LD did take a lighter course load and almost 1 year longer to complete their degree than the MS group. Eight percent and 17% of the graduates in the MS and LD groups, respectively, entered with prior college experience, while all of the academic failures entered as freshmen. The most striking finding in this study is that although there was no significant difference in graduation rate, the academic failure rate in the matched sample was almost three times higher than in the LD group. This study suggests that some of the strategies that have been developed to identify and assist potentially successful students with LD have been effective and may benefit other at-risk college students, as well.

Authors' Note

The authors express their appreciation to the Thorn River and Butz Foundations for supporting this research.

Note

Performance on tests of math calculation and application as measured by the Woodcock-Johnson Psycho-Educational Battery (Woodcock & Johnson, 1977) was in the ninth-grade range.

9. Identifying Alterable Patterns in Employment Success for Highly Successful Adults with Learning Disabilities

PAUL J. GERBER, RICK GINSBERG, AND HENRY B. REIFF

As the field of learning disabilities widens its focus to encompass individuals across the developmental continuum and begins to grapple with the issues of employability and employment, the workplace is becoming the focus of intense interest. Substantial progress was made in the schools in the 1970s and 1980s. Legislation has opened doors and created opportunities that were only wishful thinking in prior years. All of this momentum has put increasing pressure on the notion of outcomes for adults with learning disabilities.

Outcomes cannot be judged by the success of transition programs, nor can the true measure of outcomes emanate from an analysis of entry-level job placement. Ultimately, the judgment of successful outcomes must be looked at further down the vocational path, in job maintenance, employment stability, career advancement, and the attainment of leadership roles.

Reprinted, with changes, from "Identifying alterable patterns in employment success for highly successful adults with learning disabilities," by Paul J. Gerber, Rick Ginsberg, and Henry B. Reiff, *Journal of Learning Disabilities*, Vol. 25, 1992, pp. 475–487.

The literature on vocational outcomes of adults with learning disabilities is sparse, and the findings reflect the heterogeneity of the population itself. We do know that there are issues of dependency (Gerber & Reiff, 1992) and underemployment and unemployment (President's Committee on the Employment of People with Disabilities, 1990). At the same time, there are exemplars for vocational success at all levels in the workforce (Gerber & Reiff, 1992). Moreover, there are documented accounts of notable people with learning disabilities in the history of civilization (Baker, 1972) and on the current American scene.

Attempts to Investigate Success

In the 1980s a wave of researchers sought to ascertain how success and excellence had been attained in the business world (Covey, 1989; Garfield, 1986; Peters & Austin, 1985; Peters & Waterman, 1982; Price, 1984). The qualitative data in these studies were gathered from the most successful people and companies in the United States, and those data revealed that the key to success was the focus on success itself (individually or collectively) and the ability to lay a blueprint for successful endeavors.

In the area of education and psychology, a number of important investigations studied success, as well. One of the most fortuitous investigations undertaken studied persons who, before the age of 35, demonstrated the highest levels of accomplishment in specific artistic, psychomotor, or cognitive fields (Bloom, 1980, 1982; Bloom & Sosniak, 1981). The intent of the study was to gain a further understanding of the educational process, of human potential, and of the means by which potential becomes reality in modern society. The study uncovered early experiences that launched careers, discovered patterns of development common to all fields of endeavor, and sought out alterable variables of success. "Alterable variables" were special circumstances in self, situation, influence, and interaction that may have had either an individual or a cumulative effect on success and that are susceptible to change.

This line of research spawned research on overachievement in community college students (Easton & Ginsberg, 1985). This workfocused on a theoretical approach to identifying alterable patterns of success that would be transferable to others.

Another investigation focused on success in children who had been labeled "superkids" (Pines, 1979). These children were noted for outstanding achievement in such areas as academics, extracurricular activities, and leadership. In general, they had the ability to achieve at the highest levels despite overwhelming odds (e.g., extreme poverty, devastating sickness in the family, dysfunctional family system). The study identified internal psychological mechanisms for this overachievement, including determination and a strong need for a sense of control in one's environment.

In the area of disability, a small number of scholarly inquiries sought to understand the ingredients of success. Illustrative of the studies of success in adulthood were those done by Baker (1972) and Maker (1978). Baker studied famous people with disabilities in history; he found that their success was due in large part to "amazing will power to overcome adversity" (p. 30). Maker and her colleagues studied scientists with severe handicaps in order to uncover the key elements of their success. After rigorous and methodologically sound study, it was determined that success was attained by persistence (of motive and efforts), self-confidence, and strength or force of character. These findings were similar to those of a study by Terman and Oden (1947), who studied success in gifted individuals. All of these studies provided useful information to the field, but the samples of the Baker and Maker studies did not include persons with learning disabilities.

Studies Including Highly Successful Adults with Learning Disabilities

Although there are no studies focusing solely on highly successful adults with learning disabilities, two did include highly successful adults as part of their study. Rogan and Hartman (1976), in their follow-up study of former Cove School students, found that a number of subjects had gone on to highly successful careers in the military and business, and some had completed a PhD. Although the reasons for their success were not included in the research objectives of the study, it was noteworthy that the vocational outcomes for the Cove School follow-up population ranged from unemployment and semiskilled jobs to professional and managerial employment. In another study, Gerber and Reiff (1992) discovered a qualitatively different vocational, personal, and daily living approach to adulthood that facilitated and supported highly successful functioning. There was clearly a marked difference when comparing this population to adults who were moderately successful and marginally adjusted to adulthood.

Because there has been little investigation in this area, the study of success in the context of learning disabilities potentially can have great utility. The present study sought to investigate highly successful adults with learning disabilities in order to divine how vocational success was achieved. The objectives of this research were to (a) find the alterable patterns and ingredients of success, (b) delineate the ecology of successful functioning, (c) construct a model for success in adults with learning disabilities, and (d) determine if there was a distinguishable difference between the high-success and moderate-success groups in the study.

Method

Design

Retrospective interviews were used as the main source for data collection. A causal comparative, or ex post facto, type of research design was utilized to help isolate factors that are characteristic of the population of highly successful adults with learning disabilities. In this type of study, the research seeks to determine the cause of or reason for existing differences in the behavior or status of groups of individuals (Gay, 1981). The basic approach is to start with an effect (such as success) and seek possible causes.

Sample Selection. The target population was identified through a nomination process across North America. Nominations were sought from the National Network of Learning Disabled Adults, the Orton Dyslexia Society, the Association for Children with Learning Disabilities (now Learning Disabilities Association of America), a number of other related organizations, schools of education, and institutions and individuals with knowledge of and experience working with persons with learning disabilities. In all, more than 211 persons were nominated for participation, with 181 eligible for screening into the participant pool.

The project coordinator screened candidates for participation in the study. Screening was done by telephone in a scripted interview of about 40 to 50 minutes in length. The interview included collection of demographic data—age, race, gender, education, income—as well as information concerning current occupation, recognition attained in candidates' respective fields, and parents' occupation levels. Another set of questions gathered data on job satisfaction, derived from the Minnesota Satisfaction Questionnaire–Short Form (Weiss, Davis, England, & Lofquist, 1967). In addition, an inventory taken during the telephone interview was used to identify the severity of disability for each potential participant. This instrument sought information about how and when identification of the learning disability was made, and whether other disabling conditions (e.g., hearing or vision loss, physical handicap, or emotional condition) were more significant than the learning disability. Also, questions explored the severity of the learning disability at school age and currently on a 7-point scale for 12 items: listening, speaking, reading, writing, spelling, mathematical abilities, perception, coordination, impulsivity, distractibility, hyperactivity, and attention span.

With the screening data, candidates for participation in the project were placed into high-success and moderate-success groups. Success, a subjective construct, was defined across five variables: income level, job classification (derived from the Duncan Socioeconomic Index; Reiss, 1961), education level, prominence in one's field, and job satisfaction. Standards were set so that each candidate could be ranked as *high, moderate,* or *low* for each of the five criteria. For income level, a different set of standards was adopted for men and women, to reflect differential earning capacities between the genders. Then, utilizing the data from the screening, a panel of five experts in learning disabilities rated each candidate on each of the five criteria. Disagreements in ratings for any of the criteria were discussed by panel members until a consensus was reached on the appropriate rating for each candidate. To be placed in the high-success group, candidates needed a rating of *high* on four of the criteria and no ratings of *low.* The moderate-success subject pool included those with a majority of *moderate* ratings and no more than one *low* rating. In this way, we attempted to establish two clearly identifiable but distinct groups.

The final sample was selected from the pool of candidates in the two groups. We tried to control for possible confounding factors by matching participants in the high and moderate groups across several variables. These included age (within 5 years), gender, race, severity of disability (determined by our screening form and rated as *severe, moderate,* or *low* by the panel of experts), specific learning disability problem, mothers' and fathers' occupations, and parents' socioeconomic status. We worked to match two high-success participants with one moderate-success participant. We purposely had a larger sample of high-success participants due to the project's purpose of identifying key factors related to high levels of success. Thus, the final sample included a larger number of high-success participants to be interviewed, but still included sufficient numbers of moderately successful adults with learning disabilities to draw comparisons. In a few instances, we were only able to match one high-success with one moderate-success participant. Those who could not be matched across these variables were excluded from the study.

Certain quantitative information gathered during interviews was analyzed in order to ensure and further substantiate that the high- and moderate-success adult groups with learning disabilities were similar except for the degree of success obtained. As a part of the interview process, participants were asked questions from shortened versions of three questionnaires: the Rosenberg Self-Esteem Scale (Rosenberg, 1965), the Manifest Needs Questionnaire (Steers & Braunstein, 1976), and the Organizational Diagnosis Questionnaire (Preziosi, 1980). These questionnaires elicit information on self-esteem, vocational achievement motivation, and workplace relationships, respectively. The data from them showed that the two groups had similar mean scores for each of the questionnaires. Although some differences did exist in the actual scoring, the data suggested that the matching process did achieve the goal of selecting samples that were extremely similar except for the degree of vocational success achieved.

The sample comprised 71 subjects, 46 of whom were highly successful and 25 of whom were moderately successful. The participants came from 24 states and Canada. Twenty-six occupations were represented in the high-success group, while 14 were represented in the moderate group. In the highly successful group, there were 32 men and 14 women ranging in age from 29 to 67. The average age of the highly successful group was 45.5 years. The range of yearly income was $30,000 to $100,000+. Twenty-one highly successful subjects reported incomes in excess of $100,000. The educational levels of the highly successful group were as follows: Two graduated high school, 3 had some postsecondary schooling, 9 earned bachelor's degrees, 2 had a bachelor's degree and some graduate school courses, 2 had master's degrees, 1 had a master's degree plus additional graduate school courses, and 26 subjects had PhDs or MDs.

There were 16 men and 9 women in the moderately successful group. Their ages ranged from 34 to 59, and the average was 44 years. The range of income was $10,000 to $100,000+. Half of the moderately successful group earned between $40,000 and $50,000. The educational levels of the moderately successful group were as follows: One graduated high school, 1 graduated high school and attended some college courses, 1 earned an associate college degree, 4 earned bachelor's degrees, 16 earned master's degrees, and 3 received either a PhD or an MD.

Instrumentation. The interview schedule developed for this research was derived from several sources, including the available research on vocational success in persons with learning disabilities, a previous study by Gerber and Reiff (1992), discussions with educators of individuals with learning disabilities, and experts in the field. A panel of nationally known experts (specialists in the area of adults with learning disabilities and employment issues) was convened as a research advisory board to review the interview schedule as originally devised by project staff and to suggest changes and additions. Pilot interviews were conducted by project staff with six moderately or highly successful adults with learning disabilities to refine the instrument and time the interview.

The final interview schedule included approximately 130 open-ended questions across nine categories that were determined to be potentially significant for success of adults with learning disabilities. The open-ended nature of the preselected questions and the inclusion of several questions permitting the interviewees to add any information not covered by the questions on the interview schedule support our contention that all possible factors to which adults with learning disabilities might attribute their success were uncovered. The categories on the interview schedule included questions relating to success, vocation, education, family, social issues, emotional issues, the learning disability itself, daily living, and recommendations for children with learning disabilities, including ideas to help teachers, parents, employees, and employers.

Interview Process and Interviewer Training. All interviewees were contacted directly by the interviewers (including principal investigators, project coordinators, and project staff), and interviews were arranged for a time and place acceptable to both parties (typically, the place was in the interviewee's home city). Interviews were audiotaped with permission of the participant and ranged in length from approximately 3 hours to nearly 8 hours. Average length of the interviews was 4½ hours. Questioning by the interviewers followed the interview schedule prepared by project staff. The schedule included probes for certain questions, to offer assistance to the interviewee in understanding the purpose of the question. However, although interviewers were encouraged to follow up on answers given by the participants for purposes of clarification, the interviewers asked only the open-ended questions on the interview schedule. Interviewers and interviewees were not aware of whether the participants being interviewed were members of the high- or moderate-success group.

Following each interview, the interviewers transcribed it. These interview transcripts included some observational and contextual information about each interviewee and responses to each question from the interview. Thus, the interviewers did not do exact transcripts of the interviews but, rather, included only the relevant portions of answers to each question. The average length of these transcriptions was approximately 30 to 50 double-spaced typed pages. In addition, project clerical staff were asked to fully transcribe approximately 12 of the interviews (at least one for each interviewer). A reliability analysis comparing the full transcriptions with the interviewer transcripts for those interviews indicated that each interviewer did, in fact, report all appropriate information on their shortened interview transcripts.

Interviewer training was conducted by the project co-director, an expert in qualitative research methods and interview procedures. Two full-day staff meetings were devoted to interviewer training, data collection, and data preparation. Moreover, all interviewers were given background literature on conducting qualitative interviews.

Data Analysis

Analysis of the data was done in several stages. These stages amounted to several phases of data reduction in order to identify key themes and subthemes that characterized the rich descriptions collected in the interviews. The findings from the qualitative interview data met Guba and Lincoln's (1981) four criteria of validity: credibility, transferability, dependability, and confirmability.

Data were derived directly from the interview schedule and placed into low-inference categories and meta-matrices (Miles & Huberman, 1984), both within-interview and across-interview coding. Then a preliminary analysis was performed to discern patterns. Ultimately, themes and subthemes that transcended these original categories were derived and tested across all interviews and between groups (high and moderate success). This thematic analysis helped pull together large amounts of data, and the final categories and findings were drawn from subject input through the retrospective interviews. Due to the importance of verifying conclusions in this type of data analysis, project staff and consultants were involved at the various levels of analysis to test the validity of the themes discerned from the data.

The final phase of the data analysis involved incorporating comments of the advisory board, experts, interviewers, consultants, and project staff. The principal investigators and the project qualitative research consultant made a final review of the data to draw out and confirm major themes and conclusions and to finalize the model of success being developed. This resulted in an expansion and refinement of the categories and creation of the model of success for adults with learning disabilities.

Results

The data analysis performed on the interviews of the 71 successful adults with learning disabilities had three main thrusts: first, to identify patterns of success characteristic of our sample of adults with learning disabilities; second, to delineate the ecology for successful functioning to determine if we could distinguish between the high-success and the moderate-success groups and isolate those factors of high success; and, finally, given the results of the prior analyses, to develop a model of success characteristic of highly successful adults with learning disabilities.

What we discovered was a set of key themes, distinct though not necessarily mutually exclusive. In other words, the themes we discerned to characterize success for adults with learning disabilities interact very strongly with one another. A significant finding was that all the themes transcended the entire sample of adults with learning disabilities—both the high-success and the moderate-success groups. Thus, the distinction between the groups was subtle, though the analysis revealed clear differences in terms of level or degree of attainment. In each category or theme, the high-success adults with learning disabilities were more advanced or exceptional than their moderate counterparts. Although this distinction between the two groups varied in scope depending on the theme, the differences remained constant for all the identified factors.

One overriding theme characterized all of the sample's efforts geared toward success: the quest to gain control of their lives. This pursuit of control involved two sets of themes, which we refer to as "internal decisions" and "external manifestations." The internal decisions included a desire to succeed, being goal oriented, and an internal reframing of the learning disabilities ordeal into a more positive or productive experience. The external manifestations were all ways of being what we call "adaptable." Adaptability included individual persistence, a set of coping mechanisms (i.e., learned creativity), a goodness of fit between one's abilities and the environment, and a pattern or social ecology of personal support and planned experiences designed to foster success.

The model for success we developed is based on these identified themes of control, internal decisions, and external manifestations. What follows is an explanation and narrative description of these themes and their subthemes or categories. For each, distinctions are drawn between the high-success and moderate-success groups. Then, based on these descriptions, the model for vocational success for adults with learning disabilities is more fully developed.

The themes we derived emerged directly from the data collected in the retrospective interviews. No preselected categories characterize the findings. Several of the themes are quite similar. They are not mutually exclusive, as they do interact with one another; nonetheless, the themes are distinct and were clearly identifiable across all of the adults with learning disabilities we interviewed.

Control

Control is the key to success for adults with learning disabilities. This was obvious across the entire sample. Control meant making conscious decisions to take charge of one's life (internal decisions), and adapting and shaping oneself in order to move ahead (external manifestations). The adults with learning disabilities we interviewed spent their lives deciding and learning how to take control of their existence. Control was the fuel that fired their success. In the workplace, this often translated into being in control of the physical environment, but the deeper issue was more psychological or emotional.

A sad reality for many of the adults with learning disabilities was that they had experienced years of failure until they were able to take control and move on. But the need to control was paramount. Indeed, it was a necessity, given the obstacles life posed for them. Several quotes highlight this need. A high-success male dentist very succinctly explained, "I like to be in control. If things don't work out, okay, but if I lose control, I get unbelievably anxious." Similarly, a female dentist explained that "being in control makes me most confident." A vocational rehabilitation worker reiterated this point, describing the need to feel that one is "controlling one's destiny."

The degree of control attained distinguished the high-success learning disabilities group from the moderate group. There was a clear and obvious difference in the amount of control *sought* and *realized.* Ultimately, the moderately successful adults with learning disabilities did not acquire the level of control that the high-success group attained. Thus, although gaining control was still a need, and still a significant force in their lives, the internal decisions and external manifestations of the moderate-success group were not as exceptional as those of their high-success correlates. In practice, then, the degree of control they accomplished was lower.

For example, many of the moderate-success adults with learning disabilities sought control mainly to cover up their weaknesses, rather than focusing on moving ahead. This feeling or fear of being found out was common to many interviewees in both groups, but hiding the learning disability was almost an end in itself for the moderate group. Note the following statements from the moderate-success group: "I have so much fear in me about being found out . . . I need to control *that* so much." "You find that you build up a tremendous repertoire of ways to get around it (the learning disability) and avoid different issues . . . I'm never very open . . . I just want to disguise my feelings."

Along with gearing much of their control toward self-protection, the moderate group members were collectively less certain of where they were headed or what they were doing. As one woman explained, "Much of what happened to me just sort of happened." Another attributed his success largely to what he described as "luck."

Thus, although control was an overriding and meaningful characteristic for both the high-success and moderate-success adults with learning disabilities, the moderate group did not seek to gain the same degree of control as the more successful group. This difference is clarified further by developing the parallel attainment in the themes embedded in internal decisions and external manifestations.

Internal Decisions

Success for adults with learning disabilities is an evolutionary process that spans numerous years. But that process must commence with a conscious set of decisions. At the outset, these decisions may relate to simple personal matters, only later involving the striving for career excellence. Each individual must take the personal stance that he or she is going to try to gain better control of his or her existence and, ultimately, succeed in life. Simply put, success does not just happen. The beginning point is an internal, very personal set of decisions. The adult with learning disabilities must want to succeed, must set achievable goals, and must confront the learning disability so that appropriate measures may be taken to heighten the likelihood of success. These internal decisions involve what we have labeled *desire, goal orientation,* and *reframing.* Success relies heavily on recognizing and mastering these internal decisions.

1. Desire. One needs the desire to excel in order to excel. That is the essence of what we call desire. At some point in time, the high-success adults with learning disabilities decided it was time to move on. This decision is a starting point for anyone, but for those with learning disabilities, it is a far greater challenge because of all the hurdles they confront. For the high-success group we interviewed, the desire to prove themselves was very evident. A female physician said that throughout her whole life she had been driven. "Just tell me I can't do it, and I'll do it." A bank CEO explained it this way: "I'm a real believer in determination. It is three fourths of the battle. There are tons of geniuses in the world who never make it and there are lots of people with personality who don't. The difference between making it and not is determination . . . you absolutely have to stick with it."

This desire came early in life for some; for others it developed over time; but for all it was very conspicuous and very powerful. In describing this sensation, a number of individuals invoked metaphors relating to fire. The desire to them was like a burning inside:

> "I've always had a kind of burning feeling . . . kind of like being on fire to be successful."
>
> "You fight until you can't fight anymore, and then you fight some more . . . you take the hurt and turn it inward and it becomes part of the burn . . . it has to burn."
>
> "If the fires of your drive go out, you will lose your self-respect."

While the moderate-success group also displayed a desire to get ahead, it was not nearly as strong as that depicted by the high-success group. The tone of the desire expressed by the moderately successful adults with learning disabilities was much more tempered than was characteristic of the highly successful group. For example, comments such as the following were typical of the moderate subjects: "I'm not comfortable with the politics of moving upward in the field . . . I'm not comfortable with the competitive nature . . . ." "Most successful people have specific plans, and they know what they are going to do . . . Not me!" "I'm really just someone who has been plodding along."

2. Goal Orientation. Successful adults with learning disabilities consciously set goals for themselves, which is closely related to the decision concerning desire. These people need success, they are anxious about the possibility of failure, so they set explicit goals to work toward. Goals must be set for several reasons. First, goal setting allows adults with learning disabilities to have realistic, achievable aspirations. Goal setting also provides some sharper focus to individuals who have experienced great difficulty in learning and other common activities over the course of years. But, in addition, goal setting feeds on itself. Once even minimal goals are achieved, the feelings of success that are bred can be the basis for more challenging goals in the future.

For the highly successful adults with learning disabilities, goals could be either long term or short term. But the consistent characteristic is that they were set. One high-success man explained, "Successful people have a plan. You have to have a plan, goals, strategy, otherwise you are flying through the clouds and then you hit the mountain." A psychologist expressed the idea that "you should link efforts to outcomes . . . stay in your areas of strength." A businessman said, "I had my goals and set out to do them . . . I didn't care how long it would take."

The difference between the high- and moderate-success groups again was clear. The moderate-success group set more short-term goals and appeared more easily diverted from their goals. Some were even much less goal oriented than the high-success adults. And the goals set by the moderate group were much less lofty. The following remarks reflect the moderate-success goal orientation:

> "Successful people have goals. . . . Much of what happened to me just happened."
>
> "I usually have goals set for the next 4 years of my life but now I don't."
>
> "I tend to be much less goal oriented. I think it has been easy for people not to take me seriously or even for me not to take me seriously."
>
> "I didn't start with any specific goals. I didn't beat my head against the wall."

Such comments reflect the tendency on the part of the moderate-success adults with learning disabilities to have fewer clear goals and less ambitious aspirations than their high-success counterparts.

3. Reframing. Perhaps the key component of the internal decisions was a process we discerned that we call reframing. Reframing refers to the set of decisions relating to reinterpreting the learning disability experience in a more positive or productive manner. It is the recognition that the key problem the adults with learning disabilities face is not the disability itself but, rather, their inability to confront the various challenges they encounter as they learn to live with and overcome it.

We found several stages to be characteristic of this reframing process. Some individuals moved through all stages almost in unison; others moved methodically from one to the next. Clearly, the four stages interact very closely with one another. The first is the need to recognize the handicap. For many, that meant simply realizing that they did things differently, and did not have to be like everyone else. Some realized this at an early age, while for others this recognition came later in life. But, before one can begin to discover ways to successfully learn or succeed in other areas of life, a recognition of who and what one is is necessary. One successful adult explained it this way: "You are your best teacher. You have to be your best teacher. You need to find out who you are and you are not going to succeed out there if you can't look at yourself in the mirror. If you can't deal with who you are and recognize your gifts and your disadvantages, you are not going to make it." Another said, "I'm just finding out, I'm starting to realize the coping skills or the strategies. I find as I listen to other people I'm starting to learn myself how to deal with it. The beginning is just to recognize it."

As the previous quotes imply, the second stage of reframing is that a degree of *acceptance* must be attained. Certainly, recognition and acceptance are closely linked. This acceptance can involve accepting both the negative aspects (e.g., "I don't learn quickly so there is a need to work harder than others") and the positive aspects (e.g., "My disability forces me to develop other areas of strength") of the disability. But, until an individual accepts that the disability is real and that it is something he or she will always have to confront, moving ahead is impossible. Individuals must accept that despite the disability, they are still good people with something to offer. Implied here is that if someone does not accept the learning disability as real, great frustration will ensue. Several comments by the successful adults with learning disabilities capture this feeling. A director of a school for students with learning disabilities said, "I had to face myself in order to help others. This was a peak experience in my life. . . . that night I looked at myself in the mirror and said, 'You know, you're not so bad after all.'" A highly successful professor explained, "I needed to be proud of myself. As long as I was ashamed of being LD, it was difficult to succeed. It's only been since the acknowledgment and use of appropriate services [that success came]."

One aspect of accepting the disability is deciding whether to share information about the handicap with others. Some readily talked about their problem with friends and colleagues ("Sure, it's no big deal"). Others were not quite so open ("I don't wear it on my sleeve"), but they did not try to hide the fact that they were learning disabled. Still others felt it was most appropriate to keep it to themselves. Many times, this decision was based on the kind of work being performed (e.g., a doctor and a dentist were reluctant to tell their patients for fear of raising unnecessary concerns, while several individuals working with individuals with learning disabilities readily discussed their own problems as a means of inducing others to perform). But the key in terms of acceptance was that a specific and conscious decision had been made about how to deal with this issue.

With acceptance comes the third stage of reframing, the need for *understanding*. Successful adults with learning disabilities recognize and accept their weaknesses and build on their strengths. An understanding of strengths and weaknesses is required. One professor explained, "I realized in the areas I am good, I'm great. . . . In the areas I am bad, I'm terrible." A lawyer described a similar pattern, which captures all the stages described so far: "As a dyslexic, you have to accept the degree to which you will and won't succeed in life. The biggest advantage is that once you realize you can't do all these things, you become good at finding alternative solutions and at making the most of what you have. . . . I think the anger, sense of injustice, and wisdom which that situation has given me has helped me. . . ."

As is already implied in terms of the reframing process, the final stage we call *action*. All the recognition, acceptance, and understanding in the world is useless without the conscious decision to take specific action toward one's goals. The successful adults with learning disabilities all chose to do something about their circumstances that fostered their success.

Clearly, the reframing did not come easy. A psychologist explained how he was "omni-conscious" of his problems during his school years. He called himself a "JIT"—a janitor in training. One woman described parts of her youth this way: "I knew something was wrong; I was scared. I knew 'I can't do this.' I would sweat bullets, I wanted to faint and play dead. I did get sick all the time." A businessman remembered having to read aloud in class, and the emotions attached to that experience: "I had this little voice talking to me. It said that what I was saying was wrong, but the other side of my brain just kept moving and making mistakes." Similarly, a businesswoman gave this description: "I was scared. I can remember having to read out loud and we'd stand up and read and I would have such trouble reading . . . I thought my mind was processing so quickly . . . I just couldn't understand. We were reaching points in class where we were progressing to the next level. I was stumbling . . . I felt inadequate. I would take a test and there would be a word . . . Oh, my God . . . I would get everything wrong." The high-success adults weaved their way through the reframing process, despite the significant hurdles and painful experiences along the way.

All of the moderate-success adults with learning disabilities whom we interviewed reframed as well. However, they generally did not progress through all four stages to the degree that the high-success group members did. They tended to have more trouble with acceptance—sometimes even avoiding complete acceptance. Their understanding was often not as complete, and they did not take the decisive action so characteristic of the more successful adults. For example, a school director expressed: "I literally have approached life like I was a second-rate human being. Dyslexics don't feel as good about themselves as other people." Another described being, "a prisoner unto yourself, locked into yourself. . . . Success has been so brutal . . . I've been beaten up so much." A teacher talked about her desire to go back and "spit in every teacher's eye that [I] had in school." Such thoughts and feelings, though not foreign to the high-success adults with learning disabilities, were much more of a burden to the moderately successful adults. They did considerably more blaming, avoiding, and holding back than the highly successful group. Their degree of reframing was not as extensive.

External Manifestations—Adaptability

Along with the internal components of gaining control, the adults with learning disabilities exhibited or undertook certain activities that helped foster control and success. Having strong desire, setting goals, and reframing the learning disabilities experience in a more positive way are necessary beginning points. But to gain control of one's life, these internal decisions must be translated into actual behaviors, including persistence, goodness of fit with one's environment, coping behaviors we call *learned creativity,* and the support individuals and learning activities we refer to as the *social ecologies.*

Persistence. The successful adults with learning disabilities worked very hard. Desire was a necessary internal decision; its external expression came in the form of persistence. The interviewees repeatedly told us that they had to be willing to do whatever was necessary in order to accomplish something and this often meant working harder than anyone else they knew.

For the high-success group, this persistence was a way of life. They were an incredibly resilient bunch. Comments like "I overcame my problem with sheer grit and determination," "I would adapt by doing extra work," "I made accomplishments by working harder than others and gutting it out," and "I never stop trying . . . I have an incredible amount of persistence" were commonplace. Given their problems with learning, this persistence was a necessity that illuminated certain unpleasant realities about how they had to go beyond the norm in order to learn. But they did it and, ultimately, that persistence worked to their advantage.

The distinction between the moderate and high group was, again, a matter of degree. The moderately successful group were also very persistent—any level of success for someone with a learning disability requires persistence and hard work. However, they did not push with the tenacity of their more successful counterparts. The high-success group members were more driven, took many more risks, and appeared more resilient. They certainly were not as easily distracted from their goals. Although there were exceptions among the moderate-success group, collectively, they were less determined. As one moderate teacher explained in capturing this sense, "My nonassertiveness hinders my getting ahead."

Goodness of Fit. A significant element of adaptability was the goodness of fit the adults with learning disabilities sought with their environment. In other words, they tried to fit themselves to environments in which they could succeed, where their skills and abilities could be optimized. Some were in positions where they could actually create or orchestrate the environment to fit their needs.

For the adults with learning disabilities, finding work they enjoyed doing was important. The high-success group displayed astrong passion for their work. And although both the high- and moderate-success groups were very similar in terms of this goodness-of-fit issue, the key difference between the groups was related to their enthusiasm for work. Also, the high-success group would more often select work contexts wherein they could be their own boss or had the flexibility to control their destiny and make significant decisions about their work. Even as children, the successful adults with learning disabilities had sought or created environments in which they could be comfortable *and* successful. One lawyer, for example, developed his own position within the field of public law, which allowed him to define the kinds of tasks he would have to perform. A businessman started his own public relations firm, taking advantage of his strong verbal skills (his strength). Similarly, a businesswoman took advantage of what she described as her "strong personality" in deciding to embark on a sales career. Her advice captures the essence of goodness of fit: "Capitalize on your strengths . . . look at what you do best and enjoy most." Another high-success woman, a physician, suggested that she specialized in dermatology because there was little writing and the medical textbooks had lots of pictures, so "you could see it." As she explained, "one reason I like my field is that you can see it . . . it's not a guessing game."

Goodness of fit, then, was a significant adapting mechanism each of the study participants displayed. Both control and success were dependent on working in an environment that permitted these adults to shine.

Learned Creativity. The essence of adaptability was the learned creativity displayed by the high-success adults with learning disabilities. Learned creativity refers to the various strategies, techniques, and other mechanisms devised by the successful adults to enhance their ability to perform well. People with learning disabilities have invariably experienced some difficulty operating in the "regular" system, so they develop their own ways of doing things. After all, these people recognized (perhaps when they reframed) that there was little or no incentive to conform to a system that exposed their weaknesses. Success for them required that they become "quick studies," in that they had to contour their reaction to various stimuli so that they would not be embarrassed but, rather, could perform and excel. They learned to develop systems much like a blind person who sharpens other senses due to the lack of sight. The successful adults with learning disabilities came to discover that there were divergent approaches to problem solving, so they developed means to overcome obstacles related to their particular disability. They learned to take advantage of their particular areas of strength. Thus, they did not just cope, they creatively excelled.

Much of the early learned creativity for the entire sample of adults with learning disabilities was a means of manipulating the system to avoid exposing their weaknesses. The word *manipulate* appeared repeatedly in the interview transcripts. For many in the moderate-success group, this form of coping—the manipulating—was the most significant learned creativity they displayed. They consistently made statements expressing ways that they avoided exposure, for example, "I manipulate myself in such a position that I can't make a mistake." "I still feel anxious in situations where I might be found out . . . that I'm faking it." "When you're LD you become very defensive . . . you know what your weaknesses are and you want to cover them up. You find you build up a tremendous entourage of ways to get around it and avoid different issues." "I have so much fear in me about being found out, I protect."

The high-success group members often were protective, as well, especially in their formative years. And both the moderate and highly successful adults with learning disabilities used modern conveniences/technology as a means of adapting to their environment. For example, those who had problems reading and writing relied on spell checkers, word processors, tape recorders, dictaphones, and the like. Many in managerial positions (high success) relied heavily on support staff. But beyond these kinds of adapting devices, the high-success group exhibited a more sophisticated and creative scheme of coping tactics, which were essential components of their success. They more readily built upon their inborn and learned strengths. Several of the high-success adults described how developing anticipatory skills fostered their success. An engineer explained, "I create scenarios of what I will have to do under certain circumstances." A businessman boasted that he could "run rings around well-educated people because I'm faster on my feet and in my mind. They may be still thinking about it."

Many other scenarios were described that highlight the gist of this learned creativity. One high-success lawyer developed his own forms for reporting data, and he tailored its format to his abilities. He even put clients' pictures on each form to bolster his recollection of the client, due to his poor memory skills. A highly successful dentist described his self-taught lip-reading process, which helped him visualize words during conversations. A college professor explained how he invented names for towns and characters when he read.

Obviously, successful adults with learning disabilities use an array of techniques to cope with their handicap, and the high-success group used particularly creative ways to get ahead in a world that generally abhors or stifles deviations from the norm. These individuals learned early in life that success for them required such originality. So, they designed ways to learn and excel that permitted their strengths to endure.

Social Ecologies. Successful adults with learning disabilities surrounded themselves with supportive and helpful people and upgraded their skills by designing personal improvement programs. We call this support- and improvement-oriented process they developed their *social ecology.* Most of the successful adults with learning disabilities created support networks (e.g., spouse, family, friends) and consciously selected their mentors. Some were lucky: The support came from family members or close friends and thus did not have to be solicited. But having support available and actually accepting it are not always the same.

Many in our sample developed self-designed apprenticeship types of programs in order to strengthen or bolster certain skills. For some, this meant hiring people to help them—tutors, secretaries, support staff, and so forth. Several of the individuals with dyslexia in the high-success group, for example, who had written books, relied on co-authors to do the writing dictated to them. The high-success group repeatedly discussed the need for surrounding themselves with good people. Most often, personal relationships were the key for support, usually wives for men and friends for women. Several high-success individuals even discussed the mentors they had learned from along the way. But, no matter its form, support was important for guaranteeing that the adults with learning disabilities did not (as one explained) just "gather dust." As one high-success female educator described it, "it's basically that issue of knowing exactly the types of support you need . . . so it's knowing what it is you can't do and when you need to call on help to perform."

A spouse was important for many in the high-success group. For others it was a parent or a carefully chosen mentor. Occasionally it was a teacher. But the pattern we deciphered was consistent: Support and guidance are invaluable aids, and one must be willing to seek, appreciate, and accept what others can offer.

The distinction between the high- and moderate-success groups related to two factors: the degree of support utilized and the willingness to accept support. Both of these factors are no doubt linked to the degree of reframing achieved by each person. First, several in the moderate-success group utilized the support differently than the high-success adults. They did not use support in areas they personally identified as needs but, rather, relied totally on others. This high degree of dependency was not characteristic of the higher success adults.

The other difference between the groups related to individuals' willingness to seek and accept support. The high-success group did this; several in the moderate-success group did not. As one from the moderate-success group described it, if he could do it all over again, this time he would "ask for more help." Thus, although all the adults with learning disabilities agreed that support was necessary and should be encouraged, the high-success group utilized support more to their advantage, sought it out more readily, and accepted it when available.

A Model for Vocational Success

The findings derived from the analysis of more than 70 interviews of high- and moderate-success adults with learning disabilities revealed key themes that characterized this success. It remains to put these themes into a model that captures how they interact in leading to success. Figure 9.1 presents our model of vocational success for adults with learning disabilities. The model suggests that success is a function of the degree of control attained. Success itself is depicted on a continuum from low to high. High success, for the purposes of this model, is defined as we have utilized it in this study. That is, high success means having high levels in at least four of five variables—education, job satisfaction, eminence in one's field, income level, and job classification (the fifth variable cannot be considered low). Any individual, therefore, is potentially capable of achieving anywhere from a low degree of success (low across all five variables) to a high degree of success (four highs, no lows).

The degree of success depends on the degree of control achieved. Control is also depicted on a continuum. For the purposes of this model, high control refers to realizing high levels for each of the themes embedded in what we call internal decisions and external manifestations. Thus, strong desire, goal orientation, and reframing, along with strong persistence, goodness of fit, learned creativity, and social ecologies, are necessary for a high degree of control. The arrows separating control and success reflect the recognition that extraneous factors, like luck or crisis, may have an impact on one's success despite solid control. Success is never definite. But the model suggests that a high degree of control is positively related to the likelihood of a high degree of success.

The themes that make up control are those in the two boxes at the bottom of Figure 9.1. One begins with the internal decisions. These are placed in a circle and connected by broken lines to reflect that there is no clear-cut beginning point for the internal decisions, and that they all

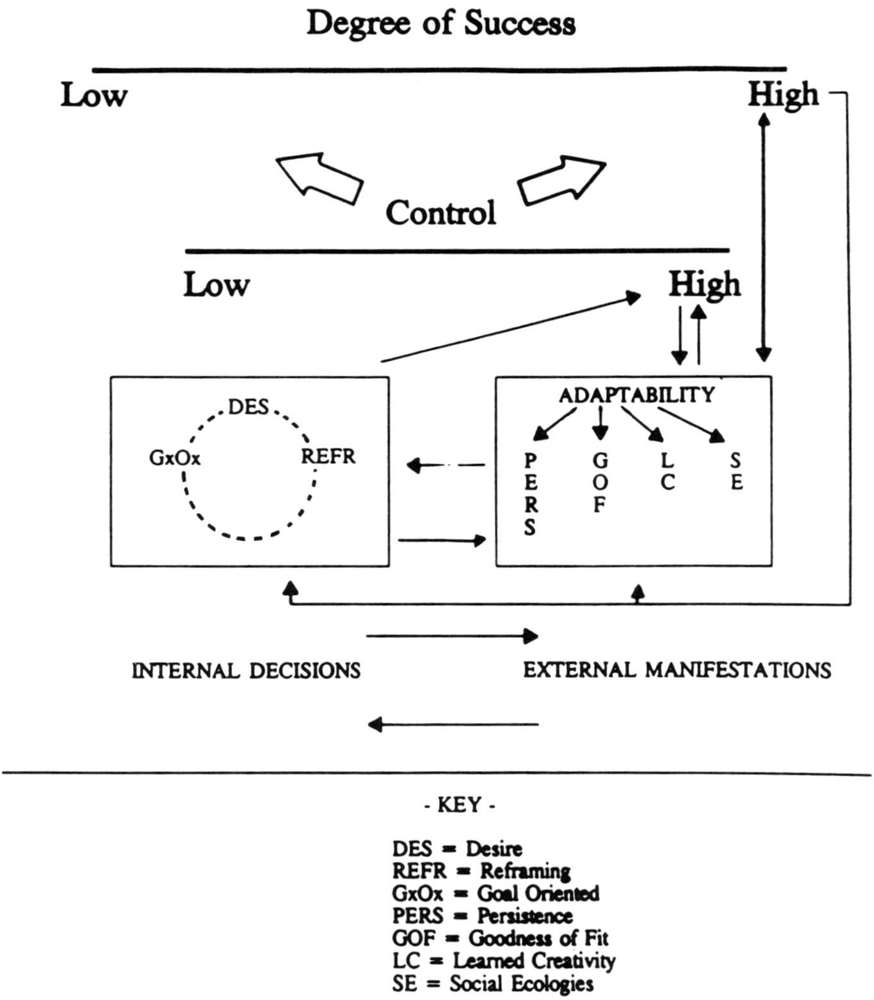

Figure 9.1 A model of vocational success for adults with learning disabilities.

are closely interrelated (the boundaries of each are very blurry). One needs strong desire, goal orientation, and reframing to achieve control (thus the solid line between the internal decisions and high control). The solid lines between the internal decisions and external manifestations reflect the fact that they do decisively affect one another. The internal decisions are precursors of the external manifestations. Similarly, the external manifestations, or adaptability, have a direct influence on stronger internal decisions (thus the solid line or loop from the external manifestations box back to the internal decisions box).

The external manifestations are all aspects of adaptability. Therefore, persistence, goodness of fit, learned creativity, and social ecologies are connected to adaptability with a solid line, though their order is not significant. The solid line between the external manifestations box and high control reflects the need for successful adapting in order to achieve high levels of control. The reciprocal solid line from high control to the external manifestations box indicates that with high levels of control, continued successful adapting will likely result. And, given that the external manifestations are reciprocally related to the internal decisions, high levels of control will provide for stronger internal decisions.

Finally, the model has a solid line between high success and the external manifestations box, and a solid line between high success and the internal decisions box. These solid lines characterize the contagious nature of success. It snowballs within a person and positively influences continued adapting (external manifestations) and more powerful internal decisions.

The rather complex nature of success depicted in this model reflects the themes derived directly from interviews with those who have achieved high levels of success. In summary, success begins with a set of internal decisions; then, highly successful adults with learning disabilities pursue several ways of adapting themselves to their disability and the world around them. Successful adapting strengthens the desire, produces more goal setting, and helps people through the maze of reframing. And, with strong adapting, high levels of control are attainable. Again, high control positively influences adapting and the internal decisions. Finally, given a high degree of control, high levels of success are most likely. And success breeds more success, conceived in this model as more control, more adaptability, and stronger internal decisions.

We believe that each of the internal decisions and external manifestations presented in the model are variables susceptible to training—in essence, they are alterable. Individuals can be taught about desire, goal orientation, and reframing, and, as a result, enhance the possibility of excelling in these areas. Similarly, people can be taught about the need for persistence, goodness of fit, learned creativity, and social support.

Although such training may not necessarily have a positive impact, learning how these themes have interacted for others' control and success may play a significant role in altering children's lives.

One caution must be noted: Success is never automatic. Even under the best of circumstances, a high degree of control may not result in high levels of success. For example, good or bad luck may influence outcomes. Yet, the model suggests that the greater the degree of control obtained, the greater the *likelihood* of success. Also implied is that lower levels of control will result in lower degrees of success.

Discussion

In this study, the investigators identified a model of success for adults with learning disabilities that has both internal and external elements. In essence, there is a dynamic interaction between the internal and external elements that produces varying degrees of successful functioning. This finding acknowledges that individuals with learning disabilities, like all individuals, can thrive best when an ecological perspective (i.e., an interactionist model of the interrelationship between an individual and his or her environment) of functioning (such as the one inherent in this study) is adopted. It also suggests that success in all forms has unique qualities to it. Thus, each of the subjects studied has his or her own formula for success (in a wide variety of forms). But there is no question that there are commonalities among all of the adults that pervade their success experiences. These commonalities were discussed in the results section.

Control is the overriding theme of the model of success constructed for adults with learning disabilities. It is from this need and desire for control that all else flows. Yet, as was said in an earlier section, the differences in the high-success group and moderate-success group were a matter of degree on the elements that make up the model of success. What should be pointed out is that there is no guarantee that one who possesses all the ingredients outlined in this model will automatically become successful. The model is not the definitive map to success. It is the belief of the investigators, however, that many of the dynamic elements posed in this model must be present if one who has a learning disability is to succeed.

What ultimately comes into question is degree of success attained in the work world. Many of the subjects in this study are the most eminent and successful persons in their fields. They also show profiles that place them on the highest points of the continuum on the elements of our model of success. Still others (most notably, many members of the comparison group) seem to have gone as far as they are able on the elements of the model and are successful in their own right. Therefore, the differences between the study groups are principally the arbitrary and subjective criteria for highly successful adults delineated by the investigators for the purposes of the study.

Questions arise regarding how alterable the elements of the model of success are. The investigators believe that all of the elements of the model are alterable. That is, they can be taught and learned, and repertoires of behavior can be altered as a result. This is true of the internal decisions and external manifestations of the model. For instance, desire can be taught, just as adaptability can.

All of the elements seem to work as a dynamic system with each other; however, further comment needs to be made regarding some of the model's elements. First, there seems to be a linkage between desire (internal process) and perseverance (external manifestation). The difference between desire and perseverance, in the opinion of the investigators, is not merely semantic, but clearly reflects the distinction between internal and external processes. The linkage places desire as not only a necessary ingredient that leads to perseverance, but also a cornerstone of successful experience.

Second, reframing seems to be a trigger mechanism for a successful learning disability experience. It hardly seems likely that persons with learning disabilities can become highly successful without thoroughly embracing the full effects of this element of the model. Reframing is a series of stages of psychological processing that provides the important linkages for all of the internal and external elements. It is thought that what happens here has a lot to do not only with success, but also with successful adjustment altogether. Further, the more one fully masters the stages of the reframing process, the more one brings to the element of learned creativity.

Learned creativity seems crucial to the level of functioning of adults with learning disabilities. The difference here is that successful reframing leads to all the possibilities that learned creativity can foster. Conversely, the failure to master the reframing process leads to learned helplessness. The former portends a life of independent functioning while the latter virtually dictates a life of dependent functioning and marginal adjustment to adulthood (Gerber & Reiff, 1992).

Third, of all the elements in the model, learned creativity may be the most difficult to learn. Many of the subjects in the study believed that learned creativity was "something that was learned over time for the purposes of survival." This element was somewhat of a gestalt of many of the elements of the model and was acquired cumulatively. In some ways it was the "proving ground of success," for it was here that alternative strategies were devised that often became the better idea or became the edge to make one fare successfully in a competitive situation. Those in the study who were in the field of business believed that it was this element that helped most in "designing a better mousetrap"; it was the centerpiece of entrepreneurial endeavors.

Fourth, it should be noted that mentors had significant representation in the social ecologies of the highly successful adults with learning disabilities. Mentors were involved much more frequently with this group than with the moderate-success group. This discovery is particularly interesting because the literature on gifted persons points out similar findings (Kauffman, Harrell, Milam, Woolverton, & Miller, 1986). Perhaps this is a significant point of coincidence with highly successful adults with learning disabilities and gifted individuals. The subjects in this study who had mentors were not necessarily gifted individuals; some were persons who officially or unofficially adopted mentors so that they could learn in nontraditional and multisensory ways (typically experientially).

The highly successful adults with learning disabilities in this study were individuals who were very well known and respected in their fields. They are new exemplars for the field of learning disabilities, which, prior to this time, proffered names on the basis of a post mortem diagnosis (Adelman & Adelman, 1987) and routinely added names of famous persons with learning disabilities to an ever-growing list. Most important, it is necessary to know that these individuals exist and that they are contributing handsomely to society.

The vast majority of the subjects in this study were educated prior to the passage of P.L. 94-142. It is noteworthy when anyone accomplishes something against the odds, but these individuals achieved success without benefiting from the special education and support services that are common in schools today. Nor were they always protected by Section 504 of the Vocational Rehabilitation Act of 1973, which adds to their accomplishment. One can only wonder what effect the new laws and newly evolving systems will mean for persons with learning disabilities in the future.

This study provides basic research on the question of success as it relates to adults with learning disabilities. It answers a set of questions that have not been asked or studied in the past. It also raises a whole new set of questions for the field—not only ones that have to do with outcomes in adulthood, but also broader questions that involve learning disabilities curricula and instruction, counseling practices, and parenting skills, to name a few.

Concluding Thoughts

This study has much to do with the study of outcomes. It also has taken a broader perspective by including in its sample adults whose ages extended well into their 60s. It was not surprising to find highly successful adults with learning disabilities doing some wondrous things in the world of work. Likewise, it was not surprising to find the wide diversity of work roles in this highly successful group. It was surprising, however, during data collection to discover the pain and agony, the trials and tribulations, that adults with learning disabilities experienced in order to become successful. Most noteworthy was the general consensus of the subjects that school had little value and relatively little connection to their success. Given that this was a pre–P.L. 94-142 sample, this sentiment is not unexpected. The ultimate question concerns successful vocational outcomes of those persons with learning disabilities who accessed the services of P.L. 94-142 and other adult services. That research remains to be done. One would intuit that in this new era of services for persons with disabilities, outcomes should eclipse or equal the accomplishments of the adults in the present sample. If not, there are important questions about the state of the art of school-age programming and transitional planning and services that need to be answered.

Authors' Note

Money to support this research project came from the U.S. Department of Education, Office of Special Education and Rehabilitation Services, National Institute on Disability and Rehabilitation Research. Project No. H133G80500.

10. Current and Future Research Priorities

ANNA GAJAR

During the late 1970s and the 1980s, in response to the mandate dictated by the Education for All Handicapped Children Act of 1975 (P.L. 94-142), the field of learning disabilities focused the majority of its research efforts on individuals with learning disabilities (LD) in primary and secondary educational environments. Most of that research was directed toward defining the characteristics of children and adolescents with learning disabilities and designing strategies, methods, and materials that would allow them to function successfully in their respective educational settings (Smith, 1989). As a result, today there is a large, sophisticated, young adult population with LD that needs services.

In essence, we are about to advance to another evolutionary stage of development in the provision of services to individuals with learning disabilities. The legislative, legal, advocacy, and basic educational groundwork was laid during the late 1970s and the 1980s, when we concentrated our efforts on the development and delivery of services to children and adolescents with LD. Our task now is to design effective, research-based intervention programs for adults with LD. The body of this chapter presents a review of current areas of research, or *what is currently known* about adults with learning disabilities, and is followed by topical sugges-

---

Reprinted, with changes, from "Adults with learning disabilities: Current and future research priorities," by Anna Gajar, *Journal of Learning Disabilities*, Vol. 25, 1992, pp. 507–519.

tions for research priorities for the 1990s. Research design and methodological suggestions are included.

Rationale

Recently, there has been a rapid rise of interest in adults with learning disabilities. This interest is reflected in the growing number of research, opinion, program, and service articles being submitted to and published in journals dealing with learning disabilities (Vogel, 1990). A number of reasons can be cited for this phenomenon, including new legislation, proposed changes in definition, enhanced advocacy networks, and federal and state funding priorities in the areas of transition and adult literacy.

Legislation. Prior to 1980, legislative direction for adults with LD was limited, due to a lack of adequate funding and social commitment to the area. However, the Rehabilitation Act of 1973 (P.L. 93-112), which emphasized services for individuals with severe disabilities, provided landmark regulations for adults with learning disabilities. Section 504 provided significant changes in training and hiring practices. Specifically, it mandated that it is illegal to discriminate against qualified individuals on the basis of their handicap. It is interesting to note that Section 504 of P.L. 93-112 is only one sentence long and reads as follows:

> No otherwise qualified handicapped individual in the United States shall, by reason of his handicap, be excluded from participation in, be denied the benefits of, or be subjected to discrimination under any program or activity receiving Federal financial assistance. (Federal Register, 1977, pp. 22683–22684)

Several additional pieces of legislation address issues affecting employment, training, community and independent living, and the civil rights of adults with learning disabilities. The 1976, 1983, and 1990 Amendments to the Education of the Handicapped Act and the 1984 Carl D. Perkins Vocational Education Act include training, employment, community, and independent living as primary areas of focus for adolescents and young adults with learning disabilities. The Americans with Disabilities Act of 1990 (P.L. 101-336) expands the nation's civil rights laws of 1964 (directed toward women and minorities) to include the 43 million Americans who have disabilities. This legislation prohibits discrimination in employment, public services, public accommodations, and transportation, and provides for telecommunications relay services for adults with disabilities.

In short, legislation passed recently and during the 1970s and 1980s has established the mandate for providing services to adults with learning disabilities. The nature of the services provided, however, must be dictated by the results of empirical research.

Definition and Advocacy. The preceding mandates were passed due, in part, to the efforts of individuals, parents, teachers, and organizations advocating for the rights of adults with disabilities. For example, a position paper of the National Joint Committee on Learning Disabilities (NJCLD) calls for a change in current definitions to include adults with learning disabilities. In addition, the NJCLD calls for programs to increase (a) professional and public awareness, (b) appropriate education, (c) vocational and employment training programs, (d) access to a range of transition programs and service options, (e) alternative programs for adults who have not attained a high school education, (f) individual involvement in program planning, (g) adherence to federal legislation and regulations, (h) *development of systematic programs of research addressing the needs of adults with learning disabilities* [my emphasis], (i) appropriate curriculum development for service providers, and (j) awareness training for mental health professionals (National Joint Committee on Learning Disabilities, 1987).

In short, due to advocacy efforts, young adults with learning disabilities are more aware of self-advocacy and are supported by a sophisticated network of external advocates, including parents, teachers, and organizations. They are currently more prepared to exercise legal and political options in order to obtain access to services. The fact remains, however, that research identifying successful programs and interventions for adults with learning disabilities has been sparse.

Transition. In a series of articles (Will, 1984a, 1984b, 1984c, 1984d, 1984e), Madeleine Will, former assistant secretary of the Offices of Special Education and Rehabilitation Services (OSERS), stated that an enormous effort would be made to "totally reorganize a system of services for disabled people in our Nation" (Will, 1984b, p. 11). She noted that recent legislation established a new priority which was "to strengthen and coordinate education, training, and support services for handicapped youth in order to foster their effective transition from school to the adult world of work and independent living" (Will, 1984b, p. 12) Wehman, Moon, Everson, Wood, and Barcus (1988) reported that "the U.S. Department of Education's Office of Special Education and Rehabilitation Services (OSERS) has made transition a major priority" (p. 2). Between 1984 and 1989 the transition initiative resulted in the establishment of 100 initial and over 180 model transition demonstration projects that served more than 18,877 persons with diverse disabilities (Lundstram

& Politiek-Haim, 1990). More than 50% of the youths served by these projects were identified as learning disabled. Lundstram and Politiek-Haim (1990), in interviews with project directors, found that directors with "research backgrounds" experienced difficulty in collecting research data "because the staff lacked an understanding of research methods (e.g., random assignment)" (p. 17). In addition, these directors had trouble satisfying the demands of the funding agency while simultaneously producing usable data. Program directors with "nonresearch backgrounds" did not know "what sort of data to collect and how to maintain a data base of information which can be analyzed to give reliable measures when evaluating the project's progress toward achieving its goals" (p. 17).

Transition has become a national priority and monies have been spent for numerous projects serving adults with learning disabilities. However, due to weak design, an absence of research priorities, and the lack of a clear understanding of research methodology, data-based results have been sparse or nonexistent.

Adult Literacy. Literacy is a national priority. As in the area of transition, the adult literacy movement has encountered a large number of individuals who have been identified or who exhibit the characteristics associated with adults with learning disabilities (Gold, 1981; Ross, 1987; Ross & Smith, 1988; Thistlewaite, 1983). A review of the adult literacy literature reveals the existence of a number of papers that express the need for services for the adult population with LD. An increasing number of opinion papers are also available (Otto, 1986). Research-based, empirical guidelines for serving this population, however, are virtually nonexistent.

A review of the results of a study of literacy and learning disabilities published on June 19, 1989, by the Learning Disabilities Association of Canada includes the following comment that is indicative of the lack of a literary research base for training adults with learning disabilities: "After interviewing numerous experts in both learning disabilities and literacy and analyzing their comments it was concluded that *it would be a mistake to assume that there exists a well established discipline of literacy instruction for adults with learning disabilities*" [my emphasis] (Learning Disabilities Association, 1990). The absence of research-based intervention programs and/or strategies in the area of literacy for adults with LD has made it imperative to define research priorities and methodological procedures for this population.

Summary. Legislation, advocacy, and the current social commitment to transition and adult literacy have provided the base for a growing interest in the provision of services to adults with LD. Successful programs, however, must be based on the results of both basic and applied research conducted across a number of individuals, settings, and domains. The following section of this chapter presents a review of the current literature dealing with adults with learning disabilities. The review provides the foundation for identifying research priorities for adults with learning disabilities.

Current Areas of Research

A review of the literature dealing with adults with LD was conducted, with more than 200 articles identified. As expected, many of the articles were either reviews of the literature or descriptive studies that could be categorized as pre–post assessment articles. A number of the reviews indicated that

1. Learning disabilities identified in childhood persist throughout the lifespan.

2. There is a pressing need for research in the area.

3. Early studies in the area were primarily concerned with the relationship of childhood characteristics (reading, language, behavior, self-concept, etc.) to adult adjustment (Balow & Bloomquist, 1965; Menkes, Rowe, & Menkes, 1967; Silver, 1969; Silver & Hagin, 1964). A number of recent studies expanded on this theme, identifying characteristics that persist into adulthood (Buchanan & Wolf, 1986; Klein, Moses, & Altman, 1988; White, Schumaker, Warner, Alley, & Deshler, 1980; White et al., 1983).

4. The self-reported characteristics and needs of adults with learning disabilities included problems in the academic (reading, spelling, arithmetic, written expression, handwriting), social, personal, and vocational domains (Hoffmann et al., 1987; White, 1985).

5. A number of researchers have studied short- and long-term memory deficits of adults with learning disabilities (Dallago & Moely, 1980; Pressley, Heisel, McCormick, & Nakamura, 1982; Torgesen & Kail, 1980; Wilhardt & Sandman, 1988; Worden, 1983). McCue, Shelly, and Goldstein (1986) found that the cognitive profiles of adults with LD were similar to those of younger students with LD. Blaha, Mandes, and Swisher (1987) found that the factor structure associated with adults with LD on the Wechsler Adult Intelligence Scale–Revised (WAIS-R) was similar to the factor structure found with children with learning disabilities on the Wechsler Intelligence Scale for Children–Revised (WISC-R).

6. Little information is available about training programs or intervention strategies. In essence, empirical studies evaluating the success of various intervention techniques are missing (Hughes & Smith, 1990).

Studies that address the adult with LD within community, postsecondary, and employment environments follow. The section concludes with a discussion of longitudinal studies in the area.

Community

There is a paucity of articles addressing the adult with learning disabilities within the community setting. Problems with family, peers, and/or community members have only been alluded to in the literature. Most of the studies deal with employment or postsecondary education. Although social and interpersonal problems experienced by adults with LD encompass many settings, they are addressed here within the community context.

Chelser (1982) reported social relationships and skills to be the major area of concern for adults with LD. Other problem areas included career counseling, concern with self-esteem and confidence, overcoming dependency on others, vocational training, job success, academics, management of personal affairs, and organizational skills. Vetter (1983) found that adults identified as learning disabled were less satisfied with their social lives, came from lower socioeconomic backgrounds, were dependent on families, and did not tend to pursue an education after high school.

Additional characteristics identified in the area of social skills include an inability to make friends (Fafard & Haubrich, 1981; Gray, 1981; White et al., 1980), discontentment with family and peer relationships (White et al., 1980), limited social contacts (Fafard & Haubrich, 1981), and symptoms of anxiety and frustration (Cox, 1977).

Postsecondary

Adults with LD are the fastest-growing group of college and/or university students with disabilities receiving services (Brill, 1987; Gajar, 1991; Gajar, Murphy, & Hunt, 1982; King, 1987). Hirschorn (1988) reported that 1.2% of the total freshman population were self-identified as learning disabled. Additional studies indicate that more than half of the 50,000 high school graduates who have been identified as learning disabled will go on to some form of postsecondary education (Mithaug, Horiuchi, & Fanning, 1985; Shaw & Shaw, 1989; White et al., 1982). "This assures that the momentum from the ten-fold increase in learning disabled college freshmen that occurred during the last decade will continue into the 1990s" (Shaw & Shaw, 1989, p. 78).

In a review of the literature pertaining to college students with learning disabilities, Hughes and Smith (1990) found that less than one third of the approximately 100 articles published over a 20-year span were data based and reported academic and cognitive performance. Empirical articles dealing with the effectiveness of treatment approaches are nonexistent. A variety of problems that adversely affect academic performance were reported. A number of the reviewed articles dealt with intellectual functioning, as well as performance in reading, math, writing, and foreign language.

The following narrative summarizes the pertinent studies in postsecondary education for adults with learning disabilities. These studies include information concerning the identification, assessment, and characteristics of university students with learning disabilities; attitudinal research; and reviews of postsecondary program and research needs.

Assessment/Identification. A number of studies dealt with issues involved in determining a severe discrepancy between potential and achievement, or with identifying cognitive and academic characteristics of postsecondary students with and without learning disabilities (Gajar, 1987a, 1987b; Gajar, Salvia, Gajria, & Salvia, 1989; Salvia, Gajar, Gajria, & Salvia, 1988; Salvia & Salvia, 1985, 1986).

In the academic and/or cognitive domain, Dalke (1988) found significant differences between LD and non-LD freshmen in all 17 clusters of the Woodcock-Johnson Psycho-Educational Test Battery. Slate, Frost, and Cross (1990), in a study of adult (LD) performance on the WAIS-R and WISC-R, found that subjects tended to obtain higher scores on the WISC-R than on the WAIS-R. Leonard (1991) found that WAIS-R results for college students did not predict academic success in postsecondary education. Faas and D'Alonzo (1990) found a significant relationship among subject WAIS-R IQ, scaled scores, and job success.

Characteristics. The academic characteristics of college students with learning disabilities indicate problems in reading (Balow & Bloomquist, 1965; Frauenheim, 1978; Frauenheim & Heckerl, 1983; Siegal, 1974; Silver & Hagin, 1964), spelling (Blalock, 1982; Frauenheim, 1978; Frauenheim & Heckerl, 1983; Weller & Strawser, 1980), listening to lectures, taking accurate notes (Alley & Deshler, 1979; Blalock, 1982; Vogel, 1985), written expression (Gajar, 1989; Gajar & Harriman, 1987), and foreign language (Gajar, 1987a). In addition, Kahn (1980) observed poor time management, difficulty in completing tasks, and poor study skills.

The social characteristics of postsecondary students with learning disabilities indicate problems such as inappropriate communication with pertinent others and lack of response to verbal cues (Blalock, 1982).

Buchanan and Wolf (1986) cited problems with self-concept. Haig and Patterson (1980) reported problems that they identified as social immaturity. Coping problems, such as withdrawal under stress, were reported by Moss and Fox (1980).

Attitudinal. The assessment of attitudes toward postsecondary students with learning disabilities has been proposed by a number of researchers (Miller, McKinley, & Ryan, 1979; Minner & Prater, 1984; Vogel, 1982; Vogel & Adelman, 1980). Minner and Prater found that the initial expectations of college faculty toward students with LD were negative. Askamit, Morris, and Leuenberger (1987) found that student service providers expressed more positive attitudes than faculty toward college students with learning disabilities. Nelson, Dodd, and Smith (1990) found that faculty in education, business, and arts and sciences, in general, were willing to provide students with accommodations. The faculties were less willing, however, to allow students to turn in tape-recorded assignments or to use a proofreader.

Program Needs. Bursuck, Rose, Cowen, and Yahaya (1989), in a survey of postsecondary education services, found that services varied a great deal from campus to campus, and that postsecondary guides to services were inaccurate and incomplete. Mangrum and Strichart (1988), in their text on college LD, stated that they had "found an insufficient number of college programs designed to specifically and comprehensively meet the needs of learning disabled students" (pp. 5–6). In short, postsecondary service providers are attempting to create model programs with little or no empirically based guidance (Barsch, 1980; Bireley & Manley, 1980; Geib, Guzzardi, & Genova, 1981).

Parks, Antonoff, Drake, Skiba, and Soberman (1987) reviewed graduate and professional schools in the United States, and found that only 24% of the respondents had developed a written plan that described services to students with LD. Services provided were at the minimum for compliance with legal mandates.

Blosser (1984) found that only 9% of directors of college disability programs were trained in special education. Norlander, Shaw, and McGuire (1990) surveyed 299 practitioners in college programs and found that the competencies perceived as most desirable were in the areas of assessment, cognitive interventions, and instruction. Administrative personnel rated management/leadership skills as most desirable. The authors proposed that a stronger link between secondary and postsecondary programs would foster effective transition planning.

Research/Program Recommendations. McGuire, Norlander, and Shaw (1990) outlined research issues in postsecondary education. These included preparation of students for postsecondary education at the secondary level of education, identification and diagnosis at the postsecondary level, flexibility in curriculum requirements (such as the often-cited foreign language requirement), research on the efficacy of varied interventions, and program evaluation.

Although many students with LD are capable of completing college and undertaking professional careers (Scheiber & Talpers, 1987), many adults with LD report that they experience social and interpersonal problems within the postsecondary community (Vogel, 1982). Consequently, counseling and/or support groups have been cited as important components of postsecondary programs (Barbaro, 1982; Bireley & Manley, 1980; Cordoni, 1980; Miller et al., 1979; Siegel, 1979; Vogel, 1982).

Employment

White et al. (1980) found that employment and unemployment rates were similar for adults with and without LD. Adults with LD, however, were employed in jobs with lower social status, expressed greater dissatisfaction with their employment situation, and expressed lower aspirations for future education or training. In a study of adult (LD) employment outcomes, Zigmond and Thornton (1985) reported an employment rate of 74.1%. This employment rate was higher than the rate documented in earlier studies.

The following narrative summarizes the studies in the area of employment. These studies contain information regarding characteristics, attitudes, and vocational rehabilitation services.

Characteristics. Gottfredson, Finucci, and Childs (1984), in a study of adult males labeled as dyslexic, found that men who were dyslexic had higher level jobs than the average man but were less likely than controls to enter jobs that required higher degrees (e.g., physician, lawyer, college faculty member). Those in high-level jobs were in professions that emphasized nonacademic, on-the-job skills (exhibited by managers or salesmen).

In a study of 65 young adults, Succimarra and Speece (1990) found that 1 year after exiting high school, 78% of the sample were employed. Most respondents relied on self and/or family and peers to secure employment, and most were single, resided at home, and engaged in various social activities. A combination of employment and social variables showed that 60% of the sample were employed and had positive perceptions of their social lives. Although the rate of employment was a positive finding, the level of employment supported a number of previous investigations finding that adults with disabilities tend to work in low-level skill positions (Carriker, 1957; Cassidy & Phelps, 1955; Hasazi, Gordon, Roe, Hull, Finck, & Salembier, 1985). The study also supported previous findings showing that adults with learning disabilities rely on family and peers for support (Mithaug et al., 1985; Vetter, 1983).

Studies reporting anecdotal or summary information about the vocational adjustment of adults with LD indicate that adults with LD have vocational adjustment problems (Blalock, 1982; Fafard & Haubrich, 1981; McCue et al., 1986; Patton & Polloway, 1982; Polloway, Smith, & Patton, 1984). Adults with learning disabilities tend to be underemployed or unemployed and are often financially dependent on parents or spouses (Cobb & Crump, 1984; Fafard & Haubrich, 1981); they manifest problems in making vocational choices, acquiring jobs, maintaining jobs, and receiving promotions (Humes, 1986). Finally, adults with LD are usually provided with job training programs that prepare them for low-level jobs (Cummings & Maddox, 1987; Sitlington, 1981).

Employer Attitudes. Brown (1989) and Siegal (1974) reported that employers demonstrate prejudices against applicants and employees with LD. Patton and Polloway (1982) reported that employers perceive adults with LD as misfits. Finally, few employers are aware of or are sensitive to the needs of adults identified as learning disabled (Thomas, 1981).

Minskoff, Sautter, Hoffmann, and Hawks (1987), in interviewing 326 employers from six states, found that most employers expressed positive attitudes toward hiring and making special allowances for individuals with handicaps. This attitude, however, was not true for employees identified as learning disabled. The authors identified three factors that might have been related to this finding: (a) employers might have more positive attitudes toward handicaps that they can see, (b) many employers have not experienced working with an adult identified as learning disabled, and (c) many employers have a limited knowledge of learning disabilities.

Vocational Rehabilitation. Rusch, McNair, and DeStefano (1988), in a study of personnel involved with federally funded transition projects, reported that a high research priority was given by these individuals to investigating the roles and responsibilities of families, teachers, rehabilitation counselors, and vocational educators in the transition planning process. Adults with learning disabilities have only recently become eligible for vocational rehabilitation services. The Rehabilitation Services Administration accepted specific learning disabilities as a medically recognizable disability in January 1981 (Gerber, 1981). However, confusion regarding assessment procedures and the necessity of meeting eligibility requirements in order to receive services has resulted in either a reluctance to serve clients with learning disabilities or the absence of services (Johnson, Bruininks, & Thurlow, 1987; Miller, Mulkey, & Kopp, 1984; Sanchez, 1984).

In their surveys of state vocational rehabilitation (VR) agencies, Miller et al. (1984) found that a relatively small number of clients with learning disabilities were being served, while Sheldon and Prout (1985) found that many problems were being posed by adults with learning disabilities. There was a lack of consistency among state VR policies regarding the diagnostic and eligibility determination processes. Only 25% of the state agencies reported having special programs, and only 12% used specific activities designed to educate prospective employers about learning disabilities or assisted employers in meeting the unique needs of the clients.

Smith (1989), in a study concerning the postschool status and vocational rehabilitation needs of a national sample of adults with learning disabilities, found that a large group of respondents were either ineligible for rehabilitation services or dissatisfied with the services that they received. In addition, respondents' knowledge of their rights in the VR application eligibility process was limited.

Minskoff, Hawks, Steidle, and Hoffmann (1989) found that adults with LD in vocational rehabilitation programs appear to constitute a homogeneous group of persons, with severe areas of deficit, including low-average general intelligence, low academic achievement (approximately at the fifth-grade level), severe language deficits, and low self-esteem.

Hursh (1984), in reviewing the vocational evaluation of adults with LD, concluded that research is needed to identify appropriate evaluation instruments and appropriate service procedures for this population. Mulkey, Kopp, and Miller (1984) suggested that the rehabilitation counselor, in consultation with the adult client, must identify appropriate vocational objectives before a vocational handicap or the success of vocational training can be determined.

Longitudinal Studies

Most longitudinal or follow-up studies in the area of adults with learning disabilities emphasize pre–post high school variables and are descriptive in nature (Edgar, Levine, & Maddox, 1986; Halpern, Close, & Nelson, 1986; Hasazi, Gordon, Roe, Hull, et al., 1985; Mithaug & Horiuchi, 1983; Mithaug et al., 1985; Wehman et al., 1985). A summary of major studies in this area is as follows:

1. Hasazi, Gordon, and Roe (1985) found that after leaving high school in Vermont, over half of the student (LD) sample were primarily employed in service occupations and had found jobs through family and friends. Employment outcomes were related to secondary vocational and training experiences.

2. Mithaug et al. (1985) found that 69% of the 1978 graduates of Colorado special education programs were employed in jobs at minimal wages. Most were living with parents and were dependent.

3. Humes and Brammer (1985), in a follow-up study of 29 individuals with learning disabilities, found that 90% were employed or in training programs. Most of these, however, were in unskilled or semiskilled jobs.

4. In a study of the postsecondary community placement of 65 students with learning disabilities, Schalock et al. (1986) found that 72% were employed (mostly less than full-time). Only 25% were living independently.

5. White et al. (1980), in a study of 47 individuals with LD, found that they held jobs at approximately the same rate as peers but their jobs carried less social status and they were less satisfied with employment.

6. Fafard and Haubrich (1981) found that most of their subjects were not employed full-time.

7. Okolo and Sitlington's (1988) summary of follow-up studies indicated that adults with LD are employed at approximately the same rate as their nondisabled peers. Employment, however, is most often part-time and at entry or minimum-wage levels.

8. In a study of the adult adjustment of 911 adults with learning disabilities, Sitlington and Frank (1990) found that only 54% of the subjects interviewed met the criteria of (a) meaningful employment, (b) independent living, (c) paying of at least a portion of their living expenses, and (d) involvement in more than one leisure activity.

9. Haring, Lovett, and Smith (1990), in a follow-up study of 64 students with LD, found that 38 of the students were incompetitive employment. Most students received few community services or little agency support after graduation; most lived with parents. "It is apparent that this sample of persons with disabilities experienced significantly higher unemployment rates than their nondisabled peers" (p. 111).

10. Edgar (1987) found that few young adults with LD move from school to successful independent living in the community.

11. A number of studies found that many students drop out of secondary special education programs (Edgar, 1987; Siegel, Deuter, Prieur, & Gaylord-Ross, 1986).

12. Finally, a number of statewide follow-up studies enumerated the difficulties young adults encounter in securing and maintaining employment (Hasazi, Gordon, & Roe, 1985; Mithaug et al., 1985).

Summary

Based on the preceding review of the current status of the literature dealing with adults with LD, a number of research priorities for the 1990s can be identified. First, the literature emphasizes the fact that learning disabilities identified in childhood have not been remediated and persist into adulthood. Additional studies are needed that identify specific samples within adult populations. Second, many of the reviewed articles were descriptive in nature and dealt mainly with sample characteristics. Few studies dealt with the effects of intervention strategies and/or training programs. Studies identifying successful intervention techniques are sorely needed. In addition, a number of domains in which adults experienced difficulties were identified by researchers and subjects. These included the cognitive, social, personal, and vocational domains. Studies dealing with successful intervention techniques within these domains are crucial. Third, research with adults with LD is viewed as relevant in a number of settings, including community, employment, and postsecondary settings, and across critical periods, such as movement from secondary to postsecondary environments or movement from employment into retirement. Few studies, however, addressed research in community environments or dealt with critical periods of older adults. Almost all of the longitudinal studies dealt with the transition from secondary to postsecondary or employment settings. Future research in a variety of settings and encompassing critical periods of an individual's life span is imperative. Finally, most studies utilized group research designs. Considering the heterogeneous nature of the population, researchers must examine alternative methodologies in future investigations. The following section deals in greater detail with the identified research priorities for the 1990s.

Research Priorities for the 1990s

Subjects

Gerber et al. (1990), in a study of adults with LD, concluded that learning disabilities are a lifelong problem and that self-reports suggest that many of the problems associated with the disability get worse over time. Based on these conclusions, it is proposed that studies on adult subjects with learning disabilities utilize two distinct populations: young adults ages 14 to 21 and adults ages 22+. This division is arbitrary and is based on the fact that young adults with learning disabilities are usually involved in the transition from secondary to postsecondary settings (Will,

1984a), while older adults with LD experience transition periods and problem areas at various times throughout their life span (Brown, 1980; Gerber, 1981; Gerber & Mellard, 1985). Researchers interested in the areas of transition and secondary education should select samples from the younger population; researchers in the area of vocational rehabilitation and adult literacy should select samples from the older adult population.

Intervention Priorities Across Settings and Domains

A number of researchers emphasized the need for identifying effective intervention strategies, designing training models, and evaluating the success of program components at both the secondary and the adult level (Cobb & Hasazi, 1987; Halpern & Benz, 1987; Kiernan & Stark, 1986; Neubert, Tilson, & Ianacone, 1989). Simpson and Umbach (1989), in a review of vocational services for adults with specific learning disabilities, proposed that, due to the heterogeneous nature of this population, case studies must be used in identification, diagnosis, intervention, and service development. A number of other researchers also supported the use of case studies in this area (Brown, 1984; Buchanan & Weller, 1984; Eldredge, 1988; Temple, 1988). The following narrative provides a blueprint for identifying effective intervention techniques within different environmental settings and across domains.

Research with adults with learning disabilities is viewed as relevant throughout the entire life span and should encompass critical periods and settings in an individual's life, including the movement from secondary to postsecondary settings, employment settings, community settings, and retirement environments. Therefore, pertinent variables that assess the probability of successful movement between and within settings need to be identified. This can be accomplished by conducting structured interviews or surveys with subjects, families, and setting professionals. Prior to assessment and intervention within the domains, systematic observations of other adults in the settings are recommended to establish normal levels of functioning. These observations may produce indications of minimal personal effectiveness in skill areas such as peer relationships, cognitive abilities, and so forth. In addition to informal techniques, norm-referenced measures may be used (when appropriate) to increase predictive capabilities.

Following the identification of pertinent variables, the assessment of subjects within the various domains may be conducted. These assessments can be used to establish the psychometric properties of the indicator battery (e.g., split half reliability, predictive validity, concurrent validity).

Postassessment is conducted to evaluate the success of intervention procedures within settings and across domains.

Intervention strategies need to be developed that address the acquisition of cognitive, social, personal, and vocational skills and competencies needed for success in community, employment, or postsecondary settings. In general, priority targets include competencies observed to be critical for independent adjustment. Treatment of these target behaviors becomes the primary emphasis for applied research.

Following assessment within settings and across domains, exemplary dependent variables are identified for each research subject. Single-subject design techniques establish the internal validity of treatment. Specific long- and short-term objectives are identified, and strategies for attaining and evaluating the achievement of each objective are defined. For example, a determined rate of reading per a specified time period may be identified as a dependent variable when an increase in reading fluency is targeted as a behavioral objective.

Independent variables are matched to the characteristics of the objectives for selected subjects. Treatment focuses on strategies for remediating or compensating for an adult's particular learning and/or behavioral problems. Strategies that have been demonstrated to be effective with other special needs groups and that incorporate cognitive and/or behavioral techniques such as mnemonic memory training, behavioral self-control, social skill training, and so forth, become exemplary independent variables.

Research Methodology

To determine the current status of adults with learning disabilities, a number of descriptive and group studies have been conducted. These studies have identified a number of characteristics of adults with learning disabilities. Because research methodology is an integral part of each of the previously cited priorities for the 1990s, and serves different purposes, the following narrative presents a discussion of the purposes, strengths, and weaknesses of descriptive/group designs, single-subject designs, and qualitative research. A comparison between single-subject and group designs is presented.

Descriptive/Group Research. Surveys, interviews, and group studies, utilizing informal and formal instruments, are conducted for the purpose of collecting data to test hypotheses or answer questions concerning the current status of the subject of study. Studies conducted with adults with learning disabilities have utilized descriptive research techniques. These have included descriptive, developmental, follow-up, and sociometric studies. This type of research is easy to conduct and fulfills the need for collecting data on the current status of the discipline.

The simplest descriptive studies include surveys, observations, or questionnaires. These merely describe the phenomena within a population. Correlational studies describe relationships between phenomena. Causal comparative research draws tentative cause/effect relationships between phenomena.

Single-Subject. Intrasubject replication designs, also referred to as single-subject research, replicate treatment effects within a subject to support the internal validity of the approach (i.e., the extent to which behavior change can be attributed to the treatment procedure). These designs are relevant in identifying successful intervention techniques for individual subjects. The adult population with learning disabilities has been identified as a heterogeneous one. The major advantage of utilizing single-subject experimental designs with adults with LD is that they allow the researcher to make precise and valid statements regarding the effectiveness of specific procedures with specific subjects when homogeneous groups are not available.

Qualitative Research. Due to the heterogeneous nature of the population with LD, a number of researchers (Eldredge, 1988; Geib et al., 1981; Simpson & Umbach, 1989; Temple, 1988) have either utilized or suggested the use of case studies or qualitative research as an alternative to group or single-subject investigations. Qualitative research involves intense data collection on many variables over an extended time period in a naturalistic setting. Data collection involves the use of interviews and both participant and nonparticipant observation techniques. Many aspects of the environment are observed in order to identify variables associated with effective or ineffective adult adjustment. A variety of strategies and instruments are utilized.

Qualitative research usually results in the formulation of hypotheses from the data to explain observed behavior. These hypotheses are tentative in nature. In this type of research, the investigator does not find support or nonsupport (as in other research) for a hypothesis. The qualitative approach is often used in anthropology (lots of data are accumulated that are usually difficult to analyze or replicate). The reader is directed to Robert B. Edgerton's (1967) book, *The Cloak of Competence,* for a more thorough understanding of the use of qualitative research with populations with handicaps.

Single-Subject Versus Group Research. Single-subject and qualitative research designs have been presented as a valuable alternative to group study for a number of reasons. First, the adult population with learning disabilities is a heterogeneous one. Individual responses to treatment are highlighted in the single-subject or case study approach. In group research, differential responses to treatment would be averaged across a number of individuals. For example, a selected strategy might substantially increase the rate of interactions between a group of subjects and peers, producing a group difference of significant magnitude to validate a program's effectiveness. The investigator, however, would be hard-pressed to determine for whom the given educational program was or was not effective. Single-subject research allows the researcher to generalize the information from adult to adult rather than from group to group (Bergin, 1966).

Second, statistical significance obtained through inferential statistics does not necessarily support the clinical or applied significance of the treatment. For example, a reduction in reliably measured negative interactions with fellow employees from 30 to 5 per day for a group of 15 individuals may be statistically significant. A number of these individuals, however, would still be considered unacceptable by fellow employees. The effectiveness of applied or single-subject research, on the other hand, is judged by the difference between the strength of an individual's behavior prior to treatment and the strength of that behavior following treatment.

Third, failure to control for variability within groups has been a major obstacle in special education research (Cronbach & Snow, 1977). Many potentially effective educational practices have not demonstrated statistical success because of differences in the characteristics of children and adolescents in the experimental groups. While some students excel through the use of specific educational practices, others show little progress. These within-group differences obscure the potential value of these procedures for some individuals.

Fourth, the single-subject or qualitative approach also minimizes the interference of between-subject differences. Single-subject designs evaluate the variability of behavior within the individual across program conditions, without relying on the presence or absence of variability between one subject and another. For example, a self-instruction program may be demonstrated to be effective in increasing on-task behavior in a job setting for an individual. In the process, no comparison is made between the individual adult worker with LD and other workers in his or her department.

The major disadvantage in the use of single-subject or qualitative research methodology for adults with learning disabilities lies in the limited confidence one may place in generalizing the findings from one individual to another (Kiesler, 1971). This can be remedied by systematic replication of single-subject designs. Replication holds several advantages over group designs. Each replication takes place in a somewhat different setting with a different treatment. Hersen and Barlow (1976) suggested that four guidelines are necessary for sound replication: First, single-case research reports should include a clear and concise description of the setting, change agents, behavior, and subjects; initial and subsequent replications should vary one of these pertinent factors. Second, investigators should identify differences across variables when contrasting systematic replications. Third, if no exceptions are found as replications proceed, wide generality of findings can be established. Fourth, systematic replications are over when all relevant replications are finished and when all relevant exceptions are identified.

An approach to increasing the external validity of single-subject and/or qualitative research designs was advanced by Bergin and Strupp (1972). The authors advocated the use of single-case studies to develop specific treatment packages potentially applicable to well-defined treatment groups. A group design could then be used to evaluate the treatment approaches, thereby increasing one's confidence in the generality of the findings.

Finally, it is likely that ideas for group research may evolve from single-subject replications or from qualitative case study designs. However, as the above discussion illustrates, it is unlikely that group designs will result in intervention procedures for specific individuals. It is also unlikely that a significant population of adults with LD with homogeneous characteristics, which can be studied as a group, will be identified in the near future.

Summary and Conclusions

A review of the literature indicates that over the past 20 years there has been an increase in interest in adults with learning disabilities. In the past, investigative efforts with this population have primarily focused on the use of survey, descriptive, and group research methodologies for the purposes of identification and diagnosis. Such research has served to define the characteristics of this population and provide basic insights into the problems faced by adults with learning disabilities. The need for services has also been identified. However, the use of single-subject and qualitative research designs to develop effective strategies to remediate and accommodate the cognitive, social, personal, and vocational problems faced by adults with LD in community employment and postsecondary settings has not been vigorously pursued. These areas have been identified as research priorities for the 1990s.

Because laws now mandate the provision of services for adults with LD, and today's population is very sophisticated in terms of advocacy, we can expect that the demand for effective services will increase. The emerging transition and adult literacy programs indicate that the field has already started responding to that need. We must establish basic guidelines for such programs through research dealing with not only the characteristics and needs of adults with LD, but also the unique characteristics and demands of the settings (community, employment, and postsecondary) with which they will be interacting. In addition, future research must direct itself to the pertinent indicators (or skills) dictated by the various domains (cognitive, social, personal, and vocational) within each setting. In short, the primary thrust of research now and in the immediate future should involve the development of data-based intervention techniques to be used in such programs and settings. Finally, we need to do research on the service delivery network to ensure that it is capable of maximizing the effective transmission of proven interventions that will facilitate the transition to adult life.

11. The Neurobiology and Neuropsychology of Adult Learning Disorders

ERIN D. BIGLER

The National Joint Committee on Learning Disabilities (NJCLD) has established a widely accepted definition of learning disabilities (for a review, see Myers & Hammill, 1990). The 1989 NJCLD statement holds that learning disabilities are "intrinsic to the individual, presumed to be due to CNS [central nervous system] dysfunction, and may occur across the life span" (p. 1). Implicit in this statement is that learning disabilities are neurologically based and may be permanent. As such, some learning disabilities will extend into adulthood. For example, Gerber et al. (1990) recently surveyed 133 adults who had achieved successful levels of adult (career)employment but who had been diagnosed learning disabled as children. Their findings suggested that in spite of these individuals' vocational success, the majority continued to have significant problems in their area of disability, and a significant number indicated that their disability even got worse. Gerber et al. summarized their results with the following statement:

> . . . problems of learning disabilities are pervasive in many areas of functioning. The present study provides ample, compelling evidence from a wide array of individuals, whose ages span the full range of adulthood, that

---

Reprinted, with changes, from "The neurobiology and neuropsychology of adult learning disorders," by Erin D. Bigler, *Journal of Learning Disabilities,* Vol. 25, 1992, pp. 488–506.

> the problems experienced during school years can be the very same problems that are experienced in adulthood. (p. 572)

The focus of this chapter is to examine learning disorders that persist into adulthood from a neuropsychological perspective. First, historical background will be reviewed that establishes the neurobiological basis for learning disabilities and how neuropsychological assessment methods can be utilized in the evaluation of the adult with learning disabilities. The next section will address some of the contemporary problematic issues that neurobiological theories of learning disabilities face. This will be followed by a section on typical neuropsychological assessment findings in the adult with learning disabilities. The chapter will conclude with separate sections on remediation and neurobiologic factors associated with psychosocial problems encountered by the adult with learning disabilities.

Historical Review and Contemporary Neurobiological and Neuropsychological Findings

Neurobiological Foundations

As reviewed by Wiederholt (1974), the term *learning disability* is a recent one. From the confluence of adult syndromes whereby a particular brain lesion (i.e., cerebrovascular accident [CVA] or stroke) resulted in some loss of acquired ability (e.g., reading) and childhood disorders whereby the child did not acquire a particular ability (e.g., reading) but in whom no detected evidence (other than the deficient ability) of brain damage existed, the concept of learning disability arose. The adult models of structural brain damage, typically based on the language-disordered patient who had suffered a CVA, were unsatisfactory for most of the childhood syndromes because of accompanying neurologic deficits (e.g., hemiplegia) associated with the CVA-induced language disorder that would not be present in childhood disorders. Oppositely, many children with prominent learning deficits displayed permanent impairment in their area of disability, despite normal cognitive functioning in most or all other areas and no outward signs of "brain damage." Accordingly, a developmental model of learning disabilities with restitution over time also was unsatisfactory, because the permanency of such a learning deficit suggested some form of permanent CNS dysfunction and not just delay.

From his first writing on the subject of reading disorders, Orton (1928) emphasized a brain dysfunction model. However, throughout his lifetime and until recently, the anatomic and physiologic base of learning disability have remained elusive. Fortunately, with refined histologic (microscopic tissue analysis) and neuroanatomic techniques, along with computer-aided electroencephalographic studies, some of the pathologic basis to learning disability is moving from the theoretical to the empirical.

In 1979 Galaburda and Kemper published their seminal neuroanatomic work on the brains of deceased individuals who were dyslexic. Galaburda has followed this up with other studies that confirmed his initial work demonstrating irregular patterns of neural development in the dyslexic brain, particularly in language and language association regions (see Galaburda, Rosen, & Sherman, 1990; Galaburda, Sherman, Rosen, Aboitiz, & Geschwind, 1985; Humphreys, Kaufmann, & Galaburda, 1990). Figure 11.1 depicts regions of the cerebral cortex that, according to Galaburda and colleagues, display aberrant development. According to adult aphasic models, many of these areas of abnormal development are not unexpected, and in fact would be in the areas predicted. However, Galaburda's research results have been the first unequivocal findings demonstrating neuropathologic substrates to likely be responsible for the reading deficit in individuals with dyslexia.

In conjunction with Galaburda's research, Duffy and colleagues (see Duffy & McAnulty, 1990) have utilized computer-assisted averaging and analysis techniques that provide a means of studying electroencephalogram (EEG) topography including sensory evoked potentials (EPs). Duffy's work, like Galaburda's, was restricted to individuals with dyslexia and displayed findingsthat would be expected (i.e., abnormal EEG patterns in dominant-hemisphere language areas), but it also demonstrated irregularitiesin areas less involved in the language process (e.g., anterior frontal regions). Duffy's results are summarized in Figure 11.2.

Galaburda's anatomic work and Duffy's electrophysiological studies provided us with the first compelling evidence demonstrating permanent structural neurological and physiological abnormalities in individuals with dyslexia (see reviews by Hynd & Semrud-Clikeman, 1989a, 1989b). These findings have now been followed up by neuroimaging confirmation in children with learning impairments, which will be discussed below. Currently, the exact effect these aberrations in structure and function have on the dyslexic brain is not completely understood, but it is apparent that as a result of these abnormalities neural transmission and interaction are disrupted. It also is evident that in individuals with dyslexia the abnormalities are not restricted to just the traditional language centers of the brain. These disrupted neurologic functions likely result in the learning deficit.

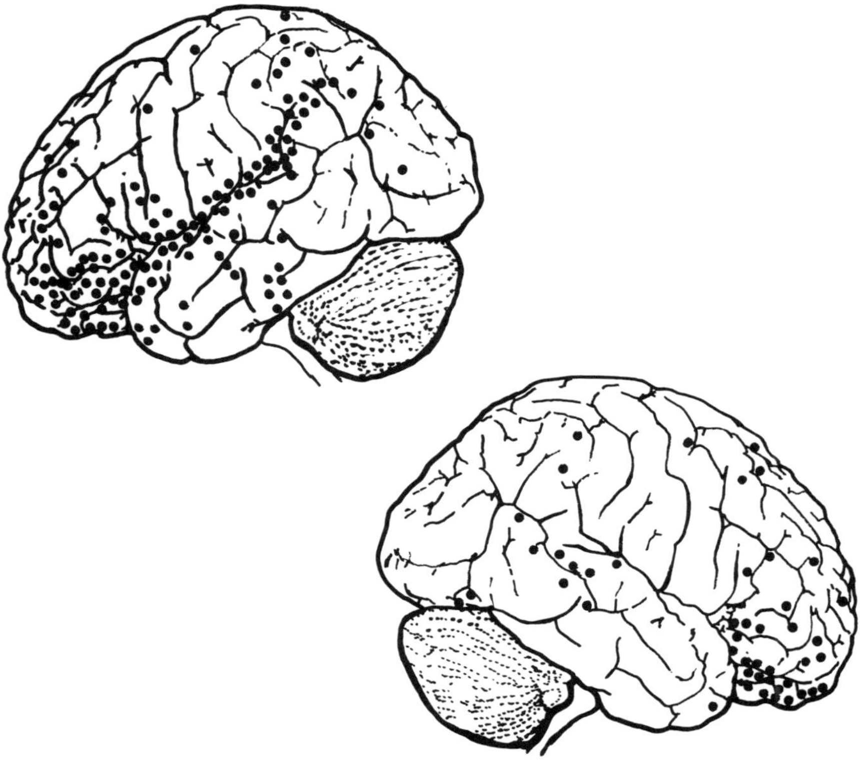

Figure 11.1 Regions of cytoarchitectonic (arrangement of cells in brain tissue) abnormalities based on postmortem gross and histological examination of the brains of four individuals with developmental dyslexia. Note that the greatest number of abnormalities are in the left hemisphere (upper left) in the peri-Sylvian region, although there are abnormalities in other regions. Adapted from "Developmental Dyslexia: Four Consecutive Patients with Cortical Anomalies" by A. M. Galaburda, G. F. Sherman, G. D. Rosen, F. Aboitiz, and N. Geschwind, 1985, *Annals of Neurology, 18*. Copyright © 1985 by Little, Brown and Company. Adapted by permission.

Neuroimaging and Metabolic Imaging in Dyslexia

As of this writing there have been three comprehensive magnetic resonance imaging (MRI) studies of individuals with dyslexia (Duara et al., 1990; Jernigan, Hesselink, Sowell, & Tallal, 1991; Larsen, Hoien, Lundberg, & Odegaard, 1990). All of them suggest an anatomic irregularity in the posterior left cerebral hemisphere when, as a group, the individuals with dyslexia are compared to controls. To date, there have been no pathologic markers or definitive indicators identified in MRI

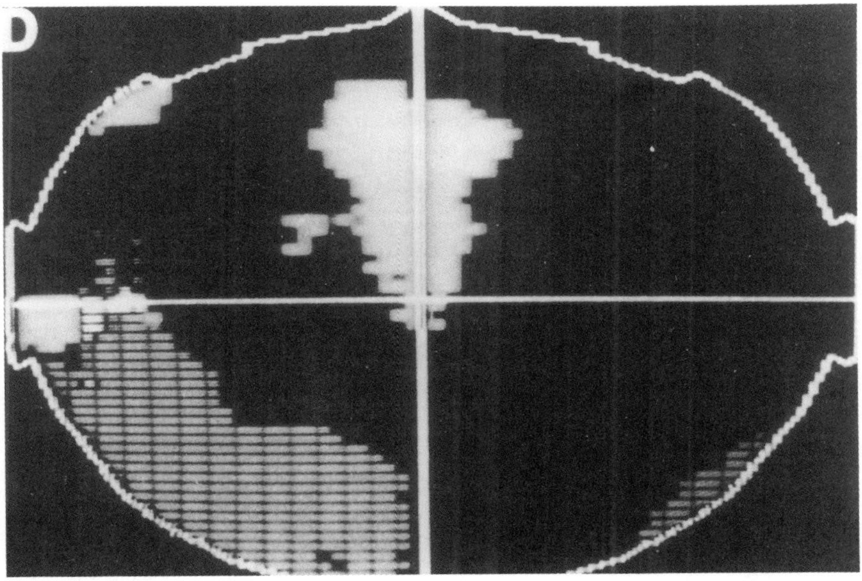

Figure 11.2 This image shows a schematic outline of the head—nose above, left ear to the left, right ear to the right, vertex (crown of the head) in the center, and occiput (back of the head) below—taken from the study by Duffy and McAnulty (1990). It represents a summary *t*-statistic (significance probability mapping) displaying all regions of between-group differences that differentiated boys with dyslexia-pure from normal readers. Regions shown reach or exceed the $p < .02$ two-tailed probability level across all EEG and/or EP states. Note that regions delineated include the classic left mid-temporal and left anterior temporal regions typically associated with language function. Note, also, the prominent bilateral medial frontal involvement. The very same regions were delineated elsewhere by blood flow studies during language functions in nondisabled subjects. Thus, Duffy and McAnulty's dyslexia-pure appears to be associated with an electrophysiological "difference" in all regions normally involved in language function, including the medial frontal region. Reprinted with permission from *Neuropsychologia,* Vol. 2, F. Duffy and G. McAnulty, "Neurophysiological Heterogeneity and the Definition of Dyslexia: Preliminary Evidence for Plasticity," Copyright © 1990, Pergamon Press Ltd.

results that are diagnostic of dyslexia in the individual case. Nonetheless, this line of research clearly implicates the presence of anatomic irregularities that are associated with the presence of dyslexia in late childhood and adulthood. This further implicates structural irregularities that are permanent and not just "developmental" in nature.

The MRI studies specify anatomic differences between nondisabled individuals and individuals with dyslexia, but there may be other regions and functional irregularities not captured by magnetic resonance imaging. For example, Flowers, Wood, and Naylor (1991), using a regional cerebral blood flow measure, demonstrated left superotemporal activation in a reading task performance. In a group of 83 adults whose childhood standardized reading scores were known, childhood reading ability was found to be inversely correlated with focal activation in posterior temporal-parietal areas of the left cerebral cortex. This finding suggests that lack of activation in these critical language areas may be associated with the presence of dyslexia and that these boundaries actually exceed some of the areas where anatomic irregularities have been identified with MRI.

Gross-Glenn et al. (1991) studied 25 adults with a familial form of dyslexia using metabolic imaging. For this group, despite a mean Full Scale IQ score of 113, the oral reading score was approximately at the ninth grade level and the spelling score was at approximately the sixth grade. (Thus, the subjects had classic features of reading and spelling disabilities.) Accordingly, this group of individuals with dyslexia showed distinct discrepancies between level of general cognitive intellectual function and achievement level, consistent with permanent learning disability. Utilizing positron emission tomography, which measures metabolic function of the brain, these researchers demonstrated significant differences in regional cerebral metabolic activity in frontal and occipital areas during reading tasks. The confluence of the Flowers et al. (1991) work with the Gross-Glenn et al. (1991) study suggests that there is a different physiological activation pattern of the brain in individuals with dyslexia compared to that of nondisabled readers. The postmortem neuroanatomy and the electrophysiology and neuroimaging findings just discussed suggest that there are significant neural organization differences between individuals with dyslexia and nondisabled readers and that these differences are not restricted to just traditional language centers of the brain.

As the above review implies, the individual with learning disabilities has a variety of underlying neurobiologic irregularities and/or abnormalities. Given these structural and physiological differences, along with known brain–behavior relationships, the neuropsychological examination between individuals with and without learning disabilities also should demonstrate significant differences. Such neuropsychological differences will be discussed below.

Neuropsychological Test Findings in Adults with Dyslexia

The topic of a neuropsychological test profile of the adult with dyslexia has been addressed by only a few studies as of this writing (Finucci, Whitehouse, Isaacs, & Childs, 1984; Mattis, French, & Rapin, 1975; Miles, 1986), and there are even fewer neuropsychological studies addressing the general area of learning disabilities in adults (see Spreen, 1989a, 1989b). Most of the work in this area has focused on children with learning disabilities (Gaddes, 1985). Fortunately, the topic of adult learning disorders recently has received attention. For example, Felton, Naylor, and Wood (1990) conducted one of the most comprehensive and rigorous studies of adults with dyslexia. In that study they examined 115 adults with well-documented childhood dyslexia. A comprehensive battery of neuropsychological tests was administered that included standardized tests of memory, visual–perceptual functioning, and various language and attention measures. In comparison to nondisabled controls, the adult subjects with dyslexia tended to perform more poorly on almost all of the neuropsychological measures. However, once intelligence and socioeconomic status were covaried and statistically controlled for, only rapid naming, phonologic awareness, and nonword reading were found to be significantly discriminating measures. In a separate longitudinal study with children, Badian, McAnulty, Duffy, and Als (1990) demonstrated that errors in phonological processing and finger localization were the best predictors for the presence and persistence of dyslexia over time. This finding, combined with those of the Felton et al. (1990) study, indicates that these phonological processing deficits are expressed early and persist into adulthood in the individual with dyslexia. DeRenzi and Lucchelli (1990) also demonstrated diminished memory performance in an individual with a reading disability. It is possible that phonological processing deficits combined with certain select deficits in memory functioning may be critical factors in certain persistent reading disorders.

In similar work, O'Donnell, Romero, and Leicht (1990) compared adults with learning disabilities with head-injured patients who were matched on IQ and gender. The adults with learning disabilities were so classified if they had a prior history of learning disorder in childhood (i.e., WRAT achievement score more than or equal to 1 standard deviation below IQ). This study also found that the group with learning disabilities did not differ from the head-injury group, and both demonstrated deficits on naming, pronunciation, and sentence interpretation. This research confirms what has been postulated by previous research (see Horn, O'Donnell, & Leicht, 1988): that there are significant neuropsychological differences between adults with learning disabilities and adults without learning deficits. The deficits tend to be somewhat nonspecific; yet, when one controls for intelligence, educational background, and some socioeconomic status variables, deficits appear to be restricted (as would be expected) to the language domain in individuals with dyslexia. From a neuropsychological perspective, such findings have implications for involvement of the left cerebral hemisphere. Yet, it is clear from the neuroanatomic and neurophysiologic research previously discussed that the neurobiologic underpinnings are not purely lateralized. Thus, some of the lateralization implications of neuropsychological research may be related to output characteristics on particular neuropsychological measures, rather than a truly lateralized deficit.

This concept of some degree of nonspecific, yet left-hemisphere–oriented, dysfunction has been supported by the recent work of Kinsbourne, Rufo, Gamzu, Palmer, and Berliner (1991), who examined a group of adults with "severe" dyslexia (reading achievement levels 2 standard deviations below a derived expected "normal" score) and compared them to age-, sex-, IQ-, and socioeconomic status–matched "recovered dyslexics" and controls on a variety of neuropsychological measures. Their findings could be grouped into four major categories: (1) adults with dyslexia demonstrating impaired verbal learning and memory, with those having the more severe form of dyslexia demonstrating the greatest impairment in verbal acquisition and retention; (2) adults with dyslexia displaying a deficient automatization of language subprocesses, such as that tapped by word fluency tasks; (3) adults with dyslexia exhibiting deficits in certain nonverbal functions, such as temporal order judgments, requiring resolution of sequential inputs cross-hemispherically; and (4) adults with dyslexia who were found to be deficient in dexterity wherein there was a deficient performance on the right body side on tasksof sequential finger and foot movements. The observation that adults with dyslexia are impaired on a variety of neuropsychological measures that are not specific only to reading implicates a nonspecific (rather than discrete) residual neurologic deficit. Furthermore, the observation that many of the deficit areas of performance are left-hemisphere–mediated has implications for more widespread left- or dominant-hemisphere dysfunction.

Problematic Issues in the Neurobiology and Neuropsychology of Adult Learning Disability

From the discussion presented above it is evident that in individuals in whom significant learning deficits persist into adulthood, underlying cerebral structure and function subserving language/learning abilities are either abnormal or organized differently compared to that of non–learning-disabled individuals. How is this reconciled with cases of considerable plasticity wherein an individual "recovers" from a significant developmental defect or abnormality? For example, Figure 11.3 depicts the CT scan of a 13-year-old girl in whom much of the occipital lobe is missing, bilaterally, secondary to surgical removal of an occipital encephalocele when this child was 4 days old. Despite this enormous bilateral defect affecting both visual cortical areas, this child developed

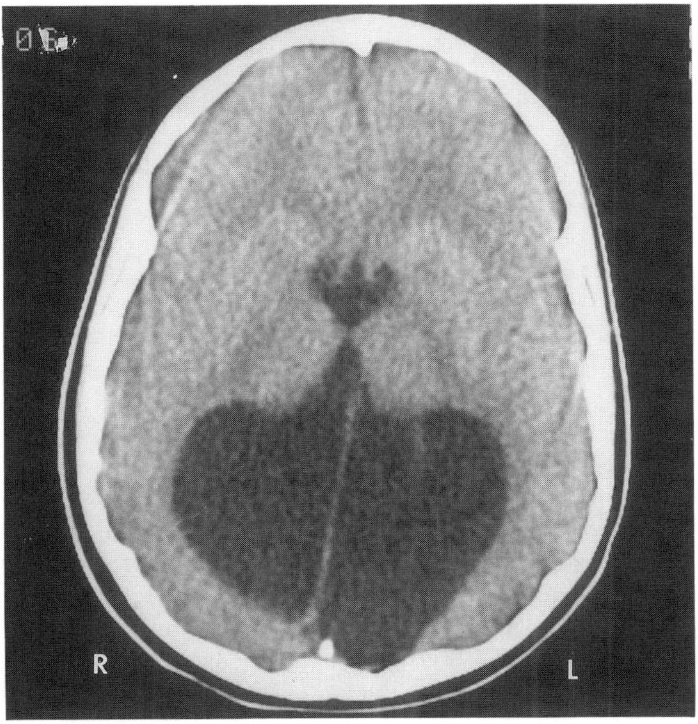

Figure 11.3 Horizontal CT scan (as if the reader were looking down on top of the subject's head) of a 13-year-old female who at 4 days of age had a large occipital encephalocele (congenital gap in the back of the head wherein part of the brain extruded into a sac) removed, which included occipital tissue. The CT demonstrates bilateral porencephaly (cavitation in the brain where the ventricle [the dark area] extends to the surface of cerebral cortex) with marked enlargement of the posterior horns bilaterally. There also appears to be agenesis of the corpus callosum. Despite the prominent visual cortical defect, the patient was capable of reading at above grade level (12th grade) and had a verbal intellectual quotient in the bright normal range (VIQ 117). Because of the visual dysgnosia she could not do the performance tests on the WISC-R but, as indicated, had no difficulty with reading. This is a case that demonstrates remarkable plasticity in the brain of a child with marked structural abnormalities that "should have" affected reading ability.

normal reading ability. In fact, when she was tested at 13 years of age, her word recognition was at the high school level (she was in the seventh grade). This represents an amazing case of cerebral plasticity and runs counter to what would be predicted concerning a permanent deficit and lack of plasticity in the adult individual with LD.

Another problematic issue for adult learning disability is the coexistence and higher frequency of learning disability with other disorders, in particular, attention-deficit/hyperactivity disorder (ADHD) and various neuropsychiatric disorders. As with learning disabilities, ADHD was once thought to be a childhood disorder (Nussbaum & Bigler, 1990). However, it is now well documented that ADHD may persist into adulthood (Zametkin et al., 1990). Each of these problematic issues will be addressed.

Learning Disabilities and Issues in Neural Plasticity

As indicated by the neuroimaging, electrophysiological, and neuropsychological studies just reviewed, the deficit in adult learning disorders is presumed to be permanent. However, in many childhood disorders of learning, the problem may be one of developmental delay, with improvement occurring over time so that a permanent neurologic deficit does not result. Also, it may be the case that some children with developmental delay or even early brain injury/damage may exhibit considerable plasticity despite the permanency of abnormal brain development or actual structural damage to the brain (Satz, 1990). This type of plasticitymost likely occurs via corollary brain systems taking over function, some form of synaptic reorganization, or new neural systems typically unrelated to a given function taking over that function (e.g., a sensory region taking over some aspects of motor function). There are some remarkable case studies of neural plasticity (see Bigler, Lowe, & Yeo, 1989).

In some cases of early brain injury and neural plasticity it may be better to have a large insult to the CNS rather than a subtle one (Kolb, 1989). Large lesions may "force" neural structures and systems into a different type of reorganization, whereas the more subtle deficits seen with learning disability may not. For example, Figure 11.4 presents another remarkable case of neural plasticity in a child with virtually no left cerebral hemisphere, yet normal intellectual and academic/language development (see Table 11.1). In contrast, Figure 11.5 depicts a "normal" MRI scan of a child with severe learning disabilities that demonstrates no lesion or area of "brain damage" (although there is a reversed asymmetry present) or any type of gross abnormality. In these two very contrasting cases, one child has a massive structural deficit wherein all traditional language centers of the left hemisphere are absent, yet develops "normal" reading and language ability (see Figure 11.4). Oppositely, the other child exhibits no gross abnormality, but has a severe learning disability (see Figure 11.5).

The question regarding neural plasticity is, why does it not work in all cases? What is unique about the neural substrate deficits in learning disability remaining in adulthood that do not permit neural restructuring

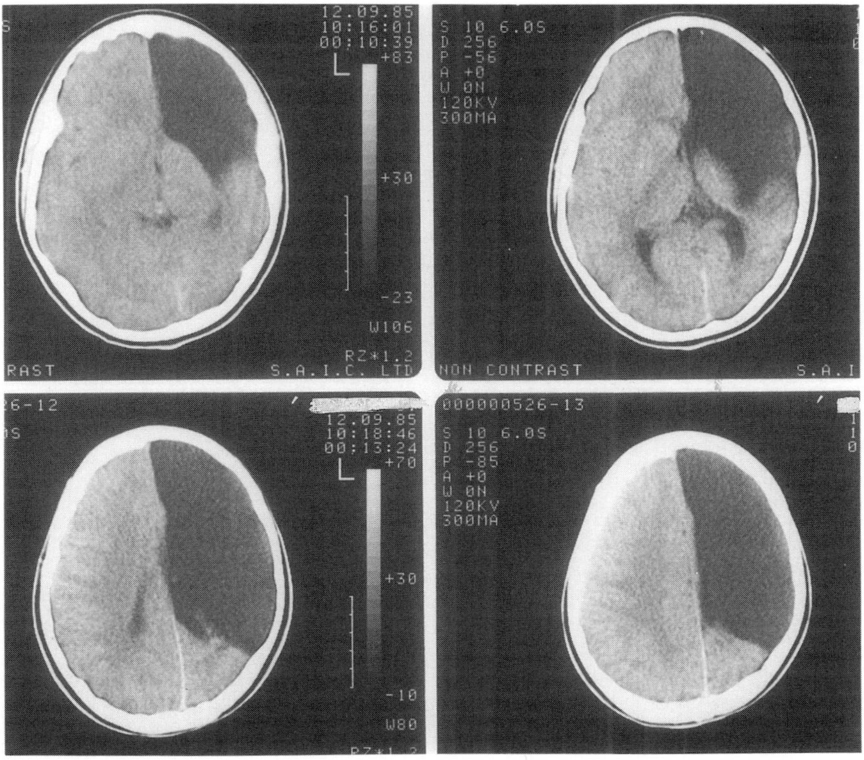

Figure 11.4 Horizontal CT scan demonstrating an enormous structural defect (dark area) in the left hemisphere (note that the picture is taken in the radiological plane, where left is on the pictorial right). This scan demonstrates complete absence of the left frontal lobe along with most of the left parietal and temporal regions. Despite such marked defects, language function developed normally, including reading, spelling, and expressive language abilities (see Table 11.1). From "Case Studies in Cerebral Plasticity" by E. Bigler and R. Naugle, 1985, *International Journal of Clinical Neuropsychology, 7.*

or reprogramming to compensate for the deficit? Obviously, in cases of persistent learning disability, neural plasticity is either absent or incompletely expressed.

In reviewing Galaburda's work, it appears that in the dyslexic brain, because of aberrant neural interconnections and a failure to develop normal asymmetries, there is a greater specialization in one brain region, the brain no longer processes certain aspects of verbal function in a normal fashion, and the brain does not display some type of intrinsic mechanism for compensation (see Galaburda et al., 1990). Galaburda (1990) suggested that the origin of these deficits may reside, in part, in an immunologic attack on the brain in utero.

TABLE 11.1
Intellectual and Academic Performance in a Child with a Massive Left-Hemisphere Porencephalic Cyst

	Wechsler Preschool and Primary Scale of Intelligence		Wechsler Intelligence Scale for Children–Revised	
	4 years 4 months	5 years 2 months	6 years 2 months	7 years 9 months
Verbal IQ	102	100	105	98
Performance IQ	100	89	98	98
Full Scale IQ	101	94	101	98
Wide Range Achievement Test				
Reading grade level	N.1[a]	1.0	1.3	4.4
Spelling grade level	N.8[a]	K.0	1.4	4.1
Arithmetic grade level	P.8[a]	K.7	K.4	2.7

[a]Based on norms for 5-year-olds.

For the adult who is truly learning disabled, the implications are that the CNS abnormalities are permanent, that there will not be sufficient plasticity within those systems to bring level of function into the normal range, and that these underlying deficits can be manifested in abnormal neurologic and neuropsychological patterns on tests sensitive to assessing cerebral dysfunction. This also implies that the CNS abnormalities will impose an upper limit or ceiling on what "recovery" of function can take place, in terms of both direct compensatory and retraining methods.

ADHD and Learning Disability

In children, learning disabilities often coexist with attention-deficit/hyperactivity disorder (Dykman & Ackerman, 1991; Murphy & Hicks-Stewart, 1991). Silver (1990) eloquently argued that although effective attention is essential to learning, disorders of attention do not equate with learning disorders or vice versa. As Silver stated, learning disability is a "neurologically based disorder that interferes with the necessary psychological processes needed to learn" (p. 397), but disorders of attention and/or hyperactivity do not represent a learning disability per se but are "related," "neurologically-based" disorders that affect the "individual's availability for learning" (p. 397). It is well documented that learning

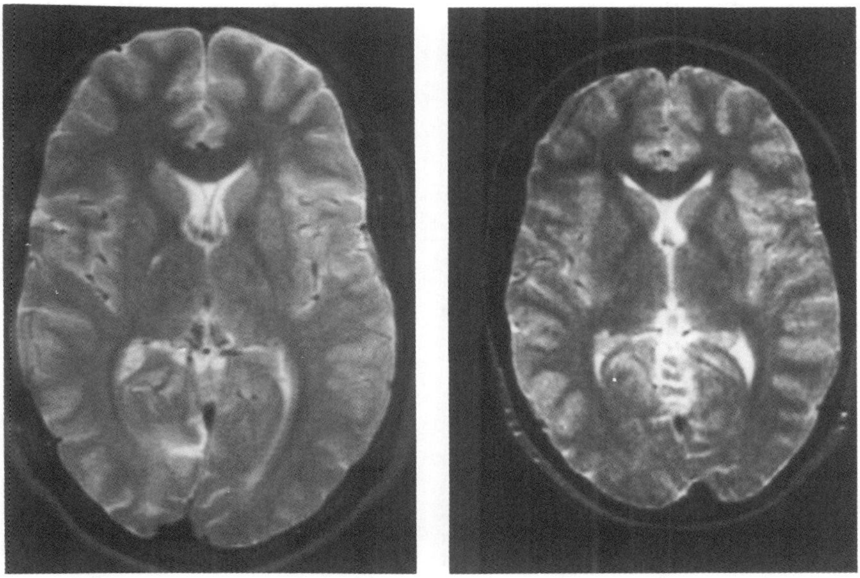

Figure 11.5 Horizontal MRI scans from a nondisabled reader (left) and a reader with dyslexia (right). These views are in the radiological plane, where left is on the viewer's right. The scan on the left depicts the "normal" hemispheric asymmetry, wherein the posterior aspect of the left hemisphere is larger. The opposite asymmetry is noted in the image on the right in the reader with dyslexia. Both individuals were right-handed. This illustration is representative of the fact that in most individuals with dyslexia no gross anatomic abnormalities or markers are found in structural imaging studies. The issue of abnormal symmetry in dyslexia remains a controversial topic (see Jernigan et al., 1991) but is clearly evident in this individual with dyslexia.

disorders and attention-deficit/hyperactivity disorder may coexist, and each may have a negative impact on the other (Bigler, 1990). Also, it now is well documented that the ADHD syndrome, or at least many of its constituent elements, persists into adulthood (Nussbaum & Bigler, 1990; Wender, 1987). This, too, has implications for "permanency."

ADHD has its own unique neural substrates that differ from, and may not overlap, what has been discussed about learning disorders. As with learning disability research, in the past there was considerable speculation as to what might be the neurobiological substrates of ADHD, but only recently has ADHD research demonstrated direct biologic linkage. To date, Lou and colleagues (Lou, Henriksen, Bruhn, Borner, & Nielsen, 1989) and Zametkin and colleagues (Zametkin et al., 1990) have come the closest to demonstrating physiological and metabolic abnormalities in individuals with ADHD (see Figure 11.6). This research suggests that diminished neuronal activity at the nigrostriatal and frontal cortical levels

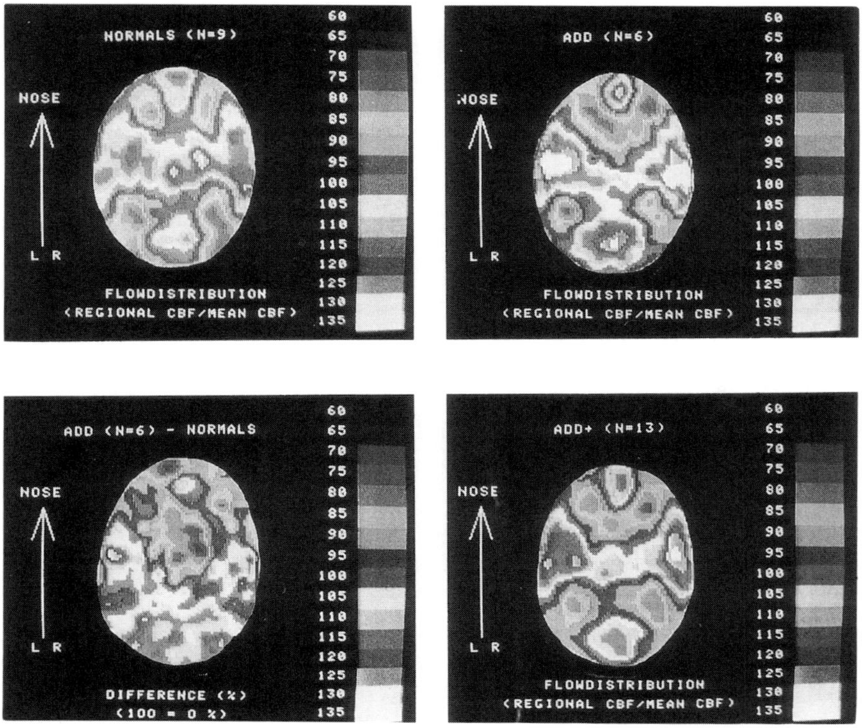

Figure 11.6 Top left, average regional cerebral blood flow (rCBF) distribution as determined by Xenon 133 inhalation and emission tomography in nine control individuals with no known neurological or learning disorder. This illustration represents the composite rCBF depicting the normal distribution of cerebral blood flow at rest. Top right, average flow distribution in six individuals with ADHD (age range 7 to 11 years). Bottom left, difference between mean flow distributions of ADHD group and control group. Bottom right, average flow distribution in ADHD with other neuropsychologic and neurologic symptoms (ADHD+) group consisting of 13 patients ranging in age from 7 to 19 years. These results suggest that in ADHD the area in striatal regions of the brain (caudate nucleus and putamen/globus pallidus complex) is hypoperfused (i.e., underactive)—depicted by the shading in the central part of the bottom left figure—and the primary sensorimotor areas were hyperperfused (i.e., overactivated)—depicted in the lateral aspects of the bottom right figure. From "Striatal Dysfunction in Attention Deficit and Hyperkinetic Disorder" by H. Lou, L. Henriksen, P. Bruhn, H. Børner, and J. Nielsen, 1989, *Archives of Neurology, 46,* p. 50. Copyright © 1989, American Medical Association. Reprinted by permission.

would be consistent with theoretical assumptions that implicated brainstem and frontal hypoarousal, and it also agrees with pharmacological models wherein stimulant medication improves attention and related cognitive functions in ADHD.

As with learning disorders in children, the majority of children with ADHD demonstrate a decrease in symptoms with age, implicating a maturation factor as part of the disorder. However, there is definitely a subgroup that displays persistence of symptoms throughout adolescence and into adulthood (Wender, 1987). In such individuals it would be presumed that permanent neurobiologic abnormalities were at the basis of the disorder. As mentioned above, ADHD and learning disability often coexist in children. This also appears to be the case with many adult learning disorders; that is, the adult with LD may have residual deficits in attention and related cognitive functions (Wender, 1987).

Neuropsychological Assessment

Because neuropsychological assessment techniques provide the most sensitive and comprehensive methods for detecting cerebral dysfunction based on behavioral and cognitive measures, the neuropsychological assessment process is well suited to examining the adult with learning disabilities. Contemporary neuropsychological assessment methods that might be utilized in the evaluation of adult learning disabilities will be discussed below.

Much of neuropsychological assessment is based on a discrepancy model, with the area of deficit performance deviating in a negative direction (i.e., worse performance) from other areas of intact or normal function or from some normed reference group (Bigler, 1988; Lezak, 1983; Matarazzo, 1990). Over the past two decades a large body of clinical neuropsychometric data has accumulated and established a normative data base for motor coordination, perceptual–motor functioning, sensory–perceptual processing, language, memory, intellectual and academic functioning, and a host of other cognitive variables (Bigler, 1988; Lezak, 1983). These data are then used for comparison purposes: The individual's performance is compared to normative data and expected levels of function given some other variable, such as IQ, educational background, or vocational status. In neuropsychology, as in most assessment disciplines, a significant discrepancy is typically thought to be something greater than 1.0 to 1.5 standard deviations from some expected level of performance. With neuropsychological assessment, when a particular performance is significantly below expectations, the implications are that a brain deficit may underlie the impaired performance. Similarly, with some neuropsychological measures, there are cutoff scores that typically reflect the impaired performance of one with brain damage or dysfunction. Thus, using the adult acquired–brain-injury model, damage to the left temporal and parietal cortical areas in a right-hand–dominant individual typically disrupts language functions in the reading, spelling, and handwriting domains. For example, the patient depicted in Figure 11.7 and Tables 11.2 and 11.3 sustained a serious traumatic injury (gunshot wound) to the left temporal lobe that resulted in a pronounced

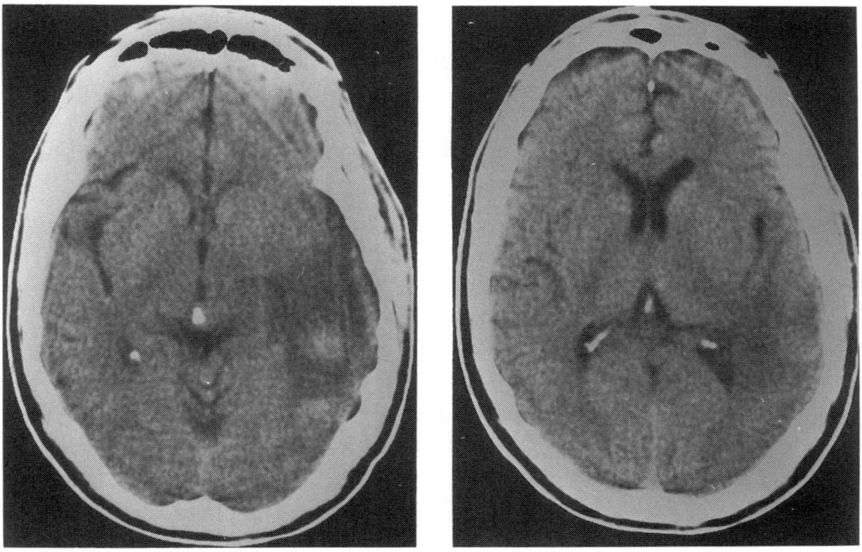

Figure 11.7 Horizontal (as if looking down on top of head) CT images in a 51-year-old male. These views are in the radiologic plane, where left is on the viewer's right. The dark shading in the mid to posterior aspect of the left hemisphere indicates damaged (necrotic) brain tissue as a result of a focal traumatic injury (gunshot wound) to the left temporal region of the brain. This resulted in an acquired dyslexia and spelling dyspraxia that are often indistinguishable from what is observed in adults with developmental dyslexia. This patient's neuropsychological data are presented in Tables 11.2 and 11.3. The reader should compare and contrast this patient's performance with that obtained from the three adults with residual reading learning disabilities as presented in Figures 11.8 and 11.9 and Tables 11.4 and 11.5.

loss of academic ability in reading and spelling but spared, in general, handwriting, visuomotor copying, arithmetic ability, and most other aspects of general cognitive functioning. Accordingly, this would be a case of acquired dyslexia. As will be demonstrated below, and as has been previously discussed (see Kinsbourne et al., 1991; O'Donnell, Kurtz, & Ramanaiah, 1983; O'Donnell et al., 1990), there are many close similarities between acquired dyslexia and residual developmental dyslexia in the adult. These similarities will be demonstrated in the cases presented below, as the above case of traumatically induced dyslexia is compared and contrasted with residual, so-called "developmental" dyslexia in three cases of adult learning disability.

In cases of pure learning disability one does not expect to find gross anatomic abnormalities on brain imaging (see Figure 11.5). However, when significant discrepancies in academic performance occur in the

TABLE 11.2
Intellectual and Achievement Results in a Patient Who Sustained a Traumatic Brain Injury to the Left Temporal-Parietal Cortex

Intellectual	
Wechsler Adult Intelligence Scale–Revised	
Full Scale IQ	97
Verbal IQ	94
Information	8
Digit Span	10
Vocabulary	7
Arithmetic	12
Comprehension	9
Similarities	6
Performance IQ	
Picture Completion	11
Picture Arrangement	8
Block Design	9
Object Assembly	8
Digit Symbol	8
Achievement	
Wide Range Achievement Test–Revised	
Reading	
Standard Score	69
Percentile	2
Grade Equivalent	4B
Spelling	
Standard Score	77
Percentile	6
Grade Equivlaent	5B
Arithmetic	
Standard Score	111
Percentile	77
Grade Equivalent	12B

context of "normal" functions in all other areas, the neuropsychological implication is that specific, and potentially focal and lateralized, neurologic deficits may underlie the learning disorder (see Kinsbourne et al., 1991). Accordingly, if the deficits are in reading, spelling, and handwriting, based on the model from adult acquired brain injury (see Figure 11.7), involvement of the dominant-hemisphere temporal-parietal regions would be implicated. Several studies (Kinsbourne et al., 1991; Lawson & Inglis, 1989; McCue, Shelly, & Goldstein, 1986; O'Donnell et al., 1983; Spreen, 1989a, 1989b) examining adults with learning disabilities have demonstrated lower verbal abilities, such as verbal intellectual functioning below performance on the Wechsler Adult Intelligence Scale (Lawson & Inglis, 1989), or diminished verbal fluency (Kinsbourne

TABLE 11.3
Neuropsychological Test Results in a Patient[a] Who Sustained a Traumatic Brain Injury to the Left Temporal-Parietal Cortex

Measure	Raw Score	Rating Standard Score	Scaled Score[c]	Clinical Rating
Motor				
Finger Oscillation				
Right	40		8	Low normal
Left	40		8	Low normal
Strength of Grip				
Right	42		10	Normal
Left	40		9	Normal
Sensory Perceptual Extinction				
Right	0		—	Normal
Left	1		—	Normal
Finger Graphesthesia				
Right	0		—	Normal
Left	0		—	Normal
Finger Gnosis				
Right	0		—	Normal
Left	0		—	Normal
Stereognosis				
Right	0		—	Normal
Left	0		—	Normal
Language[b] (Reitan-Indiana)				
Verbal		4[b]	2	Abnormal
Spatial		1[b]		Normal
Memory				
Wechsler Memory Scale				
Memory Quotient		89		Low average
Logical Memory	4		—	Abnormal
Visual Memory	13		—	Normal
Paired Associate	6		—	Abnormal
Rey Auditory Verbal Learning Test				
Trial I	2		—	Abnormal
Trial IV	6		—	Abnormal
Interference Recall	1		—	Abnormal
Recognition Recall	8			Borderline abnormal
Benton Visual Retention Test Errors	3		—	Borderline normal
General Cognition				
Raven's Coloured Progressive Matrices	32		—	Normal
Trail Making				
A	41		7	Borderline normal
B	94		7	Borderline normal

[a]Age: 45; Gender: male; education: high school; handedness: right.
[b]Score based on the Russell, Neuringer, and Goldstein (1970) scoring method.
[c]Scaled score rating based on the comprehensive norms established by Heaton, Grant, and Matthews (1991).

et al., 1991), intact nonverbal memory and problem-solving ability but impaired abilities in auditory discrimination tasks, and other verbal mediated functions (see DeRenzi & Lucchelli, 1990). Many aspects of these patterns are consistent with what is observed in childhood learning disorders (see Rourke, 1985; Rourke, Bakker, Fisk, & Strang, 1983) and implicate dysfunction in the temporal-parietal cortical areas of the dominant hemisphere. However, as previously mentioned, Kinsbourne et al.'s research suggests that the deficits extend beyond the boundaries of the temporoparietal cortex of the dominant hemisphere.

As for specific examples of the performance of adults with learning disabilities on neuropsychological measures, Tables 11.4 and 11.5 and Figures 11.8 and 11.9 present neuropsychological data on three adults with significant reading and spelling disabilities. All three individuals had no history of neurologic disease or disorder, and Case 3 had a negative MRI scan of the brain. All had been diagnosed as reading impaired in childhood and received special education treatment under the label of learning disability. However, all three clearly demonstrated the typical neuropsychological deficits associated with persistent reading and spelling disorder (see Lawson & Inglis, 1989; McCue et al., 1986; O'Donnell et al., 1983; Spreen, 1989a, 1989b). For example, as a group these three adults with residual reading/spelling learning disability displayed subtle motor findings wherein the dominant–nondominant-hand performance on finger oscillation and grip strength did not exhibit superiority of the dominant hand. (Typically, the dominant hand is 8% to 12% faster and stronger on finger oscillation, grip-strength measures, and other motor measures of dominant-hand performance; see Kinsbourne et al., 1991.) This type of finding has been interpreted as having implications for dominant-hemisphere "inefficiency" or a deficit in normal hemispheric specialization (i.e., left-hemisphere dominance for language) (see Gaddes, 1985, for a discussion). Sensory–perceptual studies likewise demonstrated subtle laterality of errors on the dominant hand in making tactile discrimination, particularly on finger graphesthesic testing. (This type of test requires the individual to perceive numbers or letters through the touch sense only, without seeing or hearing the letters or numbers.) It should be noted that Kinsbourne et al.'s research indicated that this is not a universal finding in adults, even though this deficit may have been present in childhood. Language testing revealed normal expressive language; that is, articulation and oral–facial movements were normal, but distinctly impaired reading and spelling was found and, in some cases, associated graphomotor deficits. Memory testing demonstrated normal visual memory but impaired sequential auditory processing (see performance on logical memory recall of paragraph information on Wechsler Memory Scale, Wechsler, 1945). Rote verbal memory was not affected (see normal performance on paired-associate word recall of the Wechsler Memory Scale and the Rey Auditory Verbal Learning Test [Rey, 1964], a

TABLE 11.4
WAIS-R and WRAT-R Results for Three Adults with Learning Disabilities

	Case 1 Age: 19	Case 2 Age: 30	Case 3 Age: 22	Mean
WAIS-R Results				
Full Scale IQ	95	77	99	90.3
Verbal IQ Score	85	72	97	84.6
Information	5	5	6	5.3
Digit Span	8	4	12	8.0
Vocabulary	5	5	9	6.3
Arithmetic	6	6	8	6.6
Comprehension	7	5	15	9.0
Similarities	10	5	7	7.3
Performance IQ Score	110	90	100	100.0
Picture Completion	11	9	11	10.3
Picture Arrangement	10	8	13	10.3
Block Design	13	10	13	12.0
Object Assembly	12	8	10	10.0
Digit Symbol	9	7	5	7.0
WRAT-R Results				
Reading				
Grade Equivalent	5B	C3	6E	—
Standard Score	70	52	74	65.3
Spelling				
Grade Equivalent	3B	C3	3B	—
Standard Score	61	57	60	59.3
Arithmetic				
Grade Equivalent	9B	4B	8E	—
Standard Score	89	58	88	78.3

Note. WAIS-R = Wechsler Adult Intelligence Scale–Revised; WRAT-R = Wide Range Achievement Test–Revised.

repeated-trials, 15-word list). Lastly, as is often the case with adults with a verbal learning disability, these adults had no difficulty with nonverbal visual–spatial processing, such as that tapped by the Raven Coloured Progressive Matrices (Raven, 1965). In comparing/contrasting these deficits in adult learning disability with those observed in the patient with traumatic brain injury depicted in Figure 11.7 and Tables 11.2 and 11.3, it is apparent that, in terms of neuropsychologic deficit performance, the patients are quite similar—again, the implication being that adults with reading/spelling disabilities share some common neurologic substrates with those whose reading/spelling deficits are acquired. In the case of these three adults, the locus of cerebral dysfunction based on neuropsychological test results appears to reside in frontal-temporal-parietal cortical areas of the left cerebral hemisphere.

TABLE 11.5
Neuropsychological Measure for Three Adults with Learning Disabilities

	Case 1	Case 2	Case 3	Mean
Motor				
Finger Oscillation				
Right	41	52	53	48.6
Left	37.0	49	54	46.6
Strength of Grip				
Right	55.1	48	51	51.3
Left	52.1	47	51	50.3
Sensory–Perceptual				
Extinction[a]				
Right	1	0	0	0.3
Left	0	0	0	0.0
Finger Graphesthesia				
Right	4	2	2	2.6
Left	1	2	0	1.0
Finger Gnosis				
Right	1	0	0	0.3
Left	0	0	0	0.0
Stereognosis				
Right	0	0	0	0.0
Left	0	0	0	0.0
Language (Reitan-Indiana)[a]				
Verbal	3	4	3	3.3
Spatial	1	3	1	1.6
Memory				
Wechsler Memory Scale				
MQ	92	83	97	90.6
Logical Memory	7(7)	3.5(4)	11(9.5)	7.2(6.8)
Logical Memory	13(13)	10(10)	13(13)	12(12)
Paired Associate	14.5(6/4)	17(6/3)	13(6/4)	14.8(6/3.6)
Rey Auditory Verbal Learning Test				
Trial I	6/15	4/15	6/15	
Trial IV	13/15	8/15	13/15	
Interference Recall	11/15	7/15	12/15	
Recognition Recall	15/15	12/15	15/15	
Benton Visual Retention Test				
Errors	1	NA	1	
General Cognition				
Raven CPM	34	33	34	
Trail Making				
A	29	49	50	
B	61	86	81	

Note. MQ = memory quotient; CPM = Coloured Progressive Matrices.
[a]Score based on the Russell et al. (1970) scoring method. A rating score of S1, according to Reitan and Wolfson (1985) administration protocol, is within the normal range when it is ≤1. A maximum score is 5.

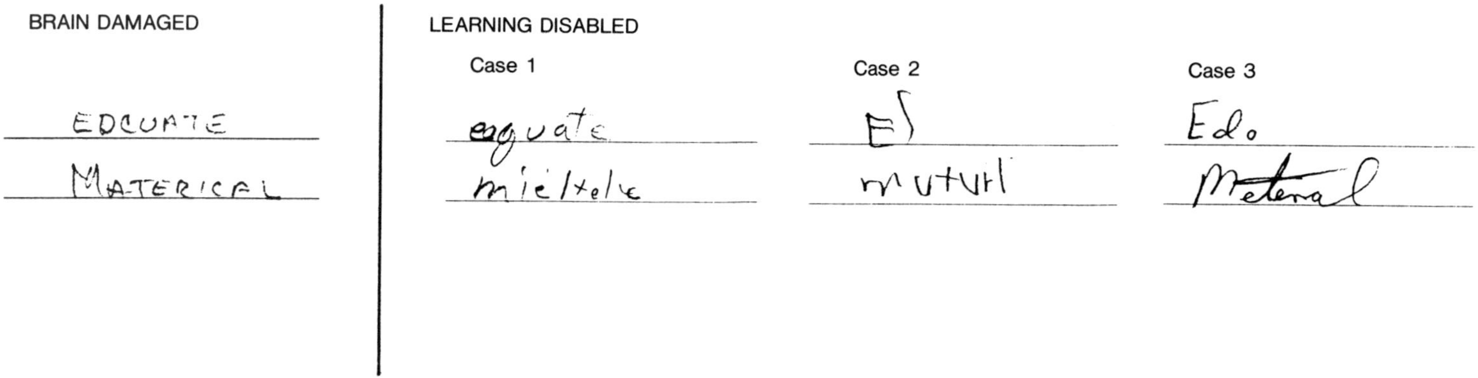

Figure 11.8 An example of spelling errors by the individual with brain damage discussed in Figure 11.7 is compared with spelling errors by the three individuals with learning disabilities (see Tables 11.4 and 11.5). The word for the top line is *educate* and for the bottom line, *material.* These words are numbers 9 and 10 on the Wide Range Achievement Test–Revised. Note that the errors in spelling are similar for the individual with traumatically induced brain injury and individuals with residual developmental reading–spelling disorder.

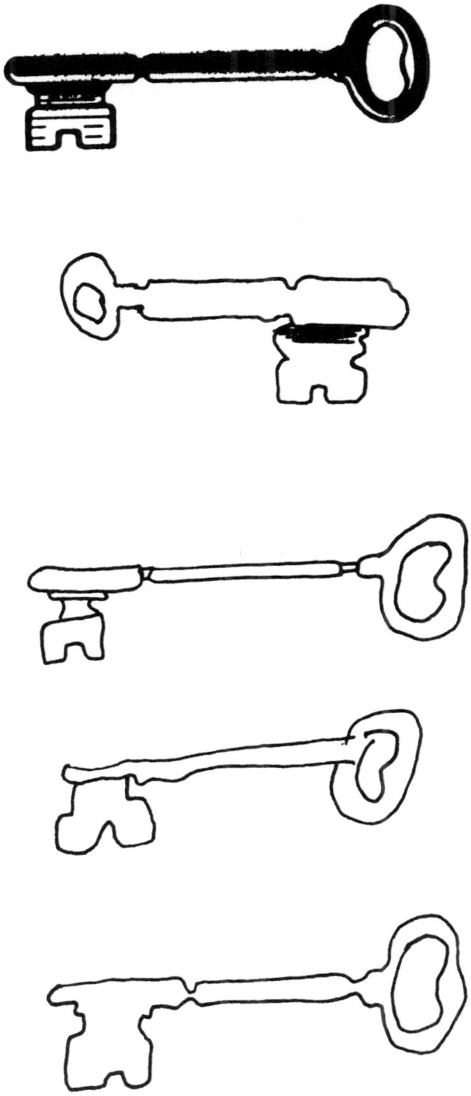

Figure 11.9 A comparison of graphomotor copying. The top figure is the stimulus figure from the Reitan-Indiana Aphasia Screening Test (Reitan & Wolfson, 1985). The reversed drawing of the key is from the individual discussed in Figure 11.7. The bottom three drawings are taken from the three adults with learning disabilities. Note that mild copying errors are present with left temporal lobe brain injury and in adult dyslexia even though visuomotor copying, per se, is not considered a language task.

One cautionary note is in order. Most of the learning disability research discussed in this chapter has focused on dyslexia. The case examples above all involve either an acquired (Figure 11.7) or developmental (Figures 11.8 and 11.9) dyslexia. Whether such neurobiologic abnormalities exist in other disorders of learning remains to be seen. However, the acquired syndromes involving visual–spatial deficits (typically involving a posterior lesion of the nondominant hemisphere) appear to be quite similar to developmental syndromes of visual–spatial impairment (see Rourke, Young, & Leenaars, 1989; Tranel, Hall, Olson, & Tranel, 1987). Accordingly, it is anticipated that neurobiologic deficits similar to those that have been identified in dyslexia will be identified in nondyslexic learning disorders.

Remediation/Treatment of Adult Learning Disorders

By their very definition, adult learning disorders suggest that traditional treatment modalities have been ineffective in remediating the deficit; otherwise, there would not be such a permanency to the deficit. This also implies that even if some effective means were developed to treat adult learning disorders, the mere fact that there is some degree of "organic" permanency imposes an upper limit on recovery or remediation. Both of these statements are, in part, accurate.

The greatest degree of brain plasticity occurs in the immature nervous system. As discussed previously, some remarkable case studies have demonstrated considerable plasticity following early brain insult. For example, the child in Figure 11.3 has virtually nooccipital cortex yet has exceptional reading skills for her age. The mechanisms that are responsible for such remarkable restitution of function are not understood at this time. Obviously, in cases such as depicted in Figures 11.3 or 11.4, the original designated structure (occipital cortex in Figure 11.3 or left hemisphere in Figure 11.4) that typically controls such functions has been supplemented or supplanted by other structures typically not directly involved in that function. These case studies also have implications for the time sequence in "recovery" of function; that is, the earlier in childhood the better (see Kolb, 1989). However, this remains a very controversial topic.

Adult brain-injury patients with damage to language centers typically never recover function back to preinjury levels (see Figures 11.10 and 11.11), but they do display varying degrees of recovery of function. So there are some built-in compensatory mechanisms that allow recovery to take place. Speculation suggests that these recovery mechanisms act via several potential pathways: (a) the damaged system (although less

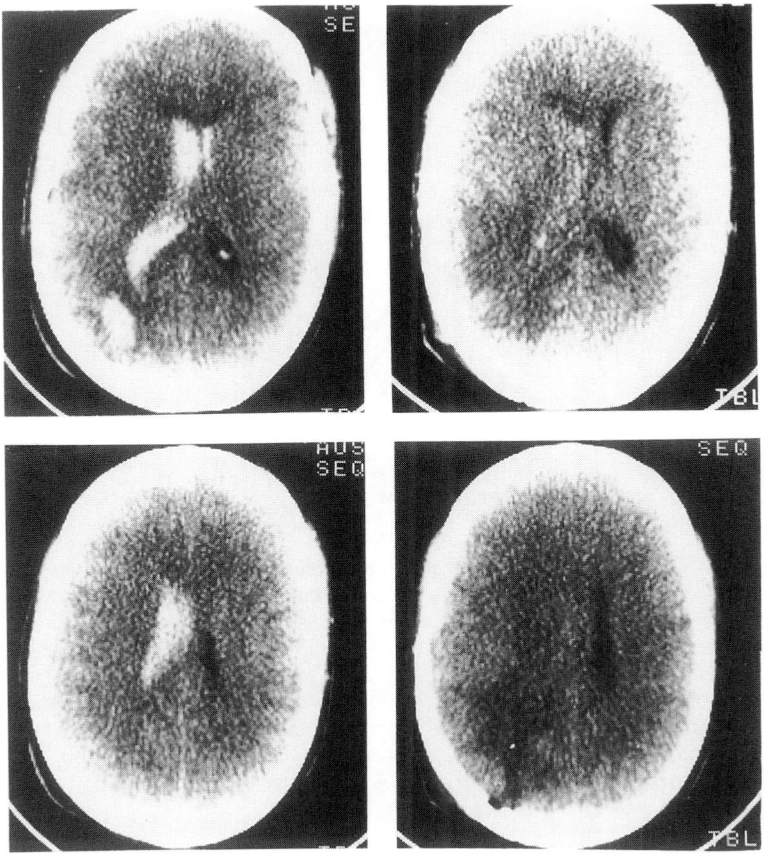

Figure 11.10 Horizontal (as if looking down on top of the head) CT in a 19-year-old college student who suffered a spontaneous rupture of an aneurysm. In these CT scans, left is on the viewer's left. The two scans in the left-hand column were taken on admission to the emergency room and depict blood (areas of white in the brain substance and ventricle) in the parietal-occipital area. The two scans in the right-hand column are at the same level as their left-column counterparts, but were taken 1 week later, following drainage of the cerebral hematoma. Note that most of the blood in the ventricle has been reabsorbed, but there are significant density changes (decreases) in the temporal-parietal-occipital areas of the dominant left hemisphere in this right-handed male. These density changes represent damaged brain tissue. As a consequence of this cerebrovascular accident, this patient became dyslexic and spelling dyspraxic. Initially, he displayed good spontaneous recovery of reading and spelling ability and actively participated in an intensive speech therapy program. By 6 months poststroke this college student was reading at the end–11th-grade level and spelling at the beginning–7th-grade level. Despite continued intensive language and academic therapies there was essentially no substantial improvement in reading or spelling (see Figure 11.11) over the next 24 months. This case demonstrates the permanency of brain injury effects on academic performance and their lack of response to traditional treatment methods.

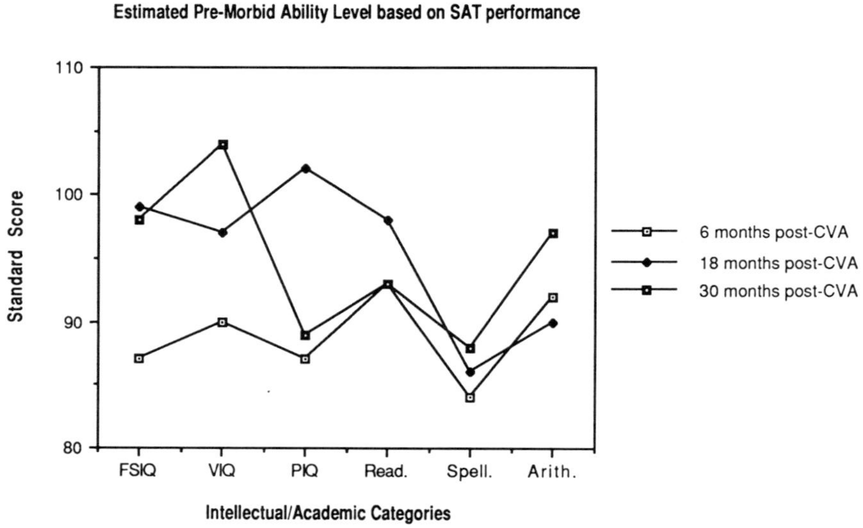

Figure 11.11 Graph depicting level of intellectual (Wechsler Adult Intelligence Scale–Revised; Wechsler, 1981) and academic (Wide Range Achievement Test–Revised; Jastak & Wilkinson, 1984) performance in the patient described in Figure 10 from 6 to 30 months poststroke. The premorbid IQ estimate (top horizontal line) is based on the patient's college SAT performance (82%). Note that, despite receiving intensive speech, cognitive, and academic therapies from the time of his stroke to 30 months poststroke, the patient's measured IQ never returns to premorbid level and there is little to no improvement in academic functioning. This case demonstrates the permanency of some brain-injury effects on academic abilities when critical language areas of the brain are affected.

efficient, it is still functioning); (b) collateral or secondary systems to the primary system taking over function; (c) other structures not directly involved in the original functions of the affected system but now taking over; or (d) compensatory systems that can approximate the same function via other systems (Bach-Y-Rita, 1990). Bach-Y-Rita demonstrated limited "recovery" of neuropsychologic function in patients that were paralyzed for 20 or more years. Thus, even the "damaged" nervous system has some capacity for recovery of function that exceeds the period of spontaneous recovery. Scheibel (1990) demonstrated significant neural plasticity in the aging nervous system, as well, thereby indicating some adaptive capacities of even the mature brain.

Applying the information gained from the brain injury as well as developmental model of neural plasticity, it appears that adults with learning disabilities are not necessarily doomed to an unalterable status as a result of these learning disabilities, but that it may take innovative and repetitive treatment strategies that, as Bach-Y-Rita (1990) would state, "unmask" inactive pathways or involve nonprimary pathways in a compensatory fashion. Along these lines, Duffy and McAnulty (1990) demonstrated electrophysiological changes that appeared to coincide with effective remediation of a prominent and persistent developmental dyslexia in a 12-year-old male. When the reading disorder was first detected at age 6, the child had augmented EEG theta, an abnormality, in the left temporal lobe that persisted through prepubescence. This type of theta irregularity has been seen with increased frequency in cases of pure dyslexia (see Figure 11.2) and implicates physiologic irregularities in dominant-hemisphere temporal lobe functioning. However, with the implementation of a comprehensive, and presumably multimodality, approach to treating the dyslexic condition at age 10, there was a steady decrease in theta that remained stable through age 12 (see Figure 11.12). Duffy and McAnulty's work suggests a dynamic and plastic relation between the brain and environment and that the more mature brain can display changes in response to therapies. Cautionary statements need to be made concerning their work, however, as it was only a case study. A large study

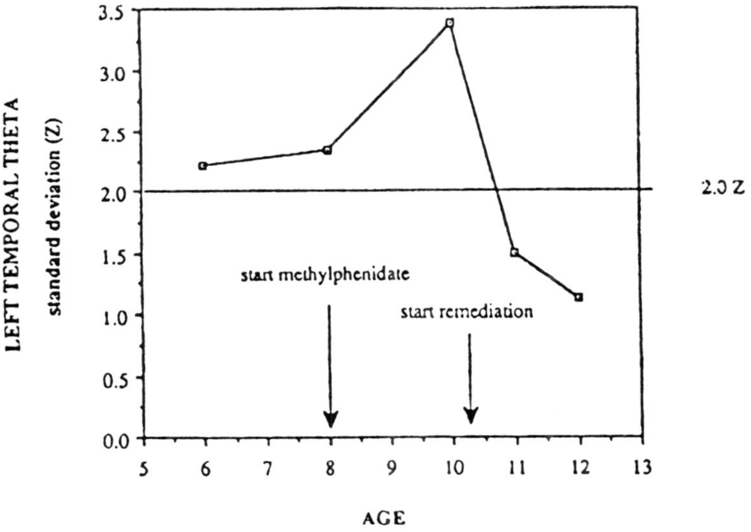

Figure 11.12 This figure shows the degree of deviation of left temporal theta (an electroencephalographic brain rhythm) from age-appropriate, normative control groups in units of standard deviation from age 6 to age 12. This boy with a condition dyslexia-plus, as defined by Duffy and McAnulty (1990), showed values above 2.0 standard deviations despite resource room schooling and methylphenidate (ages 6 to 10), both of which were ineffective in ameliorating his reading difficulty. Note the markedly diminished theta following transfer to a special school and successful remediation (ages 11 and 12). Reprinted with permission from *Neuropsychologia*, Vol. 2, F. Duffy and G. McAnulty, "Neurophysiological Heterogeneity and the Definition of Dyslexia: Preliminary Evidence for Plasticity," Copyright © 1990, Pergamon Press Ltd.

would be necessary before any final conclusions could be made, but their case study findings are most intriguing. Furthermore, this clinical observation is based on a child, not an adult. Thus, the implications for adult dyslexia and other types of learning disorders remain to be seen.

From Duffy and McAnulty's (1990) work, along with the recovery of function that has been observed in traumatic brain injury patients in response to cognitive rehabilitation therapies (see Prigatano, 1990), it appears that the key to improvement is a repetitive, multimodality approach. Obviously, many traditional educational programs and therapies have not worked with adults with learning disabilities. Innovative treatment techniques based on neurobiological assumptions underlying learning and learning disabilities are needed. This is an area that is begging for clinical research. One potentially promising method is that espoused by Bakker (see Bakker, Bouma, & Gardien, 1990). In this method a hemisphere is activated by tactile stimulation to the opposite body site (i.e., by tactually writing out letters or words on the fingers), and then a reading task is initiated. Following hemisphere activation, children in this study displayed improved text-reading accuracy. To date, this has not been tried with adults.

Neurobiologic Factors Influencing Psychosocial Functioning in the Adult with Learning Disabilities

Neuropsychological studies by Rourke and colleagues (Fuerst, Fisk, & Rourke, 1990; Rourke, 1985, 1989) have suggested a relationship between cognitive functioning and type and degree of psychosocial function/dysfunction in individuals with learning disabilities. The implication from this research is that the underlying CNS dysfunction that affects learning has a simultaneous, direct effect on personality and social function. Based on various brain-injury models, the neurobiologic determiners of human emotion are becoming better understood (see Cullum, 1989). Much of the past research on psychosocial functioning in the individual with learning disabilities has focused on self-esteem, failure, and personal rejection issues, along with a host of other psychosocial variables, as if the psychological adjustment problems were solely related to psychogenic or environmental factors. It now appears that the neurobiologic factors that induce learning impairments may be directly linked to the emotional/psychosocial problems, as well. An example of this can be found in Rourke's (1989) model of nonverbal learning disabilities and the relationship of nonverbal learning disabilities to suicide. Utilizing this model, Bigler (1989) reported several case studies of suicidal behavior in individuals with learning disabilities. Similarly, Townes et al. (1985) demonstrated a subgroup of adult individuals from a larger sample of psychiatric in-patients who manifested neuropsychological impairment and high levels of psychologic dysfunction, and who also had history of childhood learning disorders.

This entire area has not been studied with well-controlled prospective research designs; until that is done, there will be much speculation about common biologic factors as the basis of learning disability and emotional dysfunction in the adult. This will represent an important future challenge for neuropsychology and the field of learning disabilities.

Conclusions

Adults with learning disabilities have a neurologically based disorder. A variety of assessment techniques are now available for directly examining brain anatomy and physiology, and such techniques are providing the means to further establish the neurobiologic factors that underlie learning disabilities. Neuropsychological assessment techniques provide a means of identifying areas of cerebral dysfunction that may represent functional brain pathology in such adults. The neurobiologic impairments in adults with learning disabilities also may play a role in the emotional dysfunction that often coexists with learning disabilities.

12. Personal Perspectives

EDWARD A. POLLOWAY, ROSEL SCHEWEL,
AND JAMES R. PATTON

The chapters in this book have attempted to capture the flavor of the exciting directions being pursued in the relatively new field of learning disabilities in adulthood. The contributions have provided insight into a number of areas of concern within the field. While providing a sense of the state of the art, these chapters, individually and collectively, also emphatically point to future directions for research and service in postsecondary education, rehabilitative services, community adjustment, and neuropsychology.

Although we have endeavored to provide a thorough review of this field of study, this book is necessarily somewhat limited. For example, certainly, additional attention to life-span developmental models would serve to further develop the context within which we can better understand the adult with a learning disability. A more fine-grained analysis would afford a clearer picture of social relationships and, consequently, offer a perspective on how support systems of friends and family work to influence successful adjustment. Quality-of-life variables (e.g., life satisfaction) beyond the more apparent areas, such as employment, remain in

---

Reprinted, with changes, from "Learning disabilities in adulthood: Personal perspectives," by Edward A. Polloway, Rosel Schewel, and James R. Patton, *Journal of Learning Disabilities*, Vol. 25, 1992, pp. 520–522.

need of further discussion. The list of areas of inquiry that could have been added to the book is virtually boundless; nevertheless, the authors have clearly contributed to our efforts to ask the right questions and to pursue important answers.

As we reflect back on the chapters in this book as well as on our professional and personal interactions with adults who have learning disabilities, we realize how far we have collectively come—and how much more there is to be learned. Perhaps most striking is how much can be learned from persons who have grown up learning to come to grips with a disability. Certainly, each of the authors in this book has been influenced by that experience. It therefore seemed fitting to close out with some personal perspectives and reflections—not our own, but those persons' who have been identified as disabled, have been affected by our educational and community systems, and subsequently have been helped and/or hindered in their development. In order to do this, we drew on selected findings summarized in a paper that explored the challenges of learning disabilities in adulthood (Schewel, 1991).

Our effort to broaden our perspective on adults who have disabilities led Schewel (1991) to contact 51 persons who had been identified as learning disabled. Fifty of these persons reported that they had been placed in either a resource or self-contained classroom during their school years; one was not identified until adulthood. Twenty-three were between the ages of 18 and 23, 14 between the ages of 24 and 29, and 14 between the ages of 30 and 40.

This sample of adults with learning disabilities was secured in a nonrandom fashion through three sources. One county school district distributed our questionnaires to students who had completed their school LD program within the last 5 years. Other questionnaires were distributed to parents, teachers, college professors, and professionals at local meetings and statewide conferences (e.g., Learning Disabilities Association of Virginia), who then distributed them to adults with whom they were working. Further details related to the sample, the questionnaire, and the interview process are presented elsewhere (see Schewel, 1991). We focus here on selected responses obtained from these participants that may help to complete our portrait of adults with learning disabilities. In particular, three themes within the responses are most illustrative of the challenges of development: coping strategies, positive influences, and school experiences. The observations of these adults concerning how they dealt with life challenges are of significant interest. All agreed that one does not really overcome a learning disability, but that one can lead a successful life by developing coping strategies. Consequently, most of the individuals interviewed immediately identified the skills and strategies that enabled them to succeed in the workplace. Many of those strategies were learned through trial-and-error, but some participants described how they were taught specific, useful coping skills.

The importance of coping strategies becomes apparent from the words of the respondents. For example, a man who attended school before learning disabilities classes were available wrote,

> I faked my way through school because I was very bright. I resent most that no one picked up my weaknesses. Essentially I judge myself on my failures . . . [I] have always had low self-esteem. In hindsight I feel that I had low self-esteem in college . . . I was afraid to know myself. A blow to my self-esteem when I was in school was that I could not write a poem or a story . . . I could not write with a pen or pencil. The computer has changed my life. I do everything on my computer. It acts as my memory. I use it to structure my life and for all of my writing since my handwriting and written expression has always been so poor.

A bank manager noted that he also is dependent on his computer. "I depend on my computer a lot. I make a lot of lists or I'm dead in the water. I keep lists on my computer. I've developed a computer environment that handles all of my memorization."

Coping skills developed often were specifically related to occupation. A 19-year-old man who builds cabinets said, "I don't do much reading in this job. I just work with my hands. Everyone has some strengths. Some people can hardly tie a shoe. Some can read but can't do what I do. Some can work with their hands. That's me."

A deputy sheriff solves his problem by keeping two dictionaries in his squad car. "This way I am able to write my reports without errors." Similarly, another man said, "Because I'm aware of my problems I live with a dictionary. . . . Sometimes I can spell the word correctly but not have the confidence that it's correct. I'm very much a perfectionist because of my disability. I want the best . . . I check everything over." An art student uses her visual strength to advantage. "I visualize things, then I can remember them."

Finally, a professional actor explained,

> I believe that I became an actor because memorizing was for me a long-time survival skill. It was a way of pretending that I could read when I could not. Also as a dyslexic, I was accustomed to having a script prepared for me before I spoke. It seems that a lot of acting was required for survival.

Another key reflection on learning disabilities concerns the positive influences on persons who were labeled learning disabled during childhood. For example, each adult interviewed who was an active participant in a school sports program described it as having a significant influence on the development of a positive self-image while also providing a group of friends and social contacts. One stated, "I was a three-sport letterman. That saved my self-confidence." Another young man who was on a high school wrestling team believed "that was the only area that I got any confidence." A young woman expressed it this way: "Thank God for swimming. That's what kept me going." A third said, "Sports helped me make contacts. . . . I played baseball with a man who is my boss . . . so I made contacts that helped me later."

The encouragement, support, and continuous assistance by a particular family member was also cited as significantly important by many respondents. In some instances this support was advocacy for school placement and remediation, and in other instances it took the form of finding out-of-school activities in which the youngster could find success, friends, and personal satisfaction.

An example of family support follows: "My parents never said anything about my disability. They were never degrading. Mom was an advocate for me. School knees still quake when she comes around. Mom went to the schools and insisted I get the education that I need."

"My mother was an incredible help," said another young man. "She helped me with diagnosing my problem. She got me help when I needed it, then advocated for mainstreaming when I was ready. The biggest influence in my positive attitude was my mother."

A recent college graduate remembers the positive influences of both family and a tutor:

> I have an extremely supportive family who has helped me through my educational goals. I also had a tutor for eight years who helped me reach my fullest potential. My tutor was an inspiration . . . we became great friends. In high school I had to stop working with the tutor because they thought I was too dependent. My tutor built my self-confidence . . . concentrated on what I could do. I had ideas but couldn't write them so she taped them and then I listened and wrote them . . . my parents made me feel that I could learn in a different way. Dad pointed out that other people had faults. He had had school problems too, but has been a very successful business man.

Finally, these individuals' school experiences are illuminating. Unfortunately, many described at least some portion of their school experience in negative terms. One young man, a college graduate and now a congressional legislative aide, described junior high school as "wretched. I was made to feel that I was dumb. In elementary school and junior high I had a terrible self-image."

One young woman reflected this same perspective: "I get very defensive still . . . and am afraid to ask questions in fear that I will be wrong. Every teacher should remember their worst class when they were in school and realize that that's how LD kids feel all of the time."

"I remember feeling dumb . . . one teacher told me that I'd never go to college. I can't wait to go back to show her my diploma," said a

21-year-old man who was in a resource program through elementary, middle, and high school. He continued,

> I was on Ritalin for two years . . . no one knows if it did any good. I was not *too* hyperactive. Now I'm still very active but manage O.K. My LD class experiences have never been memorable . . . the majority weren't positive. LD teachers were into remediation not accommodation. Accommodation is me taking my time to get things done correctly . . . taking all the time I need. If I write very slowly I can make legible letters.

A 33-year-old woman with a college degree in finance, now employed as a stock portfolio manager, described her experience as follows: "I think of my whole school experience as being bad! Horrifying! Someone at school knocked all of the confidence out of me when I was little. I'm still always working on that. It still hurts me. I think about it a lot."

One man who dropped out of high school remembered,

> When I got to high school I really wanted to be in the choir. I finally got in it. I was so proud. Then one day at a rehearsal the choir teacher pointed me out as not being able to read the words. This really embarrassed me. I quit the choir and quit school! Now I wish I could go to community college, but I don't have the money. I'm stuck in my job (gas station) . . . I have four kids and it's rough! . . . Nothing in my school classes helped me in the job market. . . . My memory of the programs is that they just kept me going enough to pass. . . . I tried to do it but just couldn't keep up in English. I like the chance to talk about all of this . . . I've only talked about it with one other person . . . that was an art teacher years ago.

One additional observation by a 29-year-old salesman confirms this unfortunate picture:

> I was given a label that left psychological scars. I've always had a lot of determination . . . [I was] determined that this wouldn't beat me. My big life goal was to get into college and prove that my LD didn't beat me. The more away from the school environment I get, the more self-confidence I get.

Finally, one young woman summarized the three themes of coping, positive influences, and negative school experiences. She recollected her life as follows:

> I didn't finish school the normal way . . . quit college . . . traveled . . . went out West . . . stayed 4–5 years . . . was a ski bum, waitress. I knew I

wanted to do something else. . . . Moved to Chicago with a friend . . . she worked for Board of Trade. Met a guy who wanted to experiment by hiring a person with a limited education. Then he realized that I needed a college education so I went back to school . . . worked as a sales assistant. Now I am a portfolio manager.

I don't think I've ever given myself enough credit . . . 50% of the time the guy I now work for doesn't make me feel good. I'm still dealing with all of this.

When I was in school someone knocked all of my confidence out of me when I was little . . . so I'm always working on that. That can still hurt me . . . I think about it a lot . . . I think of my whole school experience as being a bad experience . . . horrifying. Thank God for swimming . . . that kept me going. This made me two-sided in my personality . . . I have lots of confidence in some situations and none in others.

I was so lucky to have a mother who was as astute as she was. . . . She encouraged me into swimming . . . also encouraged me to get into that dancing stuff. . . . She could see how frustrated I was and she was helpful. I do remember feeling different. . . . It didn't seem like anyone else was the same . . . I felt stupid, so I didn't ever want to tell anyone.

Concluding Comments

What can we learn from these observations? They provide useful insights into some of the characteristics associated with learning disabilities that persist in adulthood, the coping strategies that assist these adults in their daily lives, and influences in childhood that were sustaining during a period of demoralizing and difficult school experiences. In addition, the reflections suggest some encouraging models for individuals with learning disabilities by identifying examples of successful adjustment and highlighting strategies and experiences that affected accomplishments.

The chapters in this book, along with these brief reflections, assist in framing the nature of the problem of disabilities in adulthood as well as pointing toward possible solutions. As we work to enhance outcomes for persons with learning disabilities, it will continue to be important to be aware of the experiences of those individuals who have encountered the difficulties, the label, and the services associated with learning disabilities and to allow this awareness to guide us in ascertaining appropriate systems of support.

13. Resources for Adults with Learning Disabilities

DIANE BASSETT

As study of the field of learning disabilities has matured, so too has the understanding and acceptance of adults who manifest learning disabilities (LD). As little as 2 decades ago, it was expected that children would outgrow their learning and social difficulties and magically evolve into happy, productive adults. For many individuals, this dream has proven to be elusive. We now know that learning disabilities persist throughout the life span; this cognizance has been reflected in several definitions and policy directives (e.g., Association for Children and Adults with Learning Disabilities, 1984; National Joint Council for Learning Disabilities, 1990). Although many adults appear to have developed successful compensatory strategies to aid in coping with their disabilities (see Adelman & Vogel, 1990), researchers have recently concluded that the difficulties of adults with LD may increase in complexity and in certain situations appear to be exacerbated with age (Gerber et al., 1990; Malcolm, Polatajko, & Simons, 1990; Minskoff, Sautter, Sheldon, Steidle, & Baker, 1988; Polloway, Smith, & Patton, 1984).

As adults, individuals with learning disabilities are more likely to be unemployed or underemployed. In a survey conducted by Smith (1992) through the Learning Disability Association of America, it was found that although 75% of adults with LD were employed on either a full-time or part-time basis, nearly 25% were unemployed. Compared to the 7% unemployment rate reported nationally, it is clear that unemployment is significantly greater among adults with LD. Further, almost 45% of this employed population earned incomes of less than $7,000 per year, indicating significant underemployment as well.

There is also a growing realization that an intricate interrelationship exists between job or college success and social functioning (Barbaro, 1982). Regardless of their academic and cognitive profiles, many adults with LD have been characterized by poor self-concepts, poor communication skills, and social immaturity (Buchanan & Wolf, 1986; Gerber et al., 1990; Hoffman et al., 1987; Smith, 1988; White et al., 1983). In an earlier survey conducted by the Vocational Committee of the Association for Children and Adults with Learning Disabilities (ACLD; Chelser, 1982), adults with LD cited improvement in social skills as their most critical need.

Although many characteristics of adults with LD are manifested as deficits, some researchers have investigated factors associated with success. Gerber and Ginsberg (1990) studied successful adults and identified variables that they described as internal in nature. These include desire to excel, cognizance and acceptance of the disability, and goal orientation. They also cited external indications necessary for the success of these adults, including persistence; "goodness-of-fit" with job, school, and environment; development of adaptive/compensatory strategies; and support and resource networks. In a similar study, Speckman, Goldberg, and Herman (1992) elicited factors that advanced the success of young adults with LD. These included the acceptance of the learning disability, a proactive approach to making changes, a high level of perseverance, emotional stability and the ability to reduce stress, appropriate goal setting and self-directedness, and the presence of an effective support system. The commonalities shared by these two studies suggest that successful adults with LD know where they want to go and know how to access the determinants that can help them get there.

Adults with LD are increasingly considering postsecondary schooling and training options. Will (1984) estimated that between 250,000 and 300,000 students with disabilities leave public schools each year. The *Fifteenth Annual Report to Congress on the Implementation of the Individuals with Disabilities Education Act* (1993) indicated that over 132,000 young people with learning disabilities exited high school that year. Of this number, approximately 50% will utilize postsecondary training as compared with 80% of their nondisabled peers (Stodden & Boone, 1987). It is within this context that the need for a variety of resources for adults with LD has arisen. If these adults are to be afforded equal opportunities for success in postsecondary education, in the workplace, and in their personal lives, they must have access to those services, people, and materials that can aid them in their endeavors. Adults with LD are legally entitled to the rights and accommodations that will allow them to participate as fully contributing members of society, as outlined in governmental decrees ranging from Section 504 of the Rehabilitation Act of 1973 to the Americans with Disabilities Act of 1990 (ADA).

Service providers who work with adults with LD must have access to materials and services that can aid these adults in assessing their options for schooling, vocation, leisure and recreation, and daily living. It is critical that professionals in the field remain abreast of the current resources available both locally and nationally. This chapter presents a compendium of resources including sections on pertinent publications, postsecondary training options, associations and advocacy organizations, and employment. It is important to note that this list is not exhaustive. Furthermore, it is both natural and inevitable that in a dynamic field changes will occur related to these resources. Nevertheless, the sheer breadth of available resources indicates just how far, in a relatively short period of time, the field has developed.

RESOURCES

The following list includes publications that can be utilized by adults and youth with LD who are leaving high school; some publications are intended for use by service providers. This resource section is organized into the following subsections:

Publications
- General Interest
- Postsecondary and Higher Education
  - General Topics
  - Guides to Institutions

Newsletters

Organizations and Other Sources of Information
- Postsecondary Education and Training
- Advocacy and Professional Organizations

Publications–General Interest

Adult Basic Education and General Educational Development Programs for Disabled Adults: A Handbook for Literacy Tutors and Instructors. Library for the Blind and Physically Handicapped (1987). Available from Free Library of Philadelphia, 919 Walnut Street, Philadelphia, PA 19107; 800/222-1754; in Pennsylvania, 215/925-3213.

The Bottom Line: Basic Skills in the Workplace. U.S. Department of Education and Labor (1988). A pamphlet that discusses meeting basic literacy needs within the context of the workplace. Available free from The Office of Public Information, Employment, and Training Administration, U.S. Department of Labor, 200 Constitution Ave. NW, Room 52307, Washington, DC 20210.

Employers Guide to Learning Disabilities. By Susan Little. Designed to assist employers in learning how to comply with the Americans with Disabilities Act (ADA). Available for $3 from Learning Opportunities Program, Barat College, 700 Westleigh Road, Lake Forest, IL, 60045; 708/234-3000.

GED Test Accommodations for Candidates with Specific Learning Disabilities. Describes policies and procedures for obtaining special accommodations on the GED tests. Available free from The GED Testing Service, Special Testing, One Dupont Circle, Washington, DC 20036; 202/939-9490.

Taming the Paper Tiger. By Barbara Hemphill (1988). Provides a structure for paperwork management for individuals with LD and nondisabled people. Available from Time Out to Enjoy Inc. Publishing, 208 South LaSalle Street, Suite 1330, Chicago, IL 60604-1102.

Time Management: Strategies for Achieving Success. By Peggy A. Cvach, EdD (edited by Rhona Hartman) (December 1989). An activity paper that provides a process for setting goals, including exercises to organize time. Available free from Learning Disabilities Project, 7926 Jones Branch Drive, Suite 1100, McLean, VA 22102; 703/620-3660.

Understanding Your Learning Disability. By Cheri Warner (1988). Offers tips for becoming a better student; covers topics such as basic skills, note taking, test taking, social interactions, and organizational strategies. Available for $1 from Lisa Williams, Learning Disability Specialist, The Ohio State University at Newark, University Drive, Newark, OH 43055; 614/366-9246.

PUBLICATIONS–POSTSECONDARY

General Topics

Adults with Learning Disabilities: An Overview for the Adult Educator. By Jovita M. Ross-Gordon (1989). Presents an introduction to adults with

LD, including problems encountered, assessment and intervention issues, and future policy development. Available through the ERIC Clearinghouse on Adult, Career, and Vocational Education, Center on Education and Training for Employment, The Ohio State University, 1900 Kenny Road, Columbus, Ohio 43210-1090.

Campus Opportunities for Students with Learning Differences–2nd Edition. By Judith M. Crocker (1991–1992). Designed for high school students with LD, and their parents, as they prepare for college. Available for $3 from Octameron Associates, PO Box 3437, Alexandria, VA 22302; 703/836-5480.

College and the Learning Disabled College Student. By C. T. Mangrum and S. S. Strichart (1984). New York: Grune & Stratton. A guide for service providers to aid students with LD.

Freebie College HELPS Handbook. Handicapped and Exceptional Learners Products and Services. These products are available for little or no money from Partners in Publishing, PO Box 50347, Tulsa, OK 74150; 918/584-5906.

The K & W Guide to Colleges for the Learning Disabled (2nd ed.). By M. Kravets (1993). New York: HarperCollins. Provides perspectives of students, an admissions director, a program director, and a college graduate with learning disabilities. Describes programs and services nationally.

Learning Disabilities, Graduate School, and Careers: The Student's Perspective. By Pamela Adelman and Carol Wren (1990). Provides information on the transition from college to graduate school or a career. Available for $3 from Learning Opportunities Program, Barat College, 700 Westleigh Road, Lake Forest, IL 60045; 708/234-3000.

Postsecondary Learning Disability Unit of the University of Connecticut's A. J. Pappanikou Center on Special Education and Rehabilitation. The Center has produced a number of papers, reports, and materials regarding adolescents and adults with LD. For a listing, contact A. J. Pappanikou Center on Special Education and Rehabilitation, Publications Section, The University of Connecticut, U-64, Glenbrook Road, Storrs, CT 06269-2064.

Promoting Postsecondary Education for Students with Learning Disabilities: A Handbook for Practitioners. By L. C. Brinckerhoff, S. F. Shaw, and J. M. McGuire, Eds. (1993). Available from PRO-ED, 8700 Shoal Creek Blvd., Austin, TX 78757; 512/451-3246.

Unlocking Potential: College and Other Choices for Learning Disabled People: A Step by Step Guide. By Barbara Schieber and Jeanne Talpers (1987). Adler & Adler. Guides readers through the entire postsecondary process. Available for $12.95 from Woodbine House, 5615 Fishers Lane, Rockville, MD 20852; 800/843-7323.

Guides to Institutions

College-Level Programs for the Learning Disabled. For use by adult education programs; includes rights of students, inservice techniques, and more. Available from Partners in Publishing, PO Box 50347, Tulsa, OK 74150; 918/584-5906.

A Guide to Colleges for Learning Disabled Students. By M. Liscio (1986). Orlando; PL: Academic Press.

A Guide to Post-Secondary Educational Opportunities for the Learning Disabled. By D. M. Ridenour & J. Johnston (1981). Available from Time Out to Enjoy Inc. Publishing, 208 South LaSalle Street, Suite 1330, Chicago, IL 60604-11020.

How to Choose a College: Guide for the Student with a Disability. (1988). A joint project between AHSSPPE and HEATH Resource Center. Single copies available free from HEATH, 1 Dupont Circle, Suite 800, Washington, DC 20036.

Lovejoy's College Guide for the Learning Disabled. By C. T. Straughn (1988). New York: Monarch Press.

McGuire-Shaw Postsecondary Selection Guide for Learning Disabled College Students. Available from Special Education Center Publications, The University of Connecticut, U-64, 249 Glenbrook Road, Storrs, CT 06269-2064.

A National Directory for Four-Year Colleges, Two-Year Colleges and Post-High School Training Programs for Young People with Learning Disabilities. Available from Partners in Publishing, PO Box 50347, Tulsa, OK 74150; 918/584-5906.

Peterson's Guide to Colleges with Programs for Learning-Disabled Students (2nd ed.). By C. T. Mangrum and S. S. Strichart, Eds. (1988). Available from Peterson's Guides, 166 Bunn Drive, Princeton, NJ 08540-6008; 800/338-3282.

Newsletters

Challenge. Focuses on attention deficits in children and adults. Available for $15/year from Challenge, Inc., 42 Way of the River, West Newbury, MA 01985; 508/462-0495.

Closing the Gap. Bimonthly newsletter focusing on computers and disability. Available for $21/yr from CTG, Box 68, Henderson, MN 56044; 612/248-3294.

GED Items. A bimonthly newsletter for GED examiners and teachers. Available free from The GED Testing Service, American Council on Education, One Dupont Circle, Washington, DC 20036; 202/939-9490.

LDA Newsbriefs. A bimonthly newsletter for parents, professionals, and adults with LD. Available for $5/yr from Learning Disability Association (LDA), 4156 Library Road, Pittsburgh, PA 15234; 412/341-1515.

National Network of LD Adults Newsletter. A quarterly publication for adults with LD; includes news and resources. Available for $10/yr from the National Network of LD Adults, 808 N. 82nd Street, Suite F2, Scottsdale, AZ 85257; 602/941-5112.

Postsecondary LD Network News. Information for and about LD. Published 3 times/yr. Available for $20/yr (individuals), $30/yr (schools). Contact Dr. Stan Shaw, University of Connecticut, U-64, 249 Glenbrook Road, Storrs, CT 06269-2064; 202/486-2020.

Their World. An annual publication that depicts real-life stories about ways in which children and adults with LD cope. Available for $7 from The National Center on Learning Disabilities, 99 Park Avenue, New York, NY 10016; 212/687-7211.

Organizations and Other Sources of Information

Postsecondary Education and Training

A variety of options exists for those students who choose to pursue postsecondary education or training. Students may consider 2- or 4-year college programs, vocational education programs (both public and private), independent living programs, adult education, or job training programs. As these options are being considered, it is important for the adult with LD to visit each site of interest, meet with the director of services for students with disabilities, and carefully analyze whether the school meets the individual's needs.

College Admissions Testing. Not all colleges and universities require students to be tested with standardized measures. However, if a standardized test is required, special accommodations such as extended time, a reader, or a separate room may be arranged for the student. For further information about testing accommodations, contact the following two organizations:

- ATP Services for Handicapped Students
  CN6400, Princeton, NJ 08541-6400; 609/734-5350

- ACT Assessment "Special Testing Guide"
  Test Administration, PO Box 168, Iowa City, IA 52243; 319/337-1332

Four-Year Colleges. Four-year institutions can offer a broad array of educational options. Often, many resources are in place to help the student with LD. For further information, contact:

- Association on Higher Education and Disability (AHEAD)
  PO Box 21192, Columbus, OH 43221; 614/488-4972
- Orton Dyslexia Society
  724 York Road, Baltimore, MD 21204; 800/ABCD-123
- Learning Disabilities Association of America (LDAA)
  4156 Library Road, Pittsburgh, PA 15234; 412/341-1515

Two-Year Colleges. Many students prefer to start at a 2-year college because there are often no admissions requirements. Students can gradually build their credit hours and then transfer them to a 4-year institution if desired. For information on 2-year colleges, contact:

- American Association of Community and Junior Colleges
  One Dupont Circle NW, Washington, DC 20036; 202/293-7050
- National Center for Learning Disabilities
  99 Park Avenue, New York, NY 10016; 212/687-7211

Vocational Education. If an individual desires training in a particular trade or skill, vocational education can provide the necessary certification or degree for future employment. Also, a high school diploma or GED may not be required. For further information, contact:

- National Association of Trade and Technical Schools
  2251 Wisconsin Avenue, Washington, DC 20007; 202/333-1021
- Association of Independent Colleges and Schools
  One Dupont Circle NW, Washington, DC 20036; 202/659-2460
- National Association of Vocational Education Special Needs Personnel (NAVESNP)
  Special Needs Division, American Vocational Association, 2020 14th Street, Arlington, VA 22201; 703/522-6121

Vocational Rehabilitation. Because rehabilitation for individuals with learning disabilities is now recognized and funded by the federal Division of Vocational Rehabilitation, individuals may be able to receive training and/or education through an array of postsecondary options ranging from 4-year institutions to adult basic education programs. There is an Office of Vocational Rehabilitation located in almost every city and county in the United States. To locate these offices contact the local or state office, the local school district, or the state LDA affiliate. A listing of state offices can be obtained from the following source:

- Rehabilitation Services Administration
  330 C Street SW, Washington, DC 20202; 703/732-1282

Job Training Programs. The Job Training Partnership Act (JTPA) is funded by the federal government and operated through private industry councils. It provides training to youth and adults whose income falls below a certain level. For further information, contact:

- National Association of Private Industry Councils
  810 18th Street NW, Washington, DC 20006

Apprenticeship programs are available in many states. It is estimated that there are over 700 occupations that may be learned through an apprenticeship. Further information can be obtained from:

- U.S. Bureau of Apprenticeship and Training
  Employment and Training Administration, U.S. Department of Labor, 601 D Street NW, Washington, DC 20213

Adult Basic Education. Adult basic education (ABE) is available in most cities and counties. Many ABE programs are used to provide preparation for the GED or to assist adults in developing basic academic skills. The Department of Education in each state can provide the addresses and phone numbers of local ABE programs. Other organizations include the following:

- Laubach Literacy Action (LLA)
  PO Box 131, Syracuse, NY 13210; 315/422-9121

- Learning Resources Network
  1554 Hayes, Manhattan, KS 66502; 913/539-5376

- Literacy Hotline Contact Center
  800/228-8813
  Toll-free hotline that refers callers to nearest literacy program in their locale.

- Literacy Volunteers of America
  5795 Widewaters Parkway, Syracuse, NY 13214; 315/445-8000
  Nonprofit national organization with 400+ affiliate programs in 40 states.

Financial Aid. Financing an education can be a burden for any individual or family. Aside from the possible funding opportunities through vocational rehabilitation, little funding is available specifically for students with disabilities. A visit to the school's financial aid office may help to identify available funding. Other sourcebooks include:

- *Federal Student Aid Fact Sheet*
  U.S. Department of Education, Office of Student Financial Assistance, Washington, DC 20202; 800/433-3243

- *Financial Aid for the Disabled and Their Families*
  By Gail Ann Schlachter and R. David Walker (1988). Redwood City, CA: Reference Service Press.

- *Grants for Graduate Students*
  Peterson's Guides, 166 Bunn Drive, PO Box 2123, Princeton, NJ 08540-0008; 800/338-3282
  Available for $29.95.

- *Chronicle Student Aid Annual*
  PO Box 1190, Moravia, NY 13118-1190; 800/622-7284

Advocacy and Professional Organizations

A number of advocacy organizations exist to help adults with learning disabilities, their families, and providers who serve them. The first four agencies have been succinctly described by Dr. Stan Shaw; the other descriptions have been gleaned from HEATH Resource Center and the National Library Service for the Blind and Physically Handicapped.

HEATH Resource Center. HEATH Resource Center is federally funded through the American Council of Education. It gathers and disseminates information regarding postsecondary educational support services, policies, procedures, and adaptations in colleges and universities, vocational–technical schools, adult education programs, and independent living centers. A newsletter is published 3 times a year; there is also an excellent series of fact sheets on topical issues. HEATH publishes a resource directory and responds to requests for information.

- HEATH Resource Center
  The National Clearinghouse on Postsecondary Education for Handicapped Individuals, One Dupont Circle, Suite 670, Washington, DC 20036; 800/54-HEATH, or 202/939-9320

Association on Higher Education and Disability (AHEAD). AHEAD consists of 1,000 members in 600 institutions of higher education and is committed to promoting full participation of persons with disabilities in college. AHEAD sponsors a national Special Interest Group on learning disabilities, which publishes its own newsletter. AHEAD also holds a national conference and publishes a quarterly newsletter, a journal, and conference proceedings.

- AHEAD
  PO Box 21192, Columbus, OH 43221; 614/488-4972, FAX 614/488-1174

The Postsecondary Learning Disability Unit. The unit provides training and technical assistance and offers graduate programs (MA and PhD) to train personnel to work with adults with LD at the postsecondary level.

It also disseminates publications and offers a national training institute each June. The unit's phone number also serves as a national hotline to provide technical assistance to professionals. The unit also publishes *Postsecondary LD Network News,* which includes information on conferences, resources, and "best practices" for service providers.

- Postsecondary Learning Disability Unit
  Special Education Center, University of Connecticut, 249 Glenbrook Rd., Box U-64, Storrs, CT 06269-2064; 203/486-4036

National Network of Learning Disabled Adults (NNLDA). NNLDA provides information and referral for adults involved with or looking for support groups and networking. It acts as an advocacy organization to encourage institutions and employers to provide accommodations. NNLDA publishes a quarterly newsletter and holds an annual convention.

- National Network of Learning Disabled Adults (NNLDA)
  808 West 82nd Street, Suite F-2, Scottsdale, AZ 85257

National Association for Adults with Special Learning Needs. This new national organization will provide a professional network for adults with disabilities and will offer a newsletter, a journal, and a national conference. Its mission is to create, establish, and foster an effective national and international coalition of professionals, advocates, and consumers to serve the interests of adults with special learning needs. This organization is an associated organization of the American Association for Adult and Continuing Education (AAACE).

Attention Deficit Disorder (ADD) Association. This organization provides a national network for all ADD support groups and for individuals with ADD.

- Attention Deficit Disorder Association
  2620 Ivy Place, Toledo, OH 43613; 508/462-0495

Center for Special Education Technology. This center is operated under the aegis of the Council for Exceptional Children. It provides information about the use of technology in the education of students with disabilities.

- Center for Special Education Technology
  Council for Exceptional Children, 1920 Association Drive, Reston, VA 22091; 703/620-3660, or 800/873-8255

Council for Learning Disabilities (CLD). This organization promotes the education and welfare of individuals with LD. Publishes *Learning Disability Quarterly* and *Learning Disability Forum.*

- CLD
  Box 40303, Overland, KS 66204; 913/492-3840

Disability Rights Education and Defense Fund, Inc. (DREDF). DREDF is a legal resource center offering education, advocacy, research, policy analysis, and local referrals to callers.

- DREDF
  2212 6th Street, Berkeley, CA 94710; 415/644-2555, or 415/644-2626 (TDD)

National Center for Learning Disabilities (formerly FCLD). NCLD publishes *Their World* to increase awareness about learning disabilities.

- NCLD
  99 Park Avenue, New York, NY 10016; 212/687-7211

LAUNCH, Inc. LAUNCH provides resources for individuals with LD, coordinates efforts of other LD organizations, and provides a vehicle for communication among persons with LD through a monthly newsletter. It also offers programs to enhance social interaction.

- LAUNCH, Inc.
  Department of Special Education—ETSA, Commerce, TX 75428; 214/886-5932

Learning Disability Association (LDA). LDA (formerly ACLD) is primarily an advocacy organization for parents, professionals, and consumers involved with learning disabilities. It offers information on support groups and networking opportunities.

- LDA
  4156 Library Road, Pittsburgh, PA 15234; 412/341-1515

National Library Service for the Blind and Physically Handicapped. This program provides current books and magazines on tape, records, and in Braille for individuals whose disability prevents the use of print materials.

- National Library Service for the Blind and Physically Handicapped
  1291 Taylor Street, Washington, DC 20542; 202/287-5100, or 800/424-8567

Orton Dyslexia Society. This organization offers leadership and training for professionals and parent members who are concerned with developmental dyslexia. Chapters are located in most states.

- Orton Dyslexia Society
  724 York Road, Baltimore, MD 21204; 301/296-0232, or 800/222-3123

Partners in Publishing (PIP). PIP offers a wide variety of materials and publications on adults with LD.

- PIP
  PO Box 50347, Tulsa, OK 74150, 918/584-5906

Recording for the Blind, Inc. (RFB). Recording for the Blind lends cassette-recorded textbooks to eligible persons with LD.

- RFB
  20 Roszel Road, Princeton, NJ 08540; 609/452-0606, or 800/221-4792

Time Out to Enjoy. This nonprofit organization offers adults with LD the opportunity to network, and aims to educate the public about learning disabilities and to provide resources and referrals on various topics.

- Time Out to Enjoy
  208 South LaSalle Street, Suite 1330, Chicago, IL 60604-1102

Employment. HEATH Resources has identified three resources regarding employment issues. The first two identify publications about employment for people with disabilities. The third is designed to help employers understand learning disabilities.

- *Pathways to Employment for People with Learning Disabilities* and

- *Employment Considerations for Learning Disabled Adults*
  Available free from the President's Commission on the Employment of People with Disabilities, 1111 20th Street NW, Suite 608, Washington, DC 20036

- *For Employers . . . A Look at Learning Disabilities*
  Learning Disability Association, 4156 Library Road, Pittsburgh, PA 15234; 412/341-1515

Adults with learning disabilities are also encouraged to contact their local Division of Vocational Rehabilitation for possible employment possibilities or training.

Life Management. Throughout the country there are a growing number of independent living programs that have been established to provide supervised assistance to individuals with learning disabilities. Adults may live in apartments or dormitories where they receive guidance in daily living skills. Involvement in vocational training is a part of each program. Further information regarding independent living programs may be obtained from

- National Council of Independent Living Programs (NCILP)
  c/o Marsha Bristo, President, Access Living, 815 Van Buren, Suite 525, Chicago, IL 60607; 302/226-5900

For further information regarding specific programs, contact:

- HEATH Resource Center
  One Dupont Circle, Suite 800, Washington, DC 20036; 800/544-3284

Author's Note

The author wishes to acknowledge the generous contributions of Dr. Stan Shaw of the University of Connecticut and Rhona Hartman of HEATH Resource Center of the American Council on Education.

References

Chapter 1

Baltes, P. B., Reese, H. W., & Lipsitt, L. P. (1980). Life-span developmental psychology. Annual Review of Psychology, 31, 65–110.

Bassett, D., Polloway, E. A., & Patton, J. R. (1993). Learning disabilities: Perspectives on adult development. In P. J. Gerber & H. B. Reiff (Eds.), Learning disabilities in adulthood. Newton, MA: Butterworth-Heinemann.

Blalock, G., & Dixon, N. (1982). Improving prospects for the college-bound learning disabled. Topics in Learning & Learning Disabilities, 2(3), 69–78.

Clark, G. M., & Knowlton, H. E. (Eds.). (1987). The transition from school to adult life [Special issue]. Exceptional Children, 53(6).

Clark, G., & Kolstoe, O. P. (1990). Career development and transition education for adolescents with disabilities. Boston: Allyn & Bacon.

Cronin, M. E., & Gerber, P. J. (1982). Preparing the learning disabled adolescent for adulthood. Topics in Learning & Learning Disabilities, 2(3), 55–68.

Cronin, M. E., & Patton, J. R. (1993). Life skills instruction for all students with special needs: A practical guide for integrating real-life content into the curriculum. Austin, TX: PRO-ED.

Cronin, M. E., Patton, J. R., & Polloway, E.A. (1991). Preparing for adult outcomes: A model for developing a life skills curriculum. Manuscript submitted for publication.

Edgar, E. (1990). Education's role in improving the quality of life: Is it time to change our view of the world? Beyond Behavior, 1(1), 9–13.

Erikson, E. (1950). Childhood and society. New York: W. W. Norton.

Erikson, E. (1968). Youth, identity, and crisis. New York: Horton.

Fafard, M., & Haubrich, P. A. (1981). Vocational and social adjustment of learning disabled young adults: A follow-up study. Learning Disability Quarterly, 4, 122–130.

Gerber, P. J. (1981). Learning disabilities and eligibility for vocational rehabilitation services: A chronology of events. Learning Disability Quarterly, 4, 422–425.

Gerber, P. J., & Ginsberg, R. J. (1990). Identifying alterable patterns of success in highly successful adults with learning disabilities. Richmond: Virginia Commonwealth University.

Gould, R. L. (1978). Transformations: Growth and change in adult life. New York: Simon & Schuster.

Hammill, D. D. (1989). A brief history of learning disabilities. Austin, TX: PRO-ED.

Havighurst, R. (1972). Developmental tasks and education (3rd ed.). New York: D. McKay.

Hultsch, D., & Deutsch, F. (1981). Adult development and aging: A life-span perspective. New York: McGraw-Hill.

Keogh, B. K., Major-Kingsley, S., Omori-Gordon, H., & Reid, H. P. (1982). A system of marker variables for the field of learning disabilities. Syracuse, NY: Syracuse University Press.

Knowles, M. (1978). The adult learner: The neglected species. Houston: Gulf.

Levine, M. D. (1989). Learning disabilities at 25: The early adulthood of a maturing concept. Learning Disabilities, 1(1), 1–11.

Levinson, D. J. (1978). The seasons of a man's life. New York: Knopf.

Lieberman, M. A. (1975). Adaptive processes in later life. In N. Datan & L.H. Ginsberg (Eds.), Lifespan developmental psychology: Normative life crises. New York: Academic Press.

Ludlow, B., Luckasson, R., & Turnbull, A. (Eds.). (1988). Transitions to adult life for persons with mental retardation: Principles and practices. Baltimore: Brookes.

Patton, J. R., Cronin, M. E., Polloway, E. A., Robinson, G. A., & Hutchison, D. (1989). Curricular considerations: A life skills orientation. In G. A. Robinson, J. R. Patton, E. A. Polloway, & L. R. Sargent (Eds.), Best practices in mental retardation (pp. 21–37). Reston, VA: Division on Mental Retardation, Councilfor Exceptional Children.

Patton, J. R., & Polloway, E. A. (1982). The learning disabled: The adult years. Topics in Learning & Learning Disabilities, 2(3), 79–88.

Polloway, E. A., Patton, J. R., Epstein, M. H., & Smith, T. E. C. (1989). Comprehensive curriculum for students with mild handicaps. Focus on Exceptional Children, 21(8), 1–12.

Polloway, E. A., Smith, J. D., & Patton, J. R. (1984). Learning disabilities: An adult development perspective. Learning Disability Quarterly, 7, 179–186.

Smith, J. D. (1991). Adult development models. Unpublished manuscript, Lynchburg College, Lynchburg, VA.

Strauss, W., & Lehtinen, L. (1947). Psychopathology and education of the brain-injured child. New York: Grune & Stratton.

Trapani, C. (1990). Transition goals for adolescents with learning disabilities. Austin, TX: PRO-ED.

Vaillant, G. E. (1977). Adaptation to life. Boston: Little, Brown.

Wiederholt, J. L. (1974). Historical perspectives on the education of the learning disabled. In L. Mann & D. A. Sabatino (Eds.), The second review of special education (pp. 103–152). Philadelphia: Journal of Special Education Press.

Wiederholt, J. L., & Wolffe, K. E. (1990). Preparing problem learners for independent living. In D. D. Hammill & N. R. Bartel (Eds.), Teaching students with learning and behavior problems (5th ed., pp. 451–501). Boston: Allyn & Bacon.

Zigmond, N. (1990). Rethinking secondary school programs for students with learning disabilities. Focus on Exceptional Children, 23(1), 1–21.

CHAPTER 2

Erikson, E. (1950). Childhood and society. New York: Norton.

Erikson, E. (1963). Childhood and society (2nd ed.). New York: Norton.

Erikson, E., & Erikson, J. (1986). Vital involvement in old age. New York: Norton.

Freud, S. (1914). Psychopathology of everyday life. New York: Macmillan.

Freud, S. (1949). An outline of psychoanalysis. New York: Norton.

Hamachek, D. (1990). Evaluating self-concept and ego status in Erikson's last three psychological stages. Journal of Counseling and Development, 68, 677–683.

Kotre, J. (1984). Outliving the self: Generativity and the interpretation of lives. Baltimore: Johns Hopkins University Press.

Levinson, D., Darrow, C., Klein, E., Levinson, M., & McKee, B. (1978). The seasons of a man's life. New York: Ballantine.

Marcia, J. (1967). Ego identity status: Relationship to change in self esteem, general maladjustment and authoritarianism. Journal of Personality, 35, 118–133.

National Joint Committee on Learning Disabilities. (1994). Collective perspectives on issues affecting learning disabilities. Austin: PRO-ED.

Troll, L. (1982). Continuations: Adult development and aging. Monterey, CA: Brooks/Cole.

Vaillant, G. (1977). Adaptation to life. Boston: Little, Brown.

Chapter 3

Affleck, J., Edgar, E., Levine, P., & Kortering, L. (1989). Postschool status of students classified as mildly mentally retarded, learning disabled, or nonhandicapped: Does it get better with time? Seattle: University of Washington.

Blalock, G. (1990). The New Mexico school-to-work transition demonstration project. Final report for grant project, University of New Mexico, Albuquerque.

Blalock, G. (1993). Strategies for working with significant others. In E. A. Polloway & J. R. Patton (Eds.), Strategies for teaching learners with special needs (5th ed.). Columbus, OH: Merrill.

Blalock, G., Bassett, D. S., & Donisthorpe, L. (1989). Team strategies for integrating special needs students into vocational education programs. Unpublished manuscript, University of New Mexico, Albuquerque.

Blalock, G., Mahoney, B., & Van Dyke, R. (1992). The impact of follow-up studies on an urban district and the surrounding state. Manuscript submitted for publication.

Brandt, M. D., & Berry, J. O. (1991). Transitioning college bound students with LD. Intervention in School and Clinic, 26(5), 297–301.

Brolin, D. (1991). Life-centered career education. Reston, VA: Council for Exceptional Children.

Bruininks, R. H., Wolman, C., & Thurlow, M. L. (1989). Issues and guidelines in designing follow-up systems for special education service programs. Minneapolis: Institute on Community Integration, University of Minnesota.

Ceres Unified School District. (1988). Career education responsive to every student. Ceres, CA: Author.

Cobb, B., & Hasazi, S. B. (1987). School-aged transition services: Options for adolescents with mild handicaps. Career Development for Exceptional Individuals, 10, 15–23.

Cronin, M. E., & Patton, J. R. (1993). Life skills instruction for all students with special needs: A practical guide for integrating real-life content into the curriculum. Austin, TX: PRO-ED.

deBettencourt, L., Zigmond, N., & Thornton, H. (1989). Follow-up of postsecondary-aged rural learning disabled graduates and dropouts. Exceptional Children, 56, 40–49.

Education for All Handicapped Children Act of 1975, 20 U.S.C. § 1400 et seq.

Elksnin, L., & Elksnin, N. (1990). Using collaborative consultation with parents to promote effective vocational programming. Career Development for Exceptional Individuals, 13, 135–142.

Everson, J., Moon, S., Barcus, M., & Morton, M. V. (1987). Achieving outcomes: A guide to interagency training in transition and supported employment. Richmond, VA: Project TIE, RRTC, Virginia Commonwealth University.

Husted, D. (1992). Parent involvement in the transition process. Presentations given at University of New Mexico, Albuquerque.

Individuals with Disabilities Education Act of 1990, 20 U.S.C. § 1400 et seq.

Karpinski, M. J., Neubert, D. A., & Graham, S. (1992). A follow-along study of postsecondary outcomes for graduates and dropouts with mild disabilities in a rural setting. Journal of Learning Disabilities, 25, 376–385.

Knowlton, H. E., & Clark, G. M. (1987). Transition issues for the 1990s. Exceptional Children, 53, 562–563.

Lindsey, P., & Blalock, G. (1992). Transition to work programs in rural areas: Developing collaborative ethic. Manuscript submitted for publication.

McCue, M. (1989). The role of assessment in the vocational rehabilitation of adults with specific learning disabilities. Rehabilitation Counseling Bulletin, 33, 18–37.

Minnesota Department of Education. (1990). Interagency planning for transition in Minnesota: A resource guide. Minneapolis: University of Minnesota, Minnesota Department of Education and Institute on Community Integration.

Missouri Linc. (1991–1992). Transition planning: Statement of needs, goals and objectives. Columbia, MO: University of Missouri–Columbia.

Phillips, P. (1990). A self-advocacy plan for high school students with learning disabilities: A comparative case study analysis of students', teachers', and parents' perceptions of program effects. Journal of Learning Disabilities, 23, 466–471.

Phillips, V., & McCullough, L. (1990). Consultation-based programming: Instituting the collaborative ethic in schools. Exceptional Children, 56, 391–401.

Posthill, S. M., & Roffman, A. J. (1991). The impact of a transitional training program for young adults with learning disabilities. Journal of Learning Disabilities, 24, 619–629.

Powers, P. (1991). A guide to vocational assessment (2nd ed.). Austin, TX: PRO-ED.

Regulations Implementing IDEA Part B, 34 C.F.R. 300.341B.

Rogan, L. L., & Hartman, L. D. (1990). Adult outcome of learning disabled students ten years after initial follow-up. Learning Disabilities Focus, 5, 91–102.

Santa Fe Public Schools Special Education Department (n.d.). Individual transition plan. Santa Fe, NM: Author.

Siegel, S., Robert, M., Greener, K., Meyer, G., Halloran, W., & Gaylord-Ross, R. (1993). Career ladders for challenged youths in transition from school to adult life. Austin, TX: PRO-ED.

Sitlington, P. L., & Frank, A. R. (1990). Are adolescents with learning disabilities successfully crossing the bridge into adult life? Learning Disability Quarterly, 13, 97–111.

Sitlington, P., Frank, A., & Cooper, L. (1989). Iowa statewide follow-up study: Adult adjustment of individuals with learning disabilities. Des Moines, IA: Department of Education.

Smith, J. O. (1992). Falling through the cracks: Rehabilitation services for adults with learning disabilities. Exceptional Children, 58, 451–460.

SRI International. (1992). Youth with disabilities: How are they doing? Menlo Park, CA: Author.

Stowitschek, J. J., & Kelso, C. A. (1989). Are we in danger of making the same mistakes with ITPs as were made with IEPs? Career Development for Exceptional Individuals, 12, 139–151.

Struck, J. W. (1987). A parent handbook: Transition from school to adult life. Des Moines, IA: Drake University, Mountain Plains Regional Resource Center.

Struck, J. W. (1992, March 30). Transition planning training. Workshop conducted with Albuquerque Public Schools, Albuquerque, NM.

U.S. Department of Education. (1991). 13th annual report to Congress on the implementation of the Individuals with Disabilities Education Act. Washington, DC: Author, Office of Special Education Programs, OSERS.

University of Colorado. (1992). Colorado self-determination transition curriculum guide. Unpublished manuscript. Colorado Springs: University of Colorado, Center for Educational Research.

Webb, K. (1988). Your plan for success: A college preparation manual for students with learning disabilities. Albuquerque, NM: Author. (Available from author at 3808 Denise Court NE, Albuquerque, NM 87111)

Wehman, P. (1992). Transition for young people with disabilities: Challenges for the 1990s. Education and Training in Mental Retardation, 27, 112–118.

Zigmond, N., & Thornton, H. (1985). Follow-up of postsecondary age learning disabled graduates and dropouts. Learning Disabilities Research, 1, 50–55.

Chapter 4

Blalock, J. W. (1981). Persistent problems and concerns of young adults with learning disabilities. In W. M. Cruickshank & A. A. Silver (Eds.), Bridges to tomorrow: The best of ACLD (Vol. 2, pp. 35–55). Syracuse, NY: Syracuse University Press.

Carnevale, A. P., Gainer, L. J., & Meltzer, A. S. (1988). Workplace basics: The skills employers want (DOL Publication No. 0-225-795). Washington, DC: U.S. Government Printing Office.

Chelser, B. (1982). ACLD committee survey of LD adults. ACLD Newsbrief, 145, 1, 5.

Clark, G. M., & Kolstoe, O. P. (1990). Career development and transition education for adolescents with disabilities. Boston: Allyn & Bacon.

Cobb, R. M., & Crump, W. D. (1984). *Post-school status of young adults identified as learning disabled while enrolled in public schools: A comparison of those enrolled and not enrolled in learning disabilities programs* (Final Rep.). Washington, DC: Office of Special Education and Rehabilitation Services, Division of Educational Services. (ERIC Document Reproduction Service No. ED 253 029)

Daggett, W. R. (1988, October). *The changing nature of work—A challenge to education.* Speech presented at a meeting of the Kansas legislative and educational leaders, Topeka, KS.

deBettencourt, L., Zigmond, N., & Thornton, H. (1989). Follow-up of postsecondary-aged rural learning disabled graduates and dropouts. *Exceptional Children, 56,* 40–49.

Department of Labor. (1989). *Occupational outlook handbook.* Washington, DC: Author.

Edgar, E. (1987). Secondary programs in special education: Are many of them justifiable? *Exceptional Children, 53,* 555–561.

Fafard, M., & Haubrich, P. A. (1981). Vocational and social adjustment of learning disabled young adults: A followup study. *Learning Disability Quarterly, 4,* 122–130.

Frauenheim, J. G., & Heckerl, J. R. (1983). A longitudinal study of psychological and achievement test performance in severe dyslexic adults. *Journal of Learning Disabilities, 16,* 339–347.

Halpern, A. S. (1985). Transition: A look at the foundations. *Exceptional Children, 51,* 479–486.

Halpern, A. S. (1990). A methodological review of follow-up and follow-along studies tracking school leavers from special education. *Career Development for Exceptional Individuals, 13,* 13–27.

Halpern, A. S., Nave, G., Close, D., & Nelson, D. (1986). An empirical analysis of the dimensions of community adjustment for adults with mental retardation in semi-independent living programs. *Australia and New Zealand Journal of Developmental Disabilities, 12,* 147–157.

Hoffman, F. J., Sheldon, K. L., Minskoff, E. H., Sautter, S. W., Steidle, E. F., Baker, D. P., & Echols, L. D. (1987). Needs of learning disabled adults. *Journal of Learning Disabilities, 20,* 43–52.

Horn, W. F., O'Donnell, J. P., & Vitulano, L. D. (1983). Long-term follow-up studies of learning disabled persons. *Journal of Learning Disabilities, 16,* 542–555.

McCue, P. M., Shelley, C., & Goldstein, F. (1986). Intellectual, academic, and neuropsychological performance levels in learning disabled adults. *Journal of Learning Disabilities, 19,* 233–236.

Rogan, L. L., & Hartman, L. D. (1976). *A follow-up study of learning disabled children as adults* (Final Rep., Project No. 443Ch 60010). Washington, DC: Department of Health, Education, and Welfare.

Rogan, L. L., & Hartman, L. D. (1990). Adult outcome of learning disabled students ten years after initial follow-up. *Learning Disabilities Focus, 5,* 91–102.

Sitlington, P., Frank, A., & Cooper, L. (1989). *Iowa statewide follow-up study: Adult adjustment of individuals with learning disabilities.* Des Moines, IA: Department of Education.

Smith, D. D., Deshler, D., Hallahan, D., Lovitt, T., Robinson, S., Voress, J., & Ysseldyke, J. (1984). Minimum standards for the description of subjects in learning disabilities research reports. Learning Disability Quarterly, 7, 221–225.

Smith, T. J., & Trist, C. (1988). Training and educating the work force in the nineties: The rationale for public private collaboration. Columbus: The Ohio State University, Center on Education and Training for Employment.

Wagner, M. (1989, March). The transition experiences of youth with disabilities: A report from the National Longitudinal Transition Study. Paper presented at the meeting of the Division of Research, Council for Exceptional Children, San Francisco.

White, W. J., Schumaker, J. B., Warner, M. M., Alley, G. R., & Deshler, D. D. (1980). The current status of young adults identified as learning disabled during their school careers (Research Rep. No. 21). Lawrence: University of Kansas Institute for Research in Learning Disabilities.

Will, M. (1984, March-April). Bridges for school to working life. Programs for the handicapped. Washington, DC: Clearinghouse for the Handicapped.

William T. Grant Foundation Commission of Work, Family, and Citizenship. (1988). The forgotten half. Washington, DC: Author.

Zigmond, N., & Thornton, H. (1985). Follow-up of postsecondary age learning disabled graduates and dropouts. Learning Disabilities Research, 1, 50–55.

CHAPTER 5

Abbott, J. (1987, February). Accessing vocational education and vocational rehabilitation training and employment programs. Paper presented at the 1987 ACLD International Conference, San Antonio, TX.

American Psychiatric Association. (1987). Diagnostic and statistical manual of mental disorders (3rd ed., rev.). Washington, DC: Author.

Dowdy, C. A. (1990). Learning disability checklist. Assessment instrument submitted for publication.

Federal Register. (1977, Thursday, December 29), 65082–65085. Washington, DC.

Gerber, P. J. (1981). Learning disabilities and eligibility for vocational rehabilitation services: A chronology of events. Learning Disability Quarterly, 4, 423–425.

Gerber, P. J., Schnieders, C. A., Paradise, L. V., Reiff, H. B., Ginsberg, R. J., & Popp, P. A. (1990). Persisting problems of adults with learning disabilities: Self-reported comparisons from their school-aged and adult years. Journal of Learning Disabilities, 23, 570–573.

Hawks, R., Minkoff, E. H., Sautters, S., Sheldon, K. L., Steidle, E. F., & Hoffman, F. J. (1990). A model diagnostic battery for adults with learning disabilities in vocational rehabilitation. Learning Disabilities: A Multidisciplinary Journal, 1(3), 94–101.

Hursh, N. C. (1984). Vocational evaluation of learning disabled adults. Journal of Rehabilitation, 45–52.

Johnson, D. J., & Blalock, J. W. (1987). Adults with learning disabilities: Clinical studies. Orlando, FL: Grune & Stratton.

Koller, J. R. (1990). *Behavior questionnaire and rating scale for the learning disabled. Unpublished assessment instrument, University of Missouri, Columbia.*

Kopp, K. H., Miller, J. H., & Mulkey, S. W. (1984). *The paradox of learning disabilities: A stumbling block to rehabilitation. Journal of Rehabilitation, 50, 38–39.*

Mars, L. I. (1986). *Profile of learning disabled persons in the rehabilitation program. American Rehabilitation, 12, 10–13.*

McCue, M. (1989). *The role of assessment in the vocational rehabilitation of adults with specific learning disabilities. Rehabilitation Counseling Bulletin, 33(1), 18–37.*

McCue, P. M., Shelly, C., & Goldstein, G. (1986). *Intellectual, academic, and neuropsychological performance levels in learning disabled adults. Journal of Learning Disabilities, 19, 233–236.*

Miller, J. H., Mulkey, S. W., & Kopp, K. H. (1984). *Public rehabilitation services for individuals with specific learning disabilities. Journal of Rehabilitation, 50, 19–29.*

National Joint Committee on Learning Disabilities. (1981). *A position paper of the National Joint Committee on Learning Disabilities. Unpublished manuscript.*

National Joint Committee on Learning Disabilities. (1987). *Adults with learning disabilities: A call to action. Learning Disability Quarterly, 9, 164–167.*

Newill, B. H., Goyette, C. H., & Fogarty, T. W. (1984). *Diagnosis and assessment of the adult with specific learning disabilities. Journal of Rehabilitation, 50, 34–39.*

Patton, J. R., & Polloway, E. A. (1982). *The learning disabled: The adult years. Topics in Learning & Learning Disabilities, 2, 79–88.*

Polloway, E. E., Smith, J. D., & Patton, J. R. (1984). *Learning disabilities: An adult development perspective. Journal of Learning Disabilities, 7, 179–186.*

Prickett, J. R. (1988). *A statistical analysis of successful case closures in Iowa: Focus on learning disabilities. Journal of Job Placement, 10, 36–40.*

Rehabilitation Services Administration. (1981, July 27). *Acceptance of specific learning disabilities as a medically recognized disability program instruction. Program Information Memorandum RSA-PI-81-22, pp. 1–7.*

Rehabilitation Services Administration. (1985, January 24). *Program policy directive. Washington, DC: U.S. Office of Special Education and Rehabilitation Services.*

Rehabilitation Services Administration. (1990, September 28). *Program assistance circular 90-7. Washington, DC: U.S. Office of Special Education and Rehabilitation Services.*

Simpson, R. G., & Umbach, B. T. (1989). *Identifying and providing vocational services for adults with specific learning disabilities. Journal of Rehabilitation, 9, 49–55.*

Szymanski, E. M., King, J., Parker, R. M., & Jenkins, W. M. (1989). *The state–federal rehabilitation program: Interface with special education. Exceptional Children, 56, 70–77.*

U.S. Department of Education. (1990). *Twelfth annual report to Congress on the implementation of the Education of the Handicapped Act. Washington, DC: U.S. Office of Special Education and Rehabilitation Services.*

Vogel, S. A. (1989). *Adults with language learning disorders: Definition, diagnosis, and determination of eligibility for post-secondary and vocational rehabilitation services. Rehabilitation Education, 3, 77–90.*

Zwerlin, R. A., Smith, M., & Diffley, J. (1984). *Vocational rehabilitation for learning disabled professionals. Albertson, NY: Human Resources Center.*

Chapter 6

Academic Senate. (1990, September). Plan for accommodating the academic needs of students with disabilities. Berkeley, CA: Author.

Adelman, P. B., & Vogel, S. A. (1990). College graduates with learning disabilities: Employment attainment and career patterns. Learning Disability Quarterly, 13, 154–166.

Astin, A., Green, K., Korn, W., Schalit, M., & Berg, E. (1988). The American freshman: National norms for 1988. Los Angeles: University of California.

Aune, E. (1991). A transition model for postsecondary-bound students with learning disabilities. Learning Disabilities Research and Practice, 6, 177–187.

Ballard, J., Ramirez, B., & Zantal-Wiener, K. (1987). Public Law 94-142, Section 504, and Public Law 99-457: Understanding what they are and are not. Reston, VA: Council for Exceptional Children.

Biehl, G. R. (1978). Guide to the Section 504 self-evaluation for colleges and universities. Washington, DC: National Association of College and University Business Officers.

Brinckerhoff, L. C. (1985). Accommodations for college students with learning disabilities: The law and its implementation. In J. Gartner (Ed.), Proceedings of the eighth annual AHSSPPE conference (pp. 89–95). Columbus, OH: AHSSPPE Publications.

Brinckerhoff, L. C. (1991). Developing LD support services with minimal resources. Journal of Postsecondary Education and Disability, 9, 184–196.

Brinckerhoff, L. C., & Eaton, H. (1991, Spring). Developing a summer orientation program for college students with learning disabilities. Postsecondary LD Network News, pp. 1–3, 6.

Brinckerhoff, L. C., Shaw, S. F., & McGuire, J. M. (1990, Spring). Implementing regional consortia for postsecondary learning disability personnel. Postsecondary LD Network News, 9, 1–3.

Bruck, M. (1987). The adult outcomes of children with learning disabilities. Annals of Dyslexia, 37, 252–263.

Byron, J., & Owen, B. (1990, Winter). Metacognitive training: Bridging the gap between content and learning strategies. Postsecondary LD Network News, 8, 1–3.

Campbell A. Dinsmore v. Charles C. Pugh and the Regents of the University of California (1989).

Carlson, S. (1985). The ethical appropriateness of subject matter tutoring for learning disabled adolescents. Learning Disability Quarterly, 8, 310–314.

Carlton, P. M., & Walkenshaw, D. (1991). Diagnosis of learning disabilities in postsecondary institutions. Journal of Postsecondary Education and Disability, 9, 197–206.

Carnevale, A., Gainer, L., Metzer, A., & Holland, S. (1988). Workplace basics: The skills employers want. Training and Development Journal, 42, 22–30.

Dalke, C., & Schmitt, S. (1987). Meeting the transition needs of college-bound students with learning disabilities. Journal of Learning Disabilities, 20, 176–180.

D'Amico, R. (1989). Learning disabilities and legal responsibilities under Section 504. In Proceedings of The Next Step: An invitational symposium on learning disabilities in selective colleges (pp. 20–35). Cambridge, MA: Harvard University.

Dexter, B. L. (1982). Helping learning disabled students prepare for college. Journal of Learning Disabilities, 15, 344–346.

Education. (1990, February 9). The Wall Street Journal Reports, p. R6.

Ellis, E. S. (1990). What's so strategic about teaching teachers to teach strategies. Teacher Education and Special Education, 13, 59–62.

Evelo, S., & Price, L. (1991). The transition of students with learning disabilities: A case study. Journal of Postsecondary Education and Disability, 9, 59–62.

Gardner, J. N., & Jewler, A. J. (1985). College is only the beginning: A student guide to higher education. Belmont, CA: Wadsworth.

Greenspan, S., Apthorp, H., & Williams, P. (1991). Social competence and work success of college students with learning disabilities. Journal of Postsecondary Education and Disability, 9, 227–234.

Handicapped Requirements Handbook. (1985, September). Academic programs. Washington, DC: Federal Programs Advisory Service.

Handicapped Requirements Handbook. (1990, October). Court orders university to increase accessible transportation; strikes down auxiliary aids policy. Washington, DC: Federal Programs Advisory Service.

Hasazi, S. B., Johnson, R. E., Hasazi, J. E., Gordon, L. R., & Hull, M. (1989). Employment of youth with and without handicaps following high school: Outcome and correlates. The Journal of Special Education, 23, 243–255.

Heyward, S. M. (1990). Access to Section 504. Atlanta, GA: Heyward, Lawton, and Associates.

Heyward, S. M. (1991, June). Learning disabilities and Section 504. Paper presented at the University of Connecticut professional training institute, Hartford.

Hoffman, F. J., Sheldon, K. L., Minskoff, E. H., Sautter, S. W., Steidle, E. F., Baker, D. P., Bailey, M. B., & Echols, L. D. (1987). Needs of learning disabled adults. Journal of Learning Disabilities, 20, 143–152.

Jaschik, S. (1990, May 30). U.S. court rules that requiring multiple-choice tests may violate the rights of learning-disabled students. Chronicle of Higher Education, p. A17.

Johnson, D. J., & Blalock, J. W. (Eds.). (1987). Adults with learning disabilities: Clinical studies. New York: Grune & Stratton.

King, W., & Jarrow, J. (1990). Testing accommodations for students with disabilities. Columbus, OH: AHSSPPE Publications.

Link, T. (1989, May 5). Dyslexic student sues UC for denying extra exam time. Oakland Tribune, p. B-2.

Litt, A. V., & McGuire, J. M. (1989). Continuum of services. Storrs: The University of Connecticut Program for College Students with Learning Disabilities.

Mangrum, C. T., & Strichart, S. S. (Eds.). (1988). College and the learning disabled student (2nd ed.). Orlando, FL: Grune & Stratton.

McGuire, J. M. (1988, May). Starting off sound means college-bound. Paper presented at the meeting of the southeastern Connecticut chapter of the Association for Children and Adults with Learning Disabilities, New Haven.

McGuire, J. M. (1990, June). Program organization and management: Four year schools. Paper presented at the University of Connecticut professional training institute, Storrs.

McGuire, J. M., & Shaw, S. F. (1987). A decision making process for the college-bound student: Matching learner, institution, and program. Learning Disability Quarterly, 10, 106–111.

Mellard, D. F. (1990). The eligibility process: Identifying students with learning disabilities in California's community colleges. Learning Disabilities Focus, 5, 75–90.

Okolo, C. M., & Sitlington, P. L. (1986). The role of special education in LD adolescents' transition from school to work. Learning Disability Quarterly, 9, 141–155.

Phillips, P. (1990). A self-advocacy plan for high school students with learning disabilities: A comparative case study analysis of students', teachers', and parents' perceptions of program effectiveness. Journal of Learning Disabilities, 23, 466–471.

Rothstein, L. F. (1986). Section 504 of the Rehabilitation Act: Emerging issues for colleges and universities. Journal of College and University Law, 13, 229–265.

Rothstein, L. F. (1989). Learning disabilities in selective colleges: Legal issues c. 1990. In Proceedings of The Next Step: An invitational symposium on learning disabilities in selective colleges (pp. 36–52). Cambridge, MA: Harvard University.

Rothstein, L. F. (1990). Special education law. New York: Longman.

Salvador v. Bell, 622 F. Supp. 438 (N.D. Ill., 1985), affd, 800 F. 2nd 97 (7th Cir. 1986).

Scheiber, B., & Talpers, J. (1987). Unlocking potential: College and other choices for learning disabled people. Bethesda, MD: Adler and Adler.

Scott, S. S. (1990). Coming to terms with the "otherwise qualified" student with a learning disability. Journal of Learning Disabilities, 23, 398–405.

Scott, S. S. (1991). A change in legal status: An overlooked dimension in the transition to higher education. Journal of Learning Disabilities, 24, 459–466.

Spector, S., Decker, K., & Shaw, S. F. (1991). Independence and responsibility: An LD resource room at South Windsor High School. Intervention in School and Clinic, 26, 159–187.

Southeastern Community College v. Davis, 422 U.S. 397 (1979). (ERIC Document Reproduction Service No. ED 173 574)

U.S. Department of Education. (1987). Profile of handicapped students in postsecondary education (National Center for Education Statistics Publication No. 065-000-00375-9). Washington, DC: U.S. Government Printing Office.

United States v. Board of Trustees of the University of Alabama, 86-C-1779-S (N.D. Ala., 1988); 408 F. 2d 740 (11th Cir. 1990).

Valdes, K. A., Williamson, C. L., & Wagner, M.TA. (1990). The national longitudinal transition study of special education students. Menlo Park, CA: SRI International.

Vogel, S. A. (1982). On developing LD college programs. Journal of Learning Disabilities, 15, 518–528.

Wagner, M. (1989). Youth with disabilities during transition: An overview of descriptive findings from The National Longitudinal Transition Study. Menlo Park, CA: SRI International.

Wynne v. Tufts University School of Medicine, No. 89-1670 (1st Cir. 1990).

Ysseldyke, J. E., Thurlow, M. L., Graden, J. L., Wesson, C., Deno, S. L., & Algozzine, B. (1983). Generalizations from five years of research on assessment and decision making. Exceptional Education Quarterly, 4, 75–93.

Zigmond, N., & Thornton, H. (1985). Follow-up of postsecondary age learning disabled graduates and drop-outs. Learning Disabilities Research, 1, 50–55.

Chapter 7

Adelman, H. S., & Taylor, L. (1991). Issues and problems related to the assessment of learning disabilities. In H. L. Swanson (Ed.), Handbook on the assessment of learning disabilities (pp. 21–43). Austin, TX: PRO-ED.

Adelman, P. B., & Vogel, S. A. (1990). College graduates with learning disabilities: Employment attainment and career patterns. Learning Disability Quarterly, 13, 154–166.

Adelman, P. B., & Vogel, S. A. (1991). The learning disabled adult. In B. Wong (Ed.), Learning about learning disabilities (pp. 563–594). New York: Academic Press.

Alley, G., & Deshler, D. (1979). Teaching the learning disabled adolescent: Strategies and methods. Denver: Love Publishing.

American College Personnel Association. (1990). Statement of ethical principles and standards. Journal of College Student Development, 31, 11–16.

Americans with Disabilities Act of 1990, 42 U.S.C. §12101 et seq.

Anastasi, A. (1988). Psychological testing (7th ed.). New York: Macmillan.

Arena, J. (1982). Diagnostic Spelling Potential Test. Novato, CA: Academic Therapy.

Beirne-Smith, M., & Deck, M. D. (1989). A survey of postsecondary programs for students with learning disabilities. Journal of Learning Disabilities, 22, 456–457.

Bender, L. (1938). Bender visual-motor gestalt test. New York: American Orthopsychiatric Association.

Bireley, M., & Manley, E. (1980). The learning disabled student in a college environment: A report of Wright State University's program. Journal of Learning Disabilities, 13, 12-15.

Blackburn, J. C., & Iovacchini, E. V. (1982). Student service responsibilities of institutions to learning disabled students. College and University, 52, 208–217.

Bracken, B. A., Prasse, D., & Breene, M. (1984). Concurrent validity of the Woodcock-Johnson Psycho-Educational Battery with regular and learning disabled students. Journal of School Psychology, 22, 185–192.

Brown, J. I., Bennett, J. M., & Hanna, G. (1981). The Nelson-Denny Reading Test. Chicago: Riverside.

Bryant, B. R., Patton, J. R., & Dunn, C. (1991). Scholastic Abilities Test for Adults. Austin, TX: PRO-ED.

Bryant, B. R., & Rivera, D. D. (1992). Are standardized tests designed for adolescents appropriate for use with adults? Manuscript submitted for publication.

Buchanan, M., & Wolf, J. S. (1986). A comprehensive study of learning disabled adults. Journal of Learning Disabilities, 19, 34–38.

Bursuck, W. D., Rose, E., Cowen, S., & Yahaya, M. A. (1989). Nationwide survey of postsecondary education services for students with learning disabilities. Exceptional Children, 56, 236–245.

Carlson, S. (1985). The ethical appropriateness of subject matter tutoring for learning disabled adolescents. Learning Disability Quarterly, 8, 310–314.

Carlton, P. M., & Walkenshaw, D. (1991). Diagnosis of learning disabilities in postsecondary institutions. Journal of Postsecondary Education and Disability, 9, 197–206.

Chamberlain, P., & Medeiros-Landurand, P. (1991). Practical considerations for the assessment of LEP students with special needs. In E. V. Hamayan & J. Damico (Eds.), Limiting bias in the assessment of bilingual students (pp. 111-156). Austin, TX: PRO-ED.

Chelser, B. L. (1982). ACLD vocational committee completes survey on LD adults. ACLD Newsbriefs, 5, 20–23.

Cooper, R. J. (1987). What an admissions counselor needs to know about learning disabled students. The Journal of College Admissions, 116, 14–19.

Cordoni, B. (1982). The learning disabled college student. Journal of Learning Disabilities, 15, 599–603.

Cuenin, L. H. (1990). Use of the Woodcock-Johnson Psycho-Educational Battery with learning disabled adults. Learning Disability Quarterly, 5, 119–123.

Cummings, J. A. (1985). Review of the Woodcock-Johnson Psycho-Educational Battery. In J. F. Mitchell (Ed.), The ninth mental measurements yearbook (pp. 1759–1762). Lincoln: University of Nebraska Press.

Dalke, C. (1988). Woodcock-Johnson Psycho-Educational Test Battery profiles: A comparative study of college freshmen with and without learning disabilities. Journal of Learning Disabilities, 21, 567–570.

Dalke, C., & Schmitt, S. (1987). Meeting the transition needs of college-bound students with learning disabilities. Journal of Learning Disabilities, 20, 176–180.

Dangel, H. L., & Ensminger, E. E. (1988). The use of a discrepancy formula with LD students. Learning Disabilities Focus, 4, 24–31.

Decker, T., Polloway, E., & Decker B. (1985). Help for the LD college student. Academic Therapy, 20, 339–345.

Denton, P. H., Seybert, J. A., & Franklin, E. L. (1988). Ideas in practice: A content-based learning strategies program. Journal of Developmental Education, 11, 20–24.

Education for All Handicapped Children Act of 1975, 20 U.S C. §1400 et seq.

Estabrook, G. (1983). Test review: The Woodcock-Johnson Psycho-Educational Battery. Journal of Psychoeducational Assessment, 1, 317–319.

Evans, L. D. (1990). A conceptual overview of the regression discrepancy model for evaluation of severe discrepancy between IQ and achievement scores. Journal of Learning Disabilities, 23, 406–412.

Evelo, S., & Price, L. (1991). The transition of students with learning disabilities: A case study. Journal of Postsecondary Education and Disability, 9, 207–218.

Gajar, A. H., Murphy, J. P., & Hunt, F. M. (1982). A university program for learning disabled students. Reading Improvement, 19, 282–288.

Garnett, K., & La Porta, S. (1984). Dispelling the myths: College students with learning disabilities. New York: Hunter College Press.

Gerber, P. J., & Leiff, H. B. (1985). A growing issue for university admissions office: The learning disabled applicant. The Journal of College Admissions, 109, 9–13.

Gerber, P. J., & Mellard, D. (1985). Rehabilitation of learning disabled adults: Recommended research priorities. Journal of Rehabilitation, 51(1), 62–64.

Gerber, P. J., Schnieders, C. A., Paradise, L. V., Reiff, H. B., Ginsberg, R. J., & Popp, P. A. (1990). Persisting problems for adults with learning disabilities: Self-reported comparisons from their school-aged and adult years. Journal of Learning Disabilities, 23, 570–573.

Golden, C. J., Hammeke, T. A., & Purisch, A. D. (1980). Luria-Nebraska Neuropsychological Battery. Los Angeles: Western Psychological Services.

Goldman, R., Fristoe, M., & Woodcock, R. W. (1976). Goldman-Fristoe-Woodcock Auditory Skills Test Battery. Circle Pines, MN: American Guidance Service.

Gregg, N., & Hoy, C. (1985). A comparison of the WAIS-R and the Woodcock-Johnson Tests of Cognitive Ability with learning disabled college students. Journal of Psychoeducational Assessment, 3, 267–274.

Gregory, R. (1987). Adult intellectual assessment. Boston: Allyn & Bacon.

Greenspan, S., Apthorp, H., & Williams, P. (1991). Social competence and work success of college students with learning disabilities. Journal of Postsecondary Education and Disability, 9, 227–234.

Guralnik, D. B. (Ed.). (1984). Webster's new world dictionary. New York: Simon and Schuster.

Halpern, A. S. (1985). Transition: A look at the foundations. Exceptional Children, 51, 479–486.

Hamayan, E. V., & Damico, J. S. (1991). Limiting bias in the assessment of bilingual students. Austin, TX: PRO-ED.

Hammill, D. D. (1987). An overview of assessment practices. In D. D. Hammill (Ed.), Assessing the abilities and instructional needs of students (pp. 3–37). Austin, TX: PRO-ED.

Hammill, D. D., Brown, L., & Bryant, B. R. (1992). A consumer's guide to tests in print (2nd ed.). Austin, TX: PRO-ED.

Hammill, D. D., Brown, V., Larsen, S. C., & Wiederholt, J. L. (1988). Test of adolescent language (2nd ed.). Austin, TX: PRO-ED.

Hammill, D., & Bryant, B. R. (1992). Detroit tests of learning aptitude-Adult. Austin, TX: PRO-ED.

Hammill, D., & Larsen, S. (1988). Test of written language (2nd ed.). Austin, TX: PRO-ED.

Hammill, D. D., Leigh, J., McNutt, G., & Larsen, S. C. (1989). A new definition of learning disabilities. Learning Disability Quarterly, 4, 336–342.

Haring, K. A., Lovett, D. L., & Smith, D. D. (1990). A follow-up study of recent special education graduates of learning disabilities programs. Journal of Learning Disabilities, 23, 108–114.

Hathaway, S. R., & McKinley, J. C. (1991). Minnesota Multiphasic Personality Inventory–Revised. Minneapolis: University of Minnesota Press.

Herzog, J. E., & Falk, B. (1991). A follow-up study of vocational outcomes of young adults with learning disabilities. Journal of Postsecondary Education and Disability, 9, 216–226.

Hippolitus, P. (1987). College freshmen with disabilities preparing for employment. Washington, DC: President's Committee on Employment of the Handicapped.

Hoffmann, F. J., Sheldon, K. L., Minskoff, E. J., Sautter, S. W., Steidle, E. F., Baker, D. P., Baily, M. B., & Echols, L. D. (1987). Needs of learning disabled adults. Journal of Learning Disabilities, 20, 43–52.

Hoy, C., & Gregg, N. (1986a). Learning disabled students: An emerging population on college campuses. The Journal of College Admissions, 112 (Summer), 10–14.

Hoy, C., & Gregg, N. (1986b). The usefulness of the Woodcock-Johnson Psycho-Educational Battery cognitive cluster scores for learning disabled college students. Journal of Learning Disabilities, 19, 489–491.

Individuals with Disabilities Education Act of 1990, 20 U.S.C §1400 et seq.

Jastak, S. R., & Wilkinson, G. S. (1984). Wide range achievement test-Revised. Wilmington, DE: Jastak Assessment Systems.

Johnson, D. J. (1987). Principles of assessment and diagnosis. In D. Johnson & J. Blalock (Eds.), Adults with learning disabilities: Clinical studies (pp. 9–30). Orlando, FL: Grune & Stratton.

Johnson, D. J., & Blalock, J. (Eds.). (1987). Adults with learning disabilities: Clinical studies. Orlando, FL: Grune & Stratton.

Johnston, C. L. (1984). The learning disabled adolescent and young adult: An overview and critique of current practices. Journal of Learning Disabilities, 17, 386–391.

Kaufman, A. S. (1985). Review of the Woodcock-Johnson Psycho-Educational Battery. In J. F. Mitchell (Ed.), The ninth mental measurements yearbook (pp. 1762–1765). Lincoln: University of Nebraska Press, Buros Institute of Mental Measurements.

Kaufman, A. S. (1990). Assessing adolescent and adult intelligence. Boston: Allyn & Bacon.

Keogh, B. K. (1983). Classification, compliance and confusion. Journal of Learning Disabilities, 16, 25.

King, W. L. (1987). Students with learning disabilities and postsecondary education: National Council on Handicapped forum on higher education and students with disabilities. In D. Knapke & C. Lendman (Eds.), Capitalizing on the future (pp. 16–21). Columbus, OH: AHSSPPE.

Kramer, J. J., & Conoley, J. C. (1989). The eleventh mental measurements yearbook. Lincoln: University of Nebraska Press.

Learning Disability Update. (1986, May). Information from HEATH, 5, 2-6.

Lenz, B. K. (1992). In the spirit of strategies instruction: Cognitive and metacognitive aspects of the strategies intervention model. In S. A. Vogel (Ed.), Educational alternatives for students with learning disabilities (pp. 141–158). New York: Springer-Verlag.

Levinson, E. M. (1986). School psychology and college learning disabled students: Training and services possibilities. Psychology in the Schools, 23, 295–302.

Longo, J. (1988). The learning disabled: Challenge to postsecondary institutions. Journal of Developmental Education, 11, 10–14.

Mangrum, C. T., & Strichart, S. S. (1984). College and the learning disabled student. Orlando, FL: Grune & Stratton.

Mangrum, T., & Strichart, S. S. (1988). College opportunities. In K. A. Kavale, S. R. Forness, & M. Bender (Eds), Handbook of learning disabilities: Volume III. Programs and practices (pp. 186–197). Boston: Little, Brown.

Mann, L., Davis, C., Boyer, C., Metz, C., & Wolford, B. (1983). LD or not LD, that was the question. Journal of Learning Disabilities, 16, 14–17.

McCue, M. (1989). The role of assessment in the vocational rehabilitation of adults with specific learning disabilities. Rehabilitation Counseling Bulletin, 33, 18–37.

McGuire, J. M., Norlander, K. A., & Shaw, S. F. (1990). Postsecondary education for students with learning disabilities: Forecasting challenges for the future. Learning Disabilities Focus, 5, 69–74.

McLoughlin, J. A., & Lewis, R. B. (1981). Assessing special students (3rd ed.). Columbus, OH: Merrill.

Mellard, D. F. (1990). The eligibility process: Identifying students with learning disabilities in California's community colleges. Learning Disabilities Focus, 5, 75–90.

Mellard, D. F., & Deshler, D. D. (1984). Modeling the condition of learning disabilities on postsecondary populations. Educational Psychologist, 19, 188–197.

Mercer, C. D. (1987). Beyond traditional assessment. In S. Vaughn & C. S. Bos (Eds.), Research in learning disabilities: Issues and future directions (pp. 153–169). Boston: College-Hill.

Milberg, W. P., Hebben, N., & Kaplan, E. (1986). The Boston process approach to neuropsychological assessment. In I. Grant & K. M. Adams (Eds.), Neuropsychological assessment of neuropsychiatric disorders (pp. 65–86). New York: Oxford University Press.

National Joint Committee on Learning Disabilities. (1985). Adults with learning disabilities: A call to action. A position paper of the National Joint Committee on Learning Disabilities. Journal of Learning Disabilities, 20, 172–175.

Nelson, R., & Lignugaris-Kraft, B. (1989). Postsecondary education for students with learning disabilities. Exceptional Children, 56, 246–265.

Norlander, K. A., Shaw, S. F., & McGuire, J. M. (1990). Competencies of postsecondary education personnel serving students with learning disabilities. Journal of Learning Disabilities, 23, 426–432.

Parker, R. (1991). Occupational aptitude survey and interest schedule (2nd ed.). Austin, TX: PRO-ED.

Parks, A. W., Antonoff, S., Drake, C., Skiba, W., & Soberman, J. (1987). A survey of programs and services for learning disabled students in graduate and professional schools. Journal of Learning Disabilities, 20, 181–188.

Polloway, E. A., Smith, J. D., & Patton, J. R. (1984). Learning disabilities: An adult development perspective. Learning Disability Quarterly, 7, 179–186.

Porch, B. E. (1971). Multi-dimensional scoring in aphasia testing. Journal of Speech and Hearing Research, 14, 776–792.

Prater, G., & Minner, S. (1986). Factors inhibiting the performance of learning disabled students in postsecondary settings. Reading, Writing, and Learning Disabilities, 2, 273–277.

Raven, J. C. (1958). Raven's Standard Progressive Matrices. London: H. K. Lewis & Co.

Rehabilitation Act of 1973, 29 U.S.C. §701 et seq.

Report on Educational Research. (1990). Disabled student enrollment exploding at universities. Washington, DC: U.S. Department of Education.

Roffman, A. J., Herzog, J. E., & Wershba-Gershon, P. M. (1994). Helping young adults understand their learning disabilities. Journal of Learning Disabilities, 27, 413–419.

Rogan, L. L., & Hartman, L. D. (1990). Adult outcome of learning disabled students ten years after initial follow-up. Learning Disabilities Focus, 5, 91–102.

Rogers, T. (1991). Dyslexia: A survivor's story. Journal of Learning Disabilities, 24, 121–123.

Ross, J. M. (1987). Learning disabled adults: Who are they and what do we do with them? Lifelong Learning: An Omnibus of Practice and Research, 11(3), 4–8.

Salvia, J., & Salvia, S. A. (1985). Use of the Woodcock-Johnson Psycho-Educational Battery, Part II: Tests of achievement with a college population. Diagnostique, 11, 3–8.

Salvia, J., & Ysseldyke, J. (1991). Assessment (5th ed.). Boston: Houghton Mifflin.

Sattler, J. M. (1988). Assessment of children (3rd ed.). San Diego: Jerome M. Sattler.

Scott, S. S. (1991). A change in legal status: An overlooked dimension in the transition to higher education. Journal of Learning Disabilities, 24, 459–546.

Shaw, S. F., Norlander, K. A., & McGuire, J. M. (1987). Training leadership personnel for learning disability college programs: Preservice and inservice models. Teacher Education and Special Education, 10, 108–112.

Siperstein, G. (1988). Students with learning disabilities in college: The need for a programmatic approach to critical transitions. Journal of Learning Disabilities, 21, 431–436.

Sitlington, P. L., & Frank, A. R. (1990). Are adolescents with learning disabilities crossing the bridge into adult life? Learning Disability Quarterly, 13, 97–111.

Slate, J. R., Frost, J., & Cross, B. (1990). Comparability of WISC-R and WAIS-R scores for a sample of college students with learning disabilities. Learning Disability Quarterly, 13, 205–208.

Slate, J. R., Frost, J., & Cross, B. (1991). WAIS-R stability for college students with learning disabilities. Learning Disability Quarterly, 14, 2–6.

Smith, D. D. (1989). Teaching students with learning and behavior problems. Englewood Cliffs, NJ: Prentice-Hall.

Spekman, N. J., Goldberg, R. J., & Herman, K. L. (1992). Learning disabled children grow up: A search for factors related to success in the young adult years. Learning Disabilities Research & Practice, 7, 161–170.

Stone, G. L., & Lucas, J. (1990). Knowledge and beliefs about confidentiality on a university campus. Journal of College Student Development, 31, 437–444.

Strichart, S. S., & Mangrum, C. T. (1985). Selecting a college for the LD student. Academic Therapy, 20, 475–479.

Sweetland, R. C., & Keyser, D. J. (Eds.). (1990). Tests: A comprehensive reference for assessments in psychology, education, and business. Austin, TX: PRO-ED.

Swiercinsky, D. P. (Ed.). (1985). Testing adults: A reference guide for special psychodiagnostic assessments. Austin, TX: PRO-ED.

Swiercinsky, D. P., & Fisk, T. (1985). The adult vocational rehabilitation assessment. In D. P. Swiercinsky (Ed.), Testing adults: A reference guide for special psychodiagnostic assessments (pp. 188–199). Austin, TX: PRO-ED.

U.S. Bureau of the Census. (1990). Statistical abstract of the United States 1990. Washington, DC: U.S. Government Printing Office.

U.S. Employment Service. (1983). General aptitude test battery. Washington, DC: Author.

Vogel, S. A. (1982). On developing LD college programs. Journal of Learning Disabilities, 15, 518–528.

Vogel, S. A. (1987). Eligibility and identification considerations in postsecondary education: A new but old dilemma. In S. Vaughn & C. S. Bos (Eds.), Research in learning disabilities: Issues and future directions (pp. 121–137). Boston: College-Hill.

Wechsler, D. (1981). Wechsler adult intelligence scale–Revised. San Antonio, TX: Psychological Corp.

Wechsler, D. (1987). Wechsler memory scale–Revised. San Antonio, TX: Psychological Corp.

Wiederholt, J. L., & Bryant, B. R. (1987). Assessing the reading abilities and instructional needs of students. Austin, TX: PRO-ED.

Wiederholt, J. L., & Bryant, B. R. (1992). Gray oral reading tests (3rd ed.). Austin, TX: PRO-ED.

Wilczenski, F. L., & Gillespie-Silver, P. (1992). Challenging the norm: Academic performance of university students with learning disabilities. Journal of College Student Development, 33, 197–202.

Wood, D. M. (1991). Discrepancy formulas and classification and identification issues that affect diagnoses of learning disabilities. Psychology in the Schools, 28, 219–225.

Woodcock, R., & Johnson, M. B. (1989). Woodcock-Johnson psycho-educational battery (rev. ed.). Allen, TX: DLM/Teaching Resources.

CHAPTER 8

Adelman, P. B., & Vogel, S. A. (1990). College graduates with learning disabilities employment attainment and career patterns. Learning Disability Quarterly, 13, 154–166.

Adelman, P. B., & Vogel, S. A. (1991). The learning disabled adult. In B. Wong (Ed.), Learning about learning disabilities (pp. 563–594). New York: Academic Press.

Astin, A., Green, K., Korn, W., Schalit, M., & Berg, E. (1988). The American freshman: National norms for 1988. Los Angeles: University of California.

Bursuck, W., Rose, E., Cowen, S., & Yahaya, M. A. (1989). Nationwide survey of postsecondary education services for students with learning disabilities. Exceptional Children, 56, 236–245.

Cowen, S. E. (1985). College choice for LD students: Know your "SWIS." Academic Therapy, 21, 77–81.

Dalke, C. (1993). Making a successful transition from high school to college: A model program. In S. A. Vogel & P.B. Adelman (Eds.), Success for college students with learning disabilities: Factors related to educational attainments. New York: Springer-Verlag.

Dalke, C., & Schmitt, S. (1987). Meeting the transition needs of college-bound students with learning disabilities. Journal of Learning Disabilities, 20, 176–180.

Decker, T. W., Polloway, E. A., & Decker, B. B. (1985). Help for the learning disabled college student. Academic Therapy, 20, 339–345.

Educational Testing Service. (1977). Descriptive tests of language skills. Princeton, NJ: Author.

Faas, L. (1987). The Arizona State University Transition Research Project–Final Report. Tempe: Arizona State University.

Gajar, A., Salvia, J., Gajria, M., & Salvia, S. (1989). A comparison of intelligence achievement discrepancies between learning disabled and non-learning disabled college students. Learning Disabilities Research, 4, 119–124.

Gerber, P. J., Ginsberg, R., & Reiff, H. B. (1990). Identifying alterable patterns in employment success for highly successful adults with learning disabilities. Project # H 133 G 80500. Washington, DC: U.S. Department of Education, Office of Special Education and Rehabilitative Services.

Gregg, K. N. (1982). An investigation of the breakdown in certain aspects of the writing process with college-age learning disabled, normal, and basic writers. Unpublished doctoral dissertation, Northwestern University, Evanston, IL.

Jastak, S., & Wilkinson, G. (1984). Wide range achievement test–Revised. Wilmington, DE: Jastak Associates.

Johnson, D., & Blalock, J. (Eds.). (1987). Young adults with learning disabilities. Orlando, FL: Grune & Stratton.

Karlsen, B., Madden, R., & Gardner, E. (1977). Stanford diagnostic reading test (blue level). Chicago: Harcourt Brace Jovanovich.

Shaw, S. F., & Norlander, K. A. (1986). The special educator's role in training personnel to provide assistance to college students with learning disabilities. Teacher Education and Special Education, 9, 77–81.

Shaywitz, S. E., & Shaw, R. (1988). The admissions process: An approach to selecting learning disabled students at the most selective colleges. Learning Disabilities Focus, 3, 81–86.

Sitlington, P. L., & Frank, A. R. (1990). Are adolescents with learning disabilities successfully crossing the bridge into adult life? Learning Disability Quarterly, 13, 97–111.

U.S. Department of Education. (1987). Profile of handicapped students in postsecondary education. Washington, DC: U.S. Government Printing Office.

Vogel, S. A. (1985). Syntactic complexity in written expression of LD college writers. Annals of Dyslexia, 35, 137–157.

Vogel, S. A. (1986, March). Getting a degree with a degree of LD. Paper presented at the ACLD International Conference, New York.

Vogel, S. A. (1987, February). Making the match: The LD student and the college. Paper presented at the ACLD International Conference, San Antonio, TX.

Vogel, S. A. (1990). Gender differences in intelligence, language, visual–motor abilities, and academic achievement in students with learning disabilities: A review of the literature. Journal of Learning Disabilities, 23, 44–52.

Vogel, S. A., & Adelman, P. B. (1990). Intervention effectiveness at the postsecondary level for the learning disabled. In T. Scruggs & B. Wong (Eds.), Intervention research in learning disabilities (pp. 329–344). New York: Springer-Verlag.

Vogel, S. A., & Adelman, P. B. (Eds.). (1993). Success for college students with learning disabilities: Factors related to educational attainments. New York: Springer-Verlag.

Vogel, S. A., & Moran, M. R. (1982). Written language disorders in learning disabled college students: A preliminary report. In W. Cruickshank & J. Lerner (Eds.), The best of ACLD 1981, Volume 3: Coming of age (pp. 211–225). Syracuse, NY: Syracuse University Press.

Woodcock, R., & Johnson, M. (1977). Woodcock-Johnson psycho-educational battery. Hingham, MA: Teaching Resources Corp.

Years in college lasting longer. (1990, February). Chicago Tribune, p. C2.

Chapter 9

Adelman, K. A., & Adelman, H. S. (1987). Rodin, Patton, Edison, Wilson, Einstein: Were they really learning disabled? Journal of Learning Disabilities, 20, 270–279.

Baker, H. (1972, May). Famous persons who have been handicapped: A critical analysis. Paper presented at the Distinguished Lecture Series in Special Education and Rehabilitation, University of Southern California, Los Angeles.

Bloom, B. (1980). The new direction in educational research: Alterable variables. Phi Delta Kappan, 61, 382–385.

Bloom, B. (1982). The role of gifts and markers in the development of talent. Exceptional Children, 49, 510–522.

Bloom, B. S., & Sosniak, L. A. (1981). Talent development vs. schooling. Educational Leadership, 39, 86–94.

Covey, S. R. (1989). The seven habits of highly effective people. New York: Simon and Schuster.

Easton, J., & Ginsberg, R. (1985). Student learning process: How poorly prepared students succeed in college. Research and Teaching in Developmental Education, 1, 12–38.

Garfield, C. (1986). Peak performers. New York: Avon Books.

Gay, L. R. (1981). Educational research (2nd ed.). Columbus, OH: Merrill.

Gerber, P. J., & Reiff, H. B. (1992). Speaking for themselves: Ethnographic interviews with adults with learning disabilities. Ann Arbor: The University of Michigan Press.

Guba, E. G., & Lincoln, Y. S. (1981). Effective evaluation. San Francisco: Jossey-Bass.

Kauffman, F., Harrell, G., Milam, C., Woolverton, N., & Miller, J. H. (1986). The nature, role and influence of mentors in the lives of gifted adults. Journal of Counseling and Development, 64, 576–578.

Maker, J. (1978). The self-perceptions of successful handicapped scientists (Grant No. G00-7701[905]). Washington, DC: U.S. Department of Health, Education and Welfare, Office of Education, Bureau of the Education for the Handicapped.

Miles, M. B., & Huberman, A. M. (1984). Qualitative data analysis. Beverly Hills: Sage.

Peters, T., & Austin, N. (1985). A passion for excellence. New York: Warner Books.

Peters, T. J., & Waterman, R. H. (1982). In search of excellence: Lessons from America's best-run companies. New York: Warner Books.

Pines, M. (1979). Superkids. Psychology Today, 1, 55–63.

President's Committee on the Employment of People with Disabilities. (1990). From paternalism to productivity—Whatever it takes. Washington, DC: President's Committee on the Employability of People with Disabilities.

Preziosi, M. (1980). Organizational diagnosis questionnaire. In S. Pfeiffer & H. Jones (Eds.), The 1980 annual handbook for group facilitators (pp. 112–120). San Diego: University Associates.

Price, J. (1984). The spirit of enterprise: The best of the new entrepreneurs. New York: Random House.

Reiss, H. (1961). Duncan socioeconomic scale. Chicago: University of Chicago Press.

Rogan, L., & Hartman, L. (1976). A follow-up study of learning disabled children as adults (Final Report, Project No. 443CH600100). Washington, DC: Bureau of Education for the Handicapped, U.S. Department of Health, Education and Welfare.

Rosenberg, S. (1965). The Rosenberg self-esteem scale. In J. Paradise (Ed.), Society and the adolescent self image. Princeton, NJ: Princeton University Press.

Steers, H., & Braunstein, H. (1976). Manifest Needs Questionnaire. In the Role of achievement motivation in job design. Journal of Applied Psychology, 64, 472–479.

Terman, L. M., & Oden, M. H. (1947). The gifted child grows up: Twenty-five year follow-up of a superior group, genetic studies of genius. Stanford, CA: Stanford University Press.

Weiss, D. J., Davis, R. V., England, G. W., & Lofquist, L. H. (1967). Manual for the Minnesota Satisfaction Questionnaire: Minnesota studies in vocational rehabilitation (No. 22). Minneapolis: University of Minnesota.

Chapter 10

Alley, G. R., & Deshler, D. D. (1979). Teaching the learning disabled adolescent: Strategies and methods. Denver: Love.

Askamit, D., Morris, M., & Leuenberger, J. (1987). Preparation of student services professionals and faculty for serving learning-disabled students. Journal of College Student Personnel, 28(1), 53–59.

Balow, B., & Bloomquist, M. (1965). Young adults ten to fifteen years after severe reading disability. Elementary School Journal, 66, 44–48.

Barbaro, F. (1982). The learning disabled college student: Some considerations in setting objectives. Journal of Learning Disabilities, 15, 599–603.

Barsch, J. (1980). Community college: New opportunities for the student. Academic Therapy, 15, 467–470.

Bergin, A. E. (1966). Some implications of psychotherapy research for therapeutic practice. Journal of Abnormal Psychology, 71, 235–246.

Bergin, A. E., & Strupp, H. E. (1972). Changing frontiers in the science of psychotherapy. New York: Aldin-Atherton.

Bireley, M., & Manley, E. (1980). The learning disabled student in a college environment: A report of Wright State University's program. Journal of Learning Disabilities, 13, 13–15.

Blaha, J., Mandes, E., & Swisher, C. W. (1987). The hierarchical factor structure of the WAIS-R for learning-disabled adults. Journal of Clinical Psychology, 43(2), 280–287.

Blalock, J. W. (1982). Persistent problems and concerns of young adults with learning disabilities. In W. M. Cruickshank & A. A. Silver (Eds.), Bridges to tomorrow: The best of ACLD (Vol. 2, pp. 35–56). Syracuse, NY: Syracuse University Press.

Blosser, R. E. (1984). The roles and functions and the preparation of disabled student service directors in higher education. Dissertation Abstracts International, 45, 2396A. (University Microfilms No. 84-25, 117)

Brill, J. (1987). Learning disabled adults in postsecondary education. Washington, DC: American Council on Education.

Brown, B. (1980). Steps to independence for people with learning disabilities. Washington, DC: President's Committee for Employment of Persons with Disabilities.

Brown, D. (1989). Learning disabled adults face the world of work. In President's Committee on Employment of the Handicapped, Learning disability: Not just a problem children outgrow (pp. 4–10). Washington, DC: Government Printing Office.

Brown, J. M. (1984). A model for enhancing the transition of mildly handicapped youth into postsecondary vocational education. In J. Chadsey-Rusch (Ed.), Conference proceedings from: Enhancing Transition From School to the Workplace for Handicapped Youth (pp. 40–55). Champaign, IL: National Network for Professional Development in Vocational Special Education.

Buchanan, M., & Weller, C. (1984). The learning disabled young adult in transition from school to career. Journal of Rehabilitation, 50, 42–46.

Buchanan, M., & Wolf, J. S. (1986). A comprehensive study of learning disabled adults. Journal of Learning Disabilities, 14, 404–407.

Bursuck, W. D., Rose, E., Cowen, S., & Yahaya, M. A. (1989). Nationwide survey of postsecondary education services for students with learning disabilities. Exceptional Children, 56, 236–245.

Carriker, W. R. (1957). A comparison of post school adjustment of regular and special class retarded individuals served in Lincoln and Omaha, Nebraska, public schools (Contract No SAE 6445). Washington, DC: Department of Health, Education, and Welfare, Office of Education.

Cassidy, V. M., & Phelps, H. R. (1955). Postschool adjustment of slow learning children. Columbus: The Ohio State University, Bureau of Special and Adult Education.

Chelser, B. (1982). ACLD vocational committee completes survey on LD adult. ACLD Newsbriefs, 5(146), 20–23.

Cobb, B., & Hasazi, S. B. (1987). School-aged transition service: Options for adolescents with mild handicaps. Career Development for Exceptional Indi-viduals, 10, 15–23.

Cobb, R. M., & Crump, W. D. (1984). Post-school status of young adults identified as learning disabled while enrolled in public schools: A comparison of those enrolled and not enrolled in learning disabilities programs (Final Report). Washington, DC: Office of Special Education and Rehabilitation Services, Division of Educational Services. (ERIC Document Reproduction Service No ED 253 029)

Cordoni, B. K. (1980). A directory of college LD services. Journal of Learning Disabilities, 15, 529–534.

Cox, S. (1977). The learning disabled adult. Academic Therapy, 13, 79–86.

Cronbach, L. J., & Snow, R. E. (1977). Aptitudes and instructional methods. New York: Irvington.

Cummings, R. W., & Maddox, C. D. (1987). Holland personality types among learning disabled and non-disabled high school students. Exceptional Children, 54, 167–170.

Dalke, C. (1988). Woodcock-Johnson Psycho-Educational Test Battery profiles: A comparative study of college freshmen with and without learning disabilities. Journal of Learning Disabilities, 21, 567–570.

Dallago, M. L. L., & Moely, B. E. (1980). Free recall in boys of normal and poor reading levels as a function of task manipulations. Journal of Experimental Child Psychology, 30, 62–78.

Edgar, E. (1987). Secondary programs in special education: Are many of them justifiable? Exceptional Children, 53, 555–561.

Edgar, E., Levine, P., & Maddox, M. (1986). State-wide follow-up studies of secondary special education students in transition. Unpublished manuscript, University of Washington, Seattle.

Edgerton, R. B. (1967). The cloak of competence: Stigma in the lives of the mentally retarded. Berkeley: University of California Press.

Eldredge, J. L. (1988). A 52 year old dyslexic learns to read. Reading, Writing, and Learning Disabilities, 4, 101–106.

Faas, L. A., & D'Alonzo, B. J. (1990). WAIS-R scores as predictors of employment success and failure among adults with learning disabilities. Journal of Learning Disabilities, 23, 311–316.

Fafard, M., & Haubrich, P. (1981). Vocational and social adjustment of learning disabled young adults: A follow-up study. Learning Disability Quarterly, 4, 122–130.

Federal Register, 42(86), 22683-22684 (May 4) 1977.

Frauenheim, J. G. (1978). Academic achievement characteristics of adult males who were diagnosed as dyslexic in childhood. Journal of Learning Disabilities, 11, 476–483.

Frauenheim, J. G., & Heckerl, J. R. (1983). A longitudinal study of psychological and achievement test performance in severe dyslexic adults. Journal of Learning Disabilities, 16, 339–347.

Gajar, A. H. (1987a). Foreign language learning disabilities: The identification of predictive and diagnostic variables. Journal of Learning Disabilities, 20, 327–330.

Gajar, A. H. (1987b). Performance of learning disabled university students on the Woodcock-Johnson Psycho-Educational Battery, Part II: Tests of Achievement. Diagnostique, 12(2), 87–92.

Gajar, A. H. (1989). A computer analysis of written language variables and a comparison of compositions written by university students with and without learning disabilities. Journal of Learning Disabilities, 22, 125–130.

Gajar, A. H. (1991). University based programs. In F. R. Rusch, L. DeStefano, L. Chadsey-Rusch, L. A. Phelps, & E. Szymanski (Eds.), Transition from school to adult life. Sycamore, IL: Sycamore.

Gajar, A. H., & Harriman, N. (1987). Identifying data based procedures for written expression disabilities at the university level. Education, 107(3), 252–258.

Gajar, A. H., Murphy, J., & Hunt, F. M. (1982). A university program for learning disabled students. Reading Improvement, 19(4), 282–288.

Gajar, A. H., Salvia, J., Gajria, M., & Salvia, S. (1989). A comparison of IQ–achievement discrepancies between LD and non-LD college students. Learning Disabilities Research, 4(2), 119–124.

Geib, B. B., Guzzardi, L. R., & Genova, P. M. (1981). Intervention for adults with learning disabilities. Academic Therapy, 16, 317–325.

Gerber, P. J. (1981). Learning disabilities and eligibility for vocational rehabilitation services: A chronology of events. Learning Disability Quarterly, 4, 422–425.

Gerber, P. J., & Mellard, D. (1985). Rehabilitation of learning disabled adults: Recommended research priorities. Journal of Rehabilitation, 51, 62–64.

Gerber, P. J., Schnieders, C. A., Paradise, L. V., Reiff, H. B., Ginsberg, R. J., & Popp, P. A. (1990). Persisting problems of adults with learning disabilities: Self-reported comparisons from their school-age and adult years. Journal of Learning Disabilities, 23, 570–573.

Gold, P. C. (1981). The DL-LEA: A remedial approach for nonreaders with a language deficiency handicap. Adult Literacy and Basic Education, 5, 185–193.

Gottfredson, L. S., Finucci, J. M., & Childs, B. (1984). Explaining the adult careers of dyslexic boys: Variations in critical skills for high-level jobs. Journal of Vocational Behavior, 24, 355–373.

Gray, R. A. (1981). Services for the LD adult: A working paper. Learning Disability Quarterly, 4, 426–434.

Haig, J. H., & Patterson, B. H. (1980, March). An overview of adult learning disabilities. Paper presented at the 13th annual meeting of the Western College Reading Association, San Francisco. (ERIC Document Reproduction Service No. ED 197 563)

Halpern, A. S., & Benz, M. R. (1987). A statewide examination of secondary special education for students with mild disabilities: Implications for the high school curriculum. Exceptional Children, 54, 122–129.

Halpern, A. S., Close, D. W., & Nelson, D. J. (1986). On my own: The impact of semi-independent living programs for adults with mental retardation. Baltimore: Brookes.

Haring, K. A., Lovett, D. L., & Smith, D. D. (1990). A follow-up study of recent special education graduates of learning disabilities programs. Journal of Learning Disabilities, 23, 108–114.

Hasazi, S. B., Gordon, L. R., & Roe, C. A. (1985). Factors associated with the employment status of handicapped youth exiting high school from 1979 to 1983. Exceptional Children, 51, 455–469.

Hasazi, S. B., Gordon, L. R., Roe, C. A., Hull, M., Finck, K., & Salembier, G. (1985). A statewide follow-up in post high school employment and residential status of students labeled "mentally retarded." Education and Training of the Mentally Retarded, 20(4), 222–234.

Hersen, M., & Barlow, D. H. (1976). Single case experimental designs. New York: Pergamon Press.

Hirschorn, M. W. (1988, January 20). Freshman interest in business careers hits new level and money remains a top priority, study finds. The Chronicle of Higher Education, pp. A31, A34–36.

Hoffmann, F. J., Sheldon, K. L., Minskoff, E. H., Sautter, S. W., Steidle, E. F., Baker, D. P., Bailey, M. B., & Echols, L. D. (1987). Needs of learning disabled adults. Journal of Learning Disabilities, 20, 43–52.

Hughes, C. A., & Smith, J. O. (1990). Cognitive and academic performance of college students with learning disabilities: A synthesis of the literature. Learning Disability Quarterly, 13, 66–79.

Humes, C. W. (1986). From learner to earner. Academic Therapy, 21, 483–489.

Humes, C. W., & Brammer, G. (1985). LD career success after high school. Academic Therapy, 21, 171–176.

Hursh, N. C. (1984). Vocational evaluation of learning disabled adults. Journal of Rehabilitation, 50(2), 47–52.

Johnson, D. R., Bruininks, R. H., & Thurlow, M. L. (1987). Meeting the challenge of transition service planning through improved interagency cooperation. Exceptional Children, 53, 522–530.

Kahn, M. S. (1980). Learning problems of the secondary and junior college learning disabled student: Suggested remedies. Journal of Learning Disabilities, 13, 40–44.

Kiernan, W. E., & Stark, J. A. (1986). Employment options for adults with developmental disabilities: A conceptual model. Remedial and Special Education, 7(6), 7–11.

Kiesler, D. J. (1971). Experimental designs in psychotherapy research. In A. E. Bergin & S. L. Garfield (Eds.), Handbook of psychotherapy and behavior changes: An empirical analysis (pp. 36–74). New York: Wiley.

King, W. L. (1987). Students with learning disabilities and postsecondary education: National council on handicapped forum on higher education and students with disabilities. In D. Knapke & C. Lendman (Eds.), Capitalizing on the future (pp. 16–21). Columbus, OH: AHSSPPE.

Klein, H. B., Moses, N., & Altman, E. (1988). Communication skills of learning disabled adults as perceived by self and others. Journal of Communication Disorders, 21, 423–436.

Learning Disabilities Association. (1990). Literacy and learning disabilities: A survey. Learning Disabilities Association Newsbriefs, 25(6), 1–16.

Leonard, F. (1991). Using Wechsler data to predict success for learning disabled college students. Learning Disabilities Research & Practice, 6(1), 17–24.

Lundstram, F., & Politiek-Haim, Y. (1990). Continuing projects: Why model transition projects continue after federal funding. Unpublished manuscript, Transition Institute, University of Illinois, Champaign-Urbana.

Mangrum, C. T., & Strichart, S. S. (1988). College and the learning disabled student. Orlando, FL: Grune & Stratton.

McCue, P. M., Shelly, C., & Goldstein, G. (1986). Intellectual, academic and neuropsychological performance levels in learning disabled adults. Journal of Learning Disabilities, 19, 233–241.

McGuire, J. M., Norlander, K. A., & Shaw, S. F. (1990). Postsecondary education for students with learning disabilities: Forecasting challenges for the future. Learning Disabilities Focus, 5(2), 69–74.

Menkes, M., Rowe, J., & Menkes, J. (1967). A twenty-five year follow-up study on the hyperkinetic child with minimal brain dysfunction. Pediatrics, 39, 393–399.

Miller, C. D., McKinley, D. L., & Ryan, L. (1979). College students: Learning disabilities and services. Personnel and Guidance Journal, 58, 154–158.

Miller, J. H., Mulkey, S. W., & Kopp, K. H. (1984). Public rehabilitation services for individuals with specific learning disabilities. Journal of Rehabilitation, 50(2), 19–29.

Minner, S., & Prater, G. (1984). College teachers' expectations of LD students. Academic Therapy, 20, 225–229.

Minskoff, E. H., Hawks, R., Steidle, E. F., & Hoffmann, J. F. (1989). A homogeneous group of persons with learning disabilities: Adults with severe learning disabilities in vocational rehabilitation. Journal of Learning Disabilities, 22, 521–528.

Minskoff, E. H., Sautter, S. W., Hoffmann, F. J., & Hawks, R. (1987). Employer attitudes toward hiring the learning disabled. Journal of Learning Disabilities, 20, 53–57.

Mithaug, D. E., & Horiuchi, C. N. (1983). Colorado statewide follow-up survey of special education students. Denver: State Department of Education.

Mithaug, D., Horiuchi, C., & Fanning, P. (1985). A report on the Colorado statewide follow-up survey of special education students. Exceptional Children, 51, 397–404.

Moss, J. R., & Fox, D. L. (1980). College-level programs for the learning disabled. Tulsa, OK: Partners in Publishing.

Mulkey, S. W., Kopp, K. H., & Miller, J. H. (1984). Determining eligibility of learning disabled adults for vocational rehabilitation services. Journal of Rehabilitation, 50(2), 53–58.

National Joint Committee on Learning Disabilities. (1987). Adults with learning disabilities: A call to action. Journal of Learning Disabilities, 20, 172–174.

Nelson, J. R., Dodd, J. M., & Smith, D. J. (1990). Faculty willingness to accommodate students with learning disabilities: A comparison among academic divisions. Journal of Learning Disabilities, 23, 185–189.

Neubert, D. A., Tilson, G. P., & Ianacone, R. N. (1989). Postsecondary transition needs and employment patterns of individuals with mild disabilities. Exceptional Children, 55, 494–500.

Norlander, K. A., Shaw, S. F., & McGuire, J. M. (1990). Competencies of postsecondary education personnel serving students with learning disabilities. Journal of Learning Disabilities, 23, 426–432.

Okolo, C., & Sitlington, P. (1988). The role of special education in LD adolescents' transition from school to work. Learning Disability Quarterly, 11, 292–306.

Otto, W. (1986). Peter Johnson we salute you. Journal of Reading, 19, 700–703.

Parks, A. W., Antonoff, S., Drake, C., Skiba, W. F., & Soberman, J. (1987). A survey of programs and services for students with learning disabilities in graduate and professional schools. Journal of Learning Disabilities, 20, 181–188.

Patton, J. R., & Polloway, E. A. (1982, October). The learning disabled through the life cycle: The adult years. Paper presented at the fourth annual conference of the Council for Learning Disabilities, Kansas City, MO.

Polloway, E. A., Smith, J. D., & Patton, J. R. (1984). Learning disabilities: An adult development perspective. Learning Disability Quarterly, 7, 179–186.

Pressley, M., Heisel, B. E., McCormick, C. B., & Nakamura, G. V. (1982). Memory strategy instruction with children. In C. J. Brainerd & M. Pressley (Eds.), Progress in cognitive development research: Verbal processes in children (Vol. 2, pp. 69–72). New York: Springer-Verlag.

Ross, J. M. (1987). Learning and coping strategies used by learning disabled students participating in adult basic education and literacy programs: A final report of the 310 Special Project 87-98-7014. Pennsylvania Department of Education, Division of Adult Basic Education.

Ross, J. M., & Smith, J. O. (1988). ABE and GED staff perceptions regarding learning disabled students: A final report of the 310 Special Project 88-98-8034. Pennsylvania Department of Education, Division of Adult Basic Education.

Rusch, F. R., McNair, J., & DeStefano, L. (1988). Research priorities in secondary special education and transitional services: A national survey. Career Development for Exceptional Individuals, 11(2), 99–110.

Salvia, J., Gajar, A. H., Gajria, M., & Salvia, S. (1988). A comparison of WAIS-R profiles of college LD and normal students. Journal of Learning Disabilities, 21, 632–636.

Salvia, J., & Salvia, S. (1985). Use of the Woodcock-Johnson Psycho-Educational Battery: Tests of Achievement (Part II) with a college population. Diagnostique, 11, 3–8.

Salvia, J., & Salvia, S. (1986). Significant discrepancies between Wechsler Adult Intelligence Scale–Revised and the Woodcock-Johnson Psycho-Educational Battery, Part II: Tests of Achievement with a college population. Diagnostique, 11, 59–68.

Sanchez, S. (1984). Where do we go from here: A look to the future in rehabilitation of learning disabled persons. Journal of Rehabilitation, 50(2), 82–88.

Schalock, R., Wolzen, B., Ross, I., Elliott, B., Werbel, G., & Peterson, K. (1986). Post-secondary community placement of handicapped students: A five-year follow-up. Learning Disability Quarterly, 9, 295–303.

Scheiber, B., & Talpers, J. (1987). Unlocking potential. Bethesda, MD: Adler & Adler.

Shaw, S. F., & Shaw, S. R. (1989). Learning disability college programming: A bibliography. Journal of Postsecondary Education and Disability, 6(1), 77–85.

Sheldon, K. L., & Prout, H. T. (1985). Vocational rehabilitation and learning disabilities: An analysis of state policies. Journal of Rehabilitation, 51(1), 59–61.

Siegal, E. (1974). The exceptional child grows up. New York: Dutton.

Siegel, D. (1979). Help for learning disabled college students. American Education, 15(6), 17–21.

Siegel, S. K., Deuter, J., Prieur, J., & Gaylord-Ross, R. (1986). The community national training program. Unpublished manuscript, San Francisco State University.

Silver, A. A. (1969). More than 20 years after—A review of developmental language disability: Adult accomplishments of dyslexic boys. The Journal of Special Education, 3, 219–222.

Silver, A. A., & Hagin, R. (1964). Specific reading disability: Follow-up studies. American Journal of Orthopsychiatry, 34, 95–102.

Simpson, R. G., & Umbach, B. T. (1989). Identifying and providing vocational services by adults with specific learning disabilities. Journal of Rehabilitation, 55(3), 49–55.

Sitlington, P. L. (1981). Vocational and special education in career programming for the mildly handicapped adolescent. Exceptional Children, 47, 592–598.

Sitlington, P. L., & Frank, A. R. (1990). Are adolescents with learning disabilities successfully crossing the bridge into adult life? Learning Disability Quarterly, 13, 97–113.

Slate, J. R., Frost, J., & Cross, B. (1990). Comparability of WISC-R and WAIS-R scores for a sample of college students with learning disabilities. Learning Disability Quarterly, 13, 205–208.

Smith, J. O. (1989). Access to rehabilitation services by adults with learning disabilities. Unpublished doctoral dissertation, the Pennsylvania State University, University Park.

Succimarra, D. J., & Speece, D. L. (1990). Employment outcomes and social integration of students with mild handicaps: The quality of life two years after high school. Journal of Learning Disabilities, 23, 213–219.

Temple, C. M. (1988). Developmental dyslexia and dysgraphia persistence in middle age. Journal of Communication Disorders, 21, 189–207.

Thistlewaite, L. (1983). Teaching reading to the student who cannot read. Lifelong Learning: The Adult Years, 7(1), 5–7, 28.

Thomas, S. W. (1981). Impact of the 1981 rehabilitation regulations on vocational evaluation of the learning disabled. Vocational Evaluation and Work Adjustment Bulletin, 14, 28–31.

Torgesen, J. K., & Kail, R. J., Jr. (1980). Memory processes in exceptional children. In B. K. Keogh (Ed.), Advances in special education: Vol. 1. Basic constructs and theoretical orientations (pp. 55–99). Greenwich, CT: JAI Press.

Vetter, A. (1983). A comparison of the characteristics of learning disabled and non-learning disabled young adults (Doctoral dissertation, The University of Kansas, 1983). Dissertation Abstracts International, 44, 3359A.

Vogel, S. (1982). On developing LD college programs. Journal of Learning Disabilities, 15, 518–529.

Vogel, S. (1985). The college student with a learning disability (2nd ed.). Lake Forest, IL: Barat College.

Vogel, S. A. (1990). An overview of the special topical issue on adults with learning disabilities. Learning Disabilities Focus, 5(2), 67–68.

Vogel, S., & Adelman, P. (1980). Personnel development: College and university programs designed for learning disabled adults. CEC Quarterly, 1, 12–18.

Wehman, P., Hill, J., Hill, M., Brooke, V., Pendleton, P., & Brit, C. (1985). Competitive employment for persons with mental retardation: A follow-up six years later. Mental Retardation, 23(6), 274–281.

Wehman, P., Moon, M. S., Everson, J. M., Wood, W., & Barcus, J. M. (1988). Transition from school to work: New challenges for youth with severe disabilities. Baltimore: Brookes.

Weller, C., & Strawser, S. (1980). Detecting learning disabilities in the college-age student. Learning Disability Quarterly, 3, 87–89.

White, J., Deshler, D., Schumaker, J., Warner, M., Alley, G., & Clark, F. (1983). The effects of learning disabilities on postschool adjustment. Journal of Rehabilitation, 49, 46–50.

White, W. J. (1985). Perspectives on the education and training of learning disabled adults. Learning Disability Quarterly, 8, 231–236.

White, W. J., Alley, G. R., Deshler, D. D., Schumaker, J. A. B., Warner, M. M., & Clark, F. L. (1982). Are there learning disabilities after high school? Exceptional Children, 49, 273–274.

White, W., Schumaker, J., Warner, M., Alley, G., & Deshler, D. (1980). The current status of young adults identified as learning disabled during their school career (Research Rep. No. 21). Lawrence: University of Kansas Institute for Research in Learning Disabilities.

Wilhardt, L., & Sandman, C. A. (1988). Performance of nondisabled adults and adults with learning disabilities on a computerized multiphasic cognitive memory battery. Journal of Learning Disabilities, 21, 179–185.

Will, M. (1984a). OSERS programming for the transition of youth with disabilities: Bridges from school to working life. Washington, DC: Office of Special Education and Rehabilitation Services, U.S. Department of Education.

Will, M. (1984b). Let us pause and reflect—but not too long. Exceptional Children, 51, 11–16.

Will, M. (1984c). OSERS programming for the transition of youth with disabilities: Bridges from school to working life. Washington, DC: Office of Special Education and Rehabilitation Services.

Will, M. (1984d). Supported employment for adults with severe disabilities: An OSERS program initiative. Washington, DC: Office of Special Education and Rehabilitation Services.

Will, M. (1984e). Bridges from school to working life. Interchange, 20(5), 2–6.

Worden, P. E. (1983). Memory strategy instruction with the learning disabled. In M. Pressley & J. R. Levin (Eds.), Cognitive strategy research: Psychological foundations (pp. 33–40). New York: Springer-Verlag.

Zigmond, N., & Thornton, H. (1985). Follow-up of postsecondary age learning disabled graduates and dropouts. Learning Disabilities Research, 1(1), 50–55.

Chapter 11

Bach-Y-Rita, P. (1990). Brain plasticity as a basis for recovery of function in humans. Neuropsychologia, 28, 547–554.

Badian, N., McAnulty, G. B., Duffy, F. H., & Als, H. (1990). Prediction of dyslexia in kindergarten boys. Annals of Dyslexia, 40, 152–169.

Bakker, D. J., Bouma, A., & Gardien, C. J. (1990). Hemisphere-specific treatment of dyslexia subtypes: A field experiment. Journal of Learning Disabilities, 23, 393–456.

Bigler, E. D. (1988). Diagnostic clinical neuropsychology (rev. ed.). Austin: University of Texas Press.

Bigler, E. D. (1989). On the neuropsychology of suicide. Journal of Learning Disabilities, 22, 180–185.

Bigler, E. D. (1990). Remediating nonverbal problems associated with learning disabilities. In P. I. Myers & D. D. Hammill (Eds.), Learning disabilities (pp. 321–349). Austin, TX: PRO-ED.

Bigler, E. D., Lowe, J. R., & Yeo, R. A. (1989). Structural anomalies and neuropsychological function. In E. D. Bigler, R. A. Yeo, & E. Turkheimer (Eds.), Neuropsychological function and brain imaging (pp. 317–338). New York: Plenum Press.

Bigler, E. D., & Naugle, R. I. (1985). Case studies in cerebral plasticity. International Journal of Clinical Neuropsychology, 7, 12–23.

Cullum, C. M. (1989). Cerebral imaging and emotional correlates. In E. D. Bigler, R. A. Yeo, & E. Turkheimer (Eds.), Neuropsychological function and brain imaging (pp. 269–293). New York: Plenum Press.

DeRenzi, E., & Lucchelli, F. (1990). Developmental dysmnesia in a poor reader. Brain, 13, 1337–1345.

Duara, R., Kushch, A., Gross-Glenn, K., Barker, W. W., Jallad, B., Pascal, S., Loewenstein, D. A., Sheldon, J., Rabin, M., Levin, B., & Lubs, H. (1990). Neuroanatomic differences between dyslexic and normal readers on magnetic resonance imaging scans. Archives of Neurology, 48, 410–416.

Duffy, F. H., & McAnulty, G. (1990). Neuropsychological heterogeneity and the definition of dyslexia: Preliminary evidence for plasticity. Neuropsychologia, 28, 555–571.

Dykman, R. A., & Ackerman, P. T. (1991). Attention deficit disorder and specific reading disability: Separate but often overlapping disorders. Journal of Learning Disabilities, 24, 96–103.

Felton, R. H., Naylor, C. E., & Wood, F. B. (1990). Neuropsychological profile of adult dyslexics. Brain and Language, 39, 485–497.

Finucci, J. M., Whitehouse, C. C., Isaacs, S. D., & Childs, B. (1984). Derivation and validation of a quantitative definition of specific reading disability for adults. Developmental Medicine and Child Neurology, 26, 143–153.

Flowers, D. L., Wood, F. B., & Naylor, C. E. (1991). Regional cerebral bloodflow correlates of language processes in reading disability. Archives of Neurology, 48, 637–643.

Fuerst, D. R., Fisk, J. L., & Rourke, B. P. (1990). Psychosocial functioning of learning-disabled children: Relations between WISC verbal IQ–performance IQ discrepancies and personality subtypes. Journal of Consulting and Clinical Psychology, 58, 657–660.

Gaddes, W. H. (1985). Learning disabilities and brain function: A neuropsychological approach (2nd ed.). New York: Springer-Verlag.

Galaburda, A. M. (1990). The testosterone hypothesis: Assessment since Geschwind and Behan, 1982. Annals of Dyslexia, 40, 18–38.

Galaburda, A. M., & Kemper, T. L. (1979). Cyto-architectonic abnormalities in developmental dyslexia: A case study. Annals of Neurology, 6, 94–102.

Galaburda, A. M., Rosen, G. D., & Sherman, G. F. (1990). Individual variability in cortical organization: Its relationship to brain laterality and implications to function. Neuropsychologia, 28, 529–546.

Galaburda, A. M., Sherman, G. F., Rosen, G. D., Aboitiz, F., & Geschwind, N. (1985). Developmental dyslexia: Four consecutive patients with cortical anomalies. Annals of Neurology, 18, 222–233.

Gerber, P. J., Schneiders, C. A., Paradise, L. V., Reiff, H. B., Ginsberg, R., & Popp, P. A. (1990). Persisting problems of adults with learning disabilities: Self-reported comparisons from their school-age and adult years. Journal of Learning Disabilities, 23, 570–573.

Gross-Glenn, K., Duara, R., Barker, W. W., Lowenstein, D., Chang, J. Y., Yoshii, F., Apicella, A. M., Pascal, S., Boothe, T., Sevush, S., Jallad, B. J., Novoa, L., & Lubs, H. A. (1991). Positron emission tomographic studies during serial word-reading by normal and dyslexic adults. Journal of Clinical and Experimental Neuropsychology, 13, 531–544.

Heaton, R. K., Grant, I., & Matthews, C. G. (1991). Comprehensive norms for an expanded Halstead-Reitan Battery. Odessa, FL: Psychological Assessment Resources.

Horn, J. L., O'Donnell, J. P., & Leicht, D. J. (1988). Phonetically inaccurate spelling among learning-disabled, head-injured, and nondisabled young adults. Brain and Language, 33, 55–69.

Humphreys, P., Kaufmann, W., & Galaburda, A. M. (1990). Developmental dyslexia in women: Neuropathological findings in three patients. Annals of Neurology, 28, 727–738.

Hynd, G. W., & Semrud-Clikeman, M. (1989a). Dyslexia and neurodevelopmental pathology: Relationships to cognition, intelligence, and reading skill acquisition. Journal of Learning Disabilities, 22, 204–216.

Hynd, G. W., & Semrud-Clikeman, M. (1989b). Dyslexia and brain morphology. Psychological Bulletin, 106, 447–482.

Jastak, S., & Wilkinson, G. S. (1984). Wide range achievement test–Revised. Wilmington, DE: Jastak Associates.

Jernigan, T. L., Hesselink, J. R., Sowell, E., & Tallal, P. A. (1991). Cerebral structure on magnetic resonance imaging in language- and learning-impaired children. Archives of Neurology, 48, 539–545.

Kinsbourne, M., Rufo, D. T., Gamzu, E., Palmer, R. L., & Berliner, A. K. (1991). Neuropsychological deficits in adults with dyslexia. Developmental Medicine and Child Neurology, 33, 763–775.

Kolb, B. (1989). Brain development, plasticity, and behavior. American Psychologist, 44, 1203–1212.

Larsen, J. P., Hoien, T., Lundberg, I., & Odegaard, S. (1990). MRI evaluation of the size and symmetry of the planum temporale in adolescents with developmental dyslexia. Brain and Language, 39, 289–301.

Lawson, J. S., & Inglis, J. (1989). Learning disability in adults: A comparison of two indices of differential cognitive impairment derived from the Wechsler scales. Journal of Clinical Psychology, 45, 106–114.

Lezak, M. D. (1983). Neuropsychological assessment. New York: Oxford University Press.

Lou, H. C., Henriksen, L., Bruhn, P., Borner, H., & Nielsen, J. B. (1989). Striatal dysfunction in attention deficit and hyperkinetic disorder. Archives of Neurology, 46, 48–52.

Matarazzo, J. D. (1990). Psychological assessment versus psychological testing: Validation from Binet to the school, clinic, and courtroom. American Psychologist, 45, 999–1017.

Mattis, S., French, J. H., & Rapin, I. (1975). Dyslexia in children and young adults: Three independent neuropsychological syndromes. Developmental Medicine and Child Neurology, 17, 150–163.

McCue, P. M., Shelly, C., & Goldstein, G. (1986). Intellectual, academic and neuropsychological performance levels in learning disabled adults. Journal of Learning Disabilities, 19, 233–236.

Miles, T. R. (1986). On the persistence of dyslexic difficulties into adulthood. In G. Th. Pavlidis & D. F. Fisher (Eds.), Dyslexia: Neuropsychology and treatment. New York: Wiley.

Murphy, V., & Hicks-Stewart, K. (1991). Learning disabilities and attention deficit–hyperactivity disorder: An interactional perspective. Journal of Learning Disabilities, 24, 386–388.

Myers, P. I., & Hammill, D. D. (1990). Learning disabilities: Basic concepts, assessment practices, and instructional strategies (4th ed.). Austin, TX: PRO-ED.

National Joint Committee on Learning Disabilities (NJCLD). (1989, September 18). Letter from NJCLD to member organizations. (Topic: modifications to the NJCLD definition of learning disabilities)

Nussbaum, N. L., & Bigler, E. D. (1990). Identification and treatment of attention deficit disorder. Austin, TX: PRO-ED.

O'Donnell, J. P., Kurtz, J., & Ramanaiah, N. V. (1983). Neuropsychological test findings for normal, learning-disabled and brain damaged young adults. Journal of Consulting and Clinical Psychology, 51, 726–729.

O'Donnell, J. P., Romero, J. J., & Leicht, D. J. (1990). A comparison of language deficits in learning-disabled, head-injured, and nondisabled young adults: Results from an abbreviated aphasia screening test. Journal of Clinical Psychology, 46, 310–315.

Orton, S. (1928). Specific reading disability: Strephosymbolia. Journal of the American Medical Association, 90, 1095–1099.

Prigatano, G. P. (1990). Recovery and cognitive retraining after traumatic brain injury. In E. D. Bigler (Ed.), Traumatic brain injury: Mechanisms of damage, assessment, intervention, and outcome (pp. 273–295). Austin, TX: PRO-ED.

Raven, J. C. (1965). Guide to using the Coloured Progressive Matrices. San Antonio, TX: Psychological Corp.

Reitan, R. M., & Wolfson, D. (1985). The Halstead-Reitan neuropsychological test battery. Tucson, AZ: Neuropsychology Press.

Rey, A. (1964). L'examen clinique en psychologie. Paris: Presses Universitaires de France.

Rourke, B. P. (1985). Neuropsychology of learning disabilities: Essentials of subtype analysis. New York: Guilford Press.

Rourke, B. P. (1989). Nonverbal learning disabilities: The syndrome and the model. New York: Guilford Press.

Rourke, B. P., Bakker, D. J., Fisk, J. L., & Strang, J. D. (1983). Child neuropsychology. New York: Guilford Press.

Rourke, B. P., Young, G. C., & Leenaars, A. A. (1989). A childhood learning disability that predisposes those afflicted to adolescent and adult depression and suicide risk. Journal of Learning Disabilities, 22, 169–175.

Russell, E. W., Neuringer, C., & Goldstein, G. (1970). Assessment of brain damage: A neuropsychological key approach. New York: Wiley Interscience.

Satz, P. (1990). Developmental dyslexia: An etiological reformulation. In G. Th. Pavlidis (Ed.), Perspective on dyslexia (Vol. 1, pp. 93–117). Chichester, Sussex, England: Wiley.

Scheibel, A. B. (1990). Dendritic correlates of higher cognitive function. In A. B. Scheibel & A. F. Wechsler (Eds.), Neurobiology of higher cognitive function (pp. 239–270). New York: Guilford Press.

Silver, L. B. (1990). Attention deficit–hyperactivity disorder: Is it a learning disability or a related disorder? Journal of Learning Disabilities, 23, 394–397.

Spreen, O. (1989a). Long-term sequelae of learning disability: A review of outcome studies. In D. J. Bakker & H. van der Vlugt (Eds.), Learning disabilities: Vol. I. Neurological correlates and treatment (pp. 273–295). Amsterdam: Swets & Zeitlinger.

Spreen, O. (1989b). Learning disability, neurology, and long-term outcome: Some implications for the individual and for society. Journal of Clinical and Experimental Neuropsychology, 11, 389–408.

Townes, B. D., Martin, D. C., Nelson, D., Prosser, R., Pepping, M., Maxwell, J., Peel, J., & Preston, M. (1985). Neurobehavioral approach to classification of psychiatric patients using a competency model. Journal of Consulting and Clinical Psychology, 53, 33–42.

Tranel, D., Hall, L. E., Olson, S., & Tranel, N. N. (1987). Evidence for a right-hemisphere developmental learning disability. Developmental Neuropsychology, 3, 113–127.

Wechsler, D. A. (1945). A standardized memory scale for clinical use. Journal of Psychology, 19, 87–95.

Wechsler, D. A. (1981). Wechsler adult intelligence scale–Revised. San Antonio, TX: Psychological Corp.

Wender, P. H. (1987). The hyperactive child, adolescent, and adult: Attention deficit disorder through the lifespan. New York: Oxford University Press.

Wiederholt, J. L. (1974). Adolescents with learning disabilities: The problem in perspective. In L. Mann & A. Sabatino (Eds.), The second review of special education (pp. 103–152). Austin, TX: PRO-ED.

Zametkin, A. J., Nordahl, T. E., Gross, M., King, A. C., Semple, W. E., Rumsey, J., Hamburger, S., & Cohen, R. M. (1990). Cerebral glucose metabolism in adults with hyperactivity of childhood onset. New England Journal of Medicine, 323, 1361–1366.

Chapter 12

Schewel, R. (1991). Adults with learning disabilities: Coping skills and positive influences. Unpublished manuscript, Lynchburg College, Lynchburg, VA.

CHAPTER 13

Americans with Disabilities Act of 1990, 42 U.S.C.A. § 12101 et seq.

Adelman, P. B., & Vogel, S. A. (1990). College graduates with learning disabilities—Employment attainment and career patterns. Learning Disability Quarterly, 13, 154–162.

Association for Children and Adults with Learning Disabilities (ACLD). (1984). Definition of the condition specific learning disabilities. Pittsburgh, PA: Learning Disability Association.

Barbaro, F. (1982). The LD college student: Some considerations in setting objectives. Journal of Learning Disabilities, 15, 599–603.

Buchanan, M., & Wolf, J. (1986). A comprehensive study of learning disabled adults. Journal of Learning Disabilities, 19, 34–37.

Chelser, B. (1982). ACLD vocational committee completes survey on LD adults. ACLD Newsbrief, 5, 20–23.

Fifteenth annual report to Congress on the implementation of the Individuals with Disabilities Education Act. (1993). Washington, DC: U.S. Department of Education, Division of Innovation and Development, Office of Special Education and Rehabilitative Services.

Gerber, P. J., & Ginsberg, R. J. (1990). Identifying alterable patterns of success in highly successful adults with learning disabilities (Executive Summary). Richmond: Virginia Commonwealth University, School of Education.

Gerber, P. J., Schnieders, C. A., Paradise, L. V., Reiff, H. B., Ginsberg, R. J., & Popp, P. A. (1990). Persisting problems of adults with learning disabilities: Self-reported comparisons from their school-age and adult years. Journal of Learning Disabilities, 23, 570–573.

Hoffman, F., Sheldon, K., Minskoff, E., Sautter, S., Steidle, E., Baker, D., & Bailey, M. (1987). Needs of learning disabled adults. Journal of Learning Disabilities, 20, 43–52.

Malcolm, C. B., Polatajko, H. J., & Simons, J. (1990). A descriptive study of adults with suspected learning disabilities. Journal of Learning Disabilities, 23, 518–520.

Minskoff, E. H., Sautter, S. W., Sheldon, K. L., Steidle, E. F., & Baker, D. P. (1988). A comparison of learning disabled adults and high school students. Learning Disabilities Research, 3, 225–229.

National Joint Conference on Learning Disabilities (NJCLD). (1990). Learning disabilities: Issues on definition. In Collective perspectives on issues affecting learning disabilities: Position papers and statements (pp. 3–8). Austin, TX: PRO-ED.

Polloway, E. A., Smith, J. D., & Patton, J. R. (1984). Learning disabilities: An adult developmental perspective. Learning Disability Quarterly, 7, 179–186.

Rehabilitation Act of 1973, 29 U.S.C. 794 § 504.

Smith, J. O. (1988). Social and vocational problems of adults with learning disabilities: A review of the literature. Learning Disabilities Focus, 4, 46–58.

Smith, J. O. (1992). Falling through the cracks: Rehabilitation services for adults with learning disabilities. Exceptional Children, 58, 451–460.

Speckman, N., Goldberg, R., & Herman, K. (1992). Learning disabled children grow up: A search for factors related to success in the young adult years. Learning Disabilities Research & Practice, 7, 161–170.

Stodden, R. A., & Boone, R. (1987). Assessing transition services for handicapped youth: A cooperative interagency approach. Exceptional Children, 53, 537–545.

White, W. J., Deshler, D. D., Schumaker, J. B., Warner, M. M., Alley, G. R., & Clark, F. L. (1983). The effects of learning disabilities on postschool adjustment. Journal of Rehabilitation, 46–50.

Will, M. (1984). OSERS programming for the transition of youth with disabilities: Bridges from school to working life. Washington, DC: U.S. Department of Education, Office of Special Education and Rehabilitation Services

Contributors

Pamela B. Adelman, Barat College

Diane Bassett, University of Northern Colorado

Melissa Behrens-Blake, University of New Mexico

Erin D. Bigler, Brigham Young University

Ginger Blalock, University of New Mexico

Loring C. Brinckerhoff, Boston University

Brian Bryant, The University of Texas—Austin

Carol A. Dowdy, University of Alabama—Birmingham

Anna Gajar, Penn State

Paul J. Gerber, Virginia Commonwealth University

Rick Ginsberg, University of South Carolina

Joan M. McGuire, University of Connecticut

Carl H. Nowell, Alabama Department of Education, Division of Rehabilitation Services

James R. Patton, PRO-ED, Inc.

Edward A. Polloway, Lynchburg College

Henry B. Reiff, Western Maryland College

Rosel Schewel, Lynchburg College

Stan F. Shaw, University of Connecticut

J. David Smith, University of South Carolina

Tom E. C. Smith, University of Arkansas

Susan A. Vogel, Northern Illinois University

Warren J. White, Kansas State University

Author Index

Subject Index